"*I recently read your excellent book,* Designing Your Perfect House. *I have read numerous books on house design and building, but not found any that so effectively integrates design philosophy and practical considerations. The discussions of spatial relationships provide very good guidance. Your sidebar checklists are also very helpful. You have done an exceptionally good job. I thoroughly enjoyed the book. Good work.*"

E.J. Ritchie, Houston

"*Your book has helped me so much; it was the best investment I ever made! Your advice has been invaluable, and I just want to thank you for sharing your design knowledge with us.*"

Luci S., New Jersey

"*I like the first sentence of the Preface. Hirsch says 'This book is for people who care enough to create a house that is uniquely their own.' The important words are 'care' and 'uniquely their own,' and throughout the book he focuses on ways for homeowners to do just that—create a home that not only suits their lifestyles but one that is magical yet comfortable and livable.*

This is such a good book! I've seen many, but not one as detailed and user-friendly as Designing Your Perfect House. *Hirsch certainly is providing a guide on creating a house that becomes a home.*"

Irene Watson, *Reader Views*

"*It was a real pleasure reading your book in preparation of building our own house (in Switzerland). I loved your photos, clear examples, and easy flowing writing style.*"

RLS, Switzerland

"*I am enjoying this book a lot. I go back and forth to it. After which I had the privilege to know you Bill. Thank you for such a good book.*"

Mohamed A., UAE

"*This is a definite must-read for anyone building a house. It opened up a lot of dialogue between the two of us regarding our lifestyle and how we envision the house…the flow, the individual rooms, the light/sun, the terrace, and pool area…and the thousand other details mentioned in the book.*"

Rochelle and Steve Prystowsky

"*This book is a must-have for everyone who plans to build a home. [Hirsh's] book is an invaluable tool to guide the way.*"

Tracy Gibson

DESIGNING
Your
PERFECT
HOUSE

LESSONS FROM AN ARCHITECT

WILLIAM J. HIRSCH JR. AIA

dalsimer press

Although the author and publisher have made every effort to ensure the accuracy and completeness of information contained in this book, we assume no responsibility for errors, inaccuracies, omissions, or any inconsistency herein. Any slighting of people, places, or organizations is unintentional.

DISCLAIMER: This book is intended to express the views and opinions of the author and is neither written as, nor should be interpreted to be, professional advice regarding code compliance, safety issues, engineering, or financial issues. Readers are advised to retain locally licensed consultants and to always consult local authorities, codes, covenants, and regulations before starting any construction project.

PHOTO CREDITS: Page 41—Dan Addison/U.VA Public Affairs; Page 58—Richard Davis; Page 65—Barbara Paul Robinson and Charles Rascob Robinson; Page 101—Jim Steinhart of www.TravelPhotoBase.com; Page 161—Illustration courtesy of National Charrette Institute; All Other Photographs—William J. Hirsch Jr. AIA

1st EDITION (978-0-9798820-3-6): 1st printing 2008 • 2nd printing 2010 • 3rd printing 2012

2nd EDITION (978-0-9798820-0-5): 1st printing 2017

ISBN 978-0-9798820-0-5

LCCN 2017938089

ATTENTION CORPORATIONS, UNIVERSITIES, COLLEGES, AND PROFESSIONAL ORGANIZATIONS:
Quantity discounts are available on bulk purchases of this book for educational, gift purposes, or as premiums for increasing magazine subscriptions or renewals. Special books or book excerpts can also be created to fit specific needs. For information, please contact Dalsimer Press, Inc., 1131 7 LKS N, West End, NC 27376; (910) 400-5379.

Envision a House

Built to stand the test of time

Meant to be the home

—Matt Hirsch

Acknowledgements

Endless thanks go to my wife, Maureen, for her unwavering support and valuable suggestions. I also thank our children, Kristi, Dan, Ben, and Matt, for patiently listening to me tell them how this project was actually going to be a book some day.

I could never have written a book like this without having the chance to gain knowledge and experience. For that knowledge, I thank the former Dean of the School of Architecture at the University of Virginia, the late J. Norwood Bosserman. He stood by me when few others did. For my experience, I thank each and every one of my wonderful clients. None of the projects you see and read about in this book would have ever become a reality without them. They taught me much.

If you read this book and feel the words flow easily and clearly, you can join me in thanking my friend Michael Levin. His skills as a writing coach and advisor played a large role in achieving that end. And the expert layout, cover design, and quality of the book itself are due to the professional guidance and skills of Debi, Scott, and Cathy at About Books, Inc.

The large mirror is a treasure from the owners' years when they lived in Holland. The mantel is newly made with details and materials to match the mirror, making a unique and dramatic statement in the great room.

Anything is possible for Your Perfect House. In this example, a roofline reminiscent of French Second Empire style is combined with a southern front veranda to create a compelling and unique style all its own.

Preface

This book is for people who care enough to create a house that is uniquely their own, regardless of the size of the house or its price range.

For most people, designing and building a new house or remodeling an existing house is both a very exciting and a very scary endeavor. The thrill of creating your dream house is fantastic. But the fear of the enormity of the task and the trepidation that comes when you consider all the potential pitfalls that lie ahead often send a chill through even the most stout-hearted souls. The purpose of this book is to open your eyes to the world of architecture and to provide you with the guidance and knowledge you need so as to minimize the possibilities of anything going wrong. With some foresight and preparation, the process of designing and building your dream home can be one of the most gratifying and exhilarating experiences in your life.

Over the years, I have designed many houses of all sizes and styles for all kinds of people. In spite of the diversity of personalities, budgets, objectives, and expectations among my clients, their questions were often the same: "How do we turn our ideas into our dream house?" "How do I keep control over a process with which I have no experience?" "What do I need to watch out for?" "How do I make my dream house unique to me and not just another house?"

I had often thought I should write out these questions along with the answers, make photocopies, and pass them out to my new clients as a sort of "primer." My booklet was to be a sort of "House Design 101," meant to provide the essential background knowledge, encouragement, and warnings I think everyone should have before spending such large amounts of time and resources. What was initially going to be that small handout has turned into this book. My original plan was also to include information about the "nuts and bolts" of the actual construction, but because the topic is so large and complex, the manuscript quickly became overwhelming in size. That "nuts and bolts" material may be the topic of a future book. This book, *Designing Your Perfect House: Lessons from an Architect*, focuses on the process and philosophy of residential architectural design, plus advice about how to turn all of your ideas, dreams, and needs into the ideal house for you and your family.

The first part of this book deals primarily with what architects call architectural theory. These are concepts and principles that we work with and worry about but that often go unnoticed or at least not openly discussed or understood by the average person. Chances are you have experienced houses that "get it right" or "get it wrong." You might have wondered what makes the difference. Let me suggest that it's not just about the appointments, finishes, and features that a house might have. It's about the intangibles of good design.

These concepts aren't difficult to understand, but they are often not obvious to most people. My hope is that by identifying and discussing these topics, you will gain an awareness and appreciation for them. They are the heart of every architectural design that feels right and pleases our senses. I believe that after reading through these ideas and concepts your senses will be stimulated and you will start to see buildings in a different and clearer way.

The second part of this book deals with the pragmatic aspect of residential design. We will discuss how to take the architectural concepts, your desires, needs, and tastes and meld them together into a house that uniquely suits you and your family. We'll try to work through a process that maintains a level of control over the design and how you and your architect will work together.

As you read through these pages, I hope you will find information to bookmark, underline, and highlight that you will refer back to again and again as you go through the design process. This is not meant to be a story that you read from front to back and then hand to a friend. It is meant to be a ready reference, full of sticky notes and handwritten reminders. This book is meant to be an important tool used to get the job of designing *Your* Perfect House done right.

Throughout the book, I refer to your architect. Since I am an architect, I naturally feel that no house should be designed without one. But I realize the majority of houses built today are designed by non-architects, such as home designers, builders, or even the homeowners themselves. In such cases, this book can be even more valuable. Think of this as your "Architect in a Book."

You will see that I also refer to the architect and builder in masculine terms. I am doing this simply as a stylistic convenience. I think it goes without saying that many fine architects and builders are women. No editorial or gender-related comment is intended.

I wish you great success. Please visit my website, www.designingyourperfecthouse.com, to ask questions, post comments, or find out what's new. Also, please visit my other website, www.williamhirsch.com, to see some of my past projects.

Thanks for becoming a part of the *Your* Perfect House family.

Contents

Lesson One—Beginning the Journey   19

    The Magical, Mystical World of Feel

    Your Opinion Counts

    What Is Architecture?

    From Space to Place

    The Language of Architecture

    Architectural Grammar

Lesson Two—Making the House a Home   31

    Sequential Progressions—Our Minds Seek Order

    Designing Spaces

    Controlling Scale—Keeping It Human

    How to "People" Spaces

Lesson Three—Unifying the Design   45

    The Axis

    Symmetry and Composition

    The Golden Mean

    Breaking the Pattern for a Reason

    Angles and Curves

    Changes in Height, Light, and Scale

Changes in Materials

The Joy of Focal Points

Just Say No to Avocado

Don't Be a Slave to Examples

But My Builder Says He Can't Do That

Lesson Four—Into the Depths of Design 69

"God Is in the Details"

Thick Walls, Solid Home

Provide Something Unexpected

The Importance of Nostalgia

Zones of Retreat

Flow

Light

The Third Dimension

Lesson Five—What Will Your House Be? 87

Why Build a House?

Do I Need an Architect?

Choosing the Right Architect

The Wright Way

Interior Designer and Landscape Architect

Design/Build

Site Unseen

Lesson Six—Make Plans before Drawing Plans   109

How You Really Live

Critical Design Questions

"Green" Mansions

Sidewalk Superintendents

Lesson Seven—Choosing the Perfect Site   121

Zoning, Land Use Ordinances, and Covenants

Lot Size and Buildable Area

Orientation

Howdy, Neighbor

Slope

Views

Boulders, Trees, and Other Physical Features

Noise and Wind

Problem Lots

Reading a Site Plan

Lesson Eight—Programming the House   143

Putting Walls and Ceilings around Spaces

Why Did They Ever Call It a Living Room?

Programming Equals Learning

A Matter of Style

Balancing and Maximizing Priorities

A Reality Test

Lesson Nine—Putting Pencil to Paper   157

    Tiny Bubbles

    Where to Park?

    It's a Sequential Thing

Lesson Ten—Designing the House   169

    Designing the Site Concept—Working with the Land

    Watch the Weather

    Approaching the House by Automobile

    Creating a Sense of Arrival—SAAPE

    Sequence of Interior Spaces

    Stairways Need to Communicate Correctly

    A Stairway to Heaven

    Developing the Plan

    From Plan to House

    Some Rules of Composition

    Windows Are the Eyes and a Door Is the Mouth of the Building

    Using the Right Stuff

    Chimneys Are Spatial Markers

Lesson Eleven—Thinking through the Places
Where You Live   189

    Kitchen—The Heart of the Home

    Dining—Breaking Bread Together

    Living—What We Do between Work and Sleep

    Sleeping—Retreat from the Day

    Bathrooms—Just Functional or Luxurious?

    Entry—The Guest Starts Here

CONTENTS

Other Places—Work, Hobbies, Etc.

Don't Forget the Closets

The Doors

Trade-Offs

The "Other Guy Syndrome"

Aging with *Your* Perfect House

Design Tidbits

Lesson Twelve—Oh, Yes…the Budget   217

Face Reality

The Murkiness of Cost per Square Foot

Bang for the Buck

Elements with Significant Cost Consequences

Meet the Builder

Things to Check Out in a Builder's House

Retainage

Types of Construction Contracts

Where Do We Go from Here?

Bonus Lesson—Building Green, Naturally   235

Design a Naturally Energy Efficient House

Energy Efficient Building Materials

Indoor Air Quality and VOCs

Sustainable Design

Renewable Energy Resources

Index   261

This European-style home makes use of a symmetrical central mass to create formality. The cast limestone front door surround announces the central axis of the house. The cast limestone is repeated in the windowsills, jambs, and heads on some windows, but as we move farther from the formal center of the façade, the windows are more simply framed with natural fieldstone.

Lesson One

BEGINNING THE JOURNEY

"Architecture is frozen music."

—JOHANN WOLFGANG VON GOETHE

Recently, a new client said to me, "Bill, I want the house you design for me to be the best house you've ever designed!"

That's a natural way for people to think about their "dream" houses, and I hope all of my clients feel their house is the best house I've ever designed. But in reality, I think there is no such thing as "an architect's best house." The needs and desires of every client are unique, so it follows that each house should necessarily be unique. Your house must be responsive to your individual desires and needs, and it must be a reflection of your personality and lifestyle. Your architect's goal should not be to design *his* best house but to design the best house for *you*.

I was driving through a very high-end development of custom-designed homes with a client just the other day. She pointed out a house two doors down the street from her building lot. "I hope my new house won't be like that," she said. The house was nicely built, but it sat in an uninspiring position on the land, and the design was like something you might pull from a magazine of "1,000 House Plans." There was nothing actually wrong with the house, but there was nothing right about it either—just like so many houses that are being built today. I assured her that her house was not going to have this bland, plain-vanilla look. Her house would be something more. So, why is it that you can design a house, put all of the right parts together, and still not end up with a house that "feels right"? Something intangible, some mystical attributes and characteristics are not there. The house ends up as a sort of Frankenstein's monster. That poor creature had two arms, two legs, a head, and all of the proper

organs, but it didn't come alive until it was jolted with a bolt of lightning. And even then, there was still something wrong with the creation. It still lacked that "something." The monster lacked a soul.

A house design can share that same perplexing shortcoming. I cannot give you a set of rules to use to make sure your new house has a soul. But I can expose you to concepts of design that will open your eyes to things that will improve the design. I can help you understand the ideas of space and place. We'll look at a process to use, questions to ask yourself, and issues to consider that will help you make better choices for your house. Add all of this together, add a measure of yourself, add the abilities of an architect or house designer, and your house will certainly end up with the soul you seek.

In this book we will discuss how to select an architect and a builder. We will look at what rooms you should have in your new house, how to tally up the square footage, the pragmatic aspects of turning your wish list into the house of your dreams, the more detailed issues of planning and design, and even the budget. But instead of jumping right into that discussion of tangibles, I would like to start with the conceptual and theoretical aspects of design.

An architect's early pencil sketches help him communicate his ideas to his clients. Whether it's by means of hand-drawn sketches, computer-drawn 3D sketches or models, or physical cardboard building models, it is easier and cheaper to try out a few ideas before actual construction starts.

These topics are the subjective concepts of residential architectural design and are often intangible and theoretical. You may find yourself giving more weight to different issues than I might, and that's okay because the things that make a house feel right often have a lot to do with personal preferences and tastes. I jokingly tell my clients this is why Baskin-Robbins has 31 flavors. Not everyone likes pistachio. So please consider these topics in the context of your personal tastes and preferences.

The Magical, Mystical World of Feel

Psychologists tell us that our minds seek order out of chaos. We have an often-unspoken need to connect the things we experience with a system that orders our world. This is the root of our impulse to line things up and balance things, often symmetrically. A successful design must have a concept. It is the skeleton of the architecture. The design concept can be obvious or sublime. It can be classic or radically innovative. Design concepts can employ grid schemes, pinwheel schemes, linear schemes, or hybrids of these. One concept is not necessarily superior to another. What is important, however, is that there is a concept.

There must to be a "purposefulness" to the plan. Probably the most common of these organizing concepts in a house is the classic "four-square" plan. The primary rooms each occupy one of the four corners of a square plan. A central hallway and staircase provide the "connections" between the rooms and the upper and lower floors. Think of the classic Georgian-style house for an example. When you step through the front door of a house like this and stand in

THIS IS NOT JUST FOR BIG HOUSES

The architectural principles we discuss here apply to houses of all sizes, from tiny houses to mansions. No house is too small to be made to feel comfortable and "right." In fact, modest-sized houses are actually easier to make feel like home than large houses because of their scale.

the front hall, you immediately recognize the organizing concept. Because of this recognition, the house seems orderly and properly assembled. You feel things are in their proper place. Although Georgian may not be the style of house you prefer, there is no denying that a house like this often "feels right."

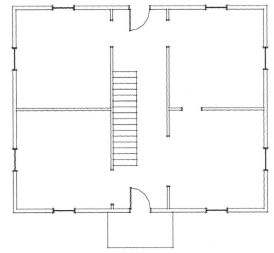

Typical Four-Square Plan. Each room occupies a corner of the house, allowing each one to have windows on two sides for better light and ventilation. Often, in the past, fireplaces were located in each room for heat, many times sharing chimneys on either side of the house. Unfortunately, many "development" homes do not have windows on the sides because neighbors are so close. In these cases residents must rely on electric lighting and air conditioning.

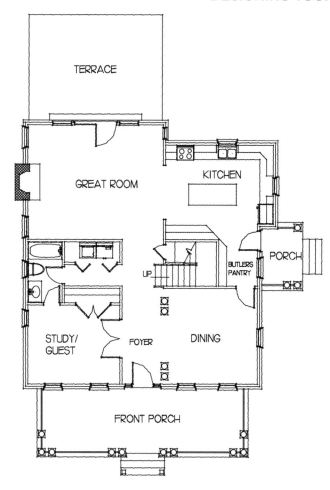

This plan is derived from the classic four-square plan. Although modified to reflect today's open living preferences, the traditional center hall is preserved, and the rooms still have windows on two sides. This house was designed for a neo-traditional community, and the garages are detached and placed at the rear of the property. Each house was designed with a sizeable front porch facing community sidewalks that promote walking and neighborly interaction.

A "spine" is an exceptionally strong organizer. We see it in a shopping mall. The main corridor is the spine, or backbone, with stores placed on either side. The same thing is true of a typical city street with buildings, stores, or houses along it and smaller side streets branching off from the main spine. Larger houses with more than four rooms on the main floor often employ a "spine" concept. A house like this might still have the center foyer, but another "crossing" hall that intersects the foyer at a right angle organizes the arrangement of the other spaces that do not connect directly with the foyer. This is a more complex organization than the "four-square" plan, but it is still readily understandable, and order prevails. Various rooms can then be placed on either side of the crossing hall.

It is best to avoid a "crazy-quilt" plan, in which spaces are plopped down almost randomly with no overriding concept of how they fit together. Our brains need to find a reason why things are where they are. More often than not, this is a subconscious realization. A house designed with an understandable concept offers clarity and comfort. You walk into the house and say to yourself, "Ah, I know what this house is all about."

I am not suggesting you will actually utter these words, but your "inner self" will feel this way, and that is a good feeling. In a house without a logical plan—one with scattered and seemingly random spaces and chaotic relationships of one space to another—you could find yourself mentally wandering aimlessly, never quite able to make conceptual order out of what you are seeing and experiencing,

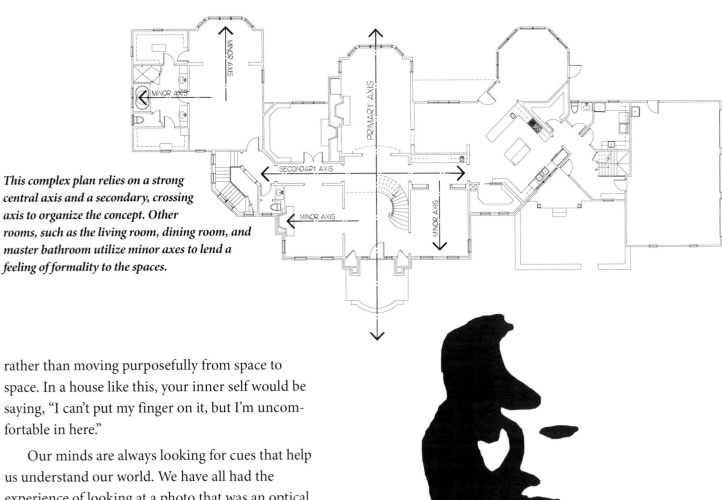

This complex plan relies on a strong central axis and a secondary, crossing axis to organize the concept. Other rooms, such as the living room, dining room, and master bathroom utilize minor axes to lend a feeling of formality to the spaces.

rather than moving purposefully from space to space. In a house like this, your inner self would be saying, "I can't put my finger on it, but I'm uncomfortable in here."

Our minds are always looking for cues that help us understand our world. We have all had the experience of looking at a photo that was an optical illusion and then, all of a sudden, the picture made sense. Our brains were seeking patterns in the chaos. At some point, the "aha!" phenomenon, as psychologists call it, kicks in: "Aha—here we go! Now I see it!" This sensation that the things we see make sense is also what you want to achieve in *Your* Perfect House. This is the most important aspect of what makes a house "feel right."

Can you see the woman's face? Can you switch your mind around and see the man playing a saxophone? Try to "feel" your brain sorting the marks on the paper, trying to make sense of them and then perceiving either the woman's face or the horn player. This is a simple illustration of the "Aha!" phenomenon. It happens when our minds seek order from chaos.

Your Opinion Counts

When you look at the design that your architect creates, if it seems disjointed or possessed of two person-alities, say so. Do your best to evaluate and critique the design as it develops. Discuss your concerns with your architect if things don't seem to be just right. Tell him if you don't understand parts of the design. He can explain things again, draw additional sketches, and even build models, both cardboard and computer-generated ones. Do not let your silence be interpreted as approval unless you truly do approve. Remember, this is the subjective part. Trust your judgment. Trust your tastes.

Even the best architect's best idea may not fit with his other ideas or with all of your ideas. Don't tell yourself, "My architect drew it, so it must be right." Don't be intimidated. Don't be afraid to say, "I just don't get it. Please explain it to me."

"Live" your way through the design. Trace the way you would travel from the public spaces through the private spaces in your house. You can ask yourself, "Is this the appropriate next place, considering where I am right now?" Think about how you will use each room while looking at the plans and sketches. Try your best to imagine yourself living in the spaces that are only lines on paper.

This unusual plan stems from the homeowner's fondness for octagonal-shaped rooms and the twenty-mile view from the rear of the house. Situated on a high, steep bluff, the octagonal room shapes give nearly every room a panoramic view as far as the eye can see.

At the same time, you can always ask, "Do things have to be the way they have always been?" In other words, just because most houses are designed in a particular way doesn't mean yours has to be designed that way, too. Don't be afraid to be inventive. After all, we are talking about *Your* Perfect House.

It's perfectly fine for you to say things like this. It may feel like you are making more work for your architect, but my bet is he will be happy to have your input. I find that I depend on client feedback. Many great ideas are born out of the interaction of an architect and the client. If your house design doesn't work for you and you don't say so, your architect will never know. He wants you to be happy with his work. His goal is to design a great house for you.

What Is Architecture?

It might seem simple, but the precise definition of "architecture" has often been debated. During my days as an architectural student at the University of Virginia, we would often critique buildings and try to determine whether they rose to the level of being called "architecture." The consensus was that Monticello easily qualified, but the standard tract house did not. This was certainly a lofty and esoteric definition of the term. Others might argue that any man-made structure should qualify as architecture, no matter how basic or mundane.

I like to define "architecture" based on what it does rather than what it is. Architecture carves out individual spaces from the enormity of the universe. This is done by creating edges and points that define a space. What separates architecture from the mere act of enclosure is the purposefulness of the act. A random or accidental creation of space achieved by erecting walls and roof to keep the rain out fails to become architecture if it is done without willful planning and intent. The missing link in non-architecture is a thoughtfulness about the way a building is constructed and how it shapes and defines your life.

Architecture lays a special claim to parts of space, the "insides," and separates and defines them apart from all of the rest, the "outsides." Some of the "insides" might actually occur outside, or at least partially outside. A backyard terrace is obviously outside, but when delineated and defined by architectural features, such as stone paving and a low garden wall edging the perimeter, the terrace is separated and claimed from the rest of the yard. As such, it has had architecture applied to it, if you will, based on our definition. It is not simply a haphazard arrangement of furniture in the middle of the lawn. The quality and character of this space are influenced by the details of its surfaces, edges, and orientation. These are a few of the elements we manipulate when we design architecture, and the success of the architecture is dependent on the skillful use of these elements.

From Space to Place

Space is a word architects toss around casually, but it deserves some clarification. There are three kinds of spaces.

First, there is "boundless space." This is all space that is undefined. It has no edges. It includes all space with edges too immense or distant to influence us. The sky is boundless space. The open ocean has edges, but we cannot "feel" them except one at a time. Because we cannot perceive its limits, we see it as endlessness.

The second kind of space is "defined space." This is a space that has discernable edges and is separated from the rest of space. Caves, canyons, and valleys are examples of defined spaces that have been created by natural forces. I call these defined spaces because you know when you are in them and you know when you have left them. Vertical elements like trees define a space around them, as in a mountain glade. The dimensions of that space are proportionate to the height and breadth of the trees. The defined space extends beyond the reach of the branches but eventually yields to the boundless space around it. Think about when you walk through the woods and feel a strong sense of being "in" the space of the forest. That space has been defined by the trees. Cut down the trees, and the space disappears.

The third kind of space is "architectural space." This is a space that has been purposefully defined by people. The edges of architectural spaces are defined by man-made or man-manipulated elements such as columns, walls, floors, ceilings, or other material alterations of an area. Conscious, thoughtful design and planning determine the nature of these spaces. Most of our lives involve interactions with architectural space. They influence us in many significant ways, yet we take them for granted, and many people do not understand the impact architectural spaces have on how we feel, who we are, and how we live.

A space can take on a higher status. It can become a "place." A place is a space that is memorable. Places are spaces you care about. These are spaces that stand apart from the rest. Architectural spaces become memorable through the architectural characteristics that define them. Qualities of scale, appropriateness for people, aesthetics, and visual impact are among the many components that give a place its character and feel. The purpose of a space can make it a place. The Oval Office in the White House is a good example of a place with enormous historic significance. The unique oval shape of this splendid room makes it memorable and gives it a special importance without being ostentatious. Incidentally, George Washington had two rooms at Mount Vernon altered to include bowed ends so he could greet guests while standing in the middle as they circled around him. Thomas Jefferson designed two oval meeting rooms in the main floor of the Rotunda at the University of Virginia. Oval rooms were seen as being democratic because no person could be placed at a more important position in the room than anyone else. It's only fitting that the most well-known room in our democracy is defined by that very shape.

When we design a house, we manipulate spaces. We determine their shape, size, edges, lighting, and other details, and we design the connections between spaces, controlling how they interact. But the real truth of architecture is the actual perception of the physical form and what it says about the way we live. During design and construction, we attend to the individual parts of the building, such as walls, floors, and staircases, but when a building is finished, we actually respond to the spaces that the physical parts of the building define and create.

The Language of Architecture

Language is a means of communication. One arrangement of a group of letters can mean something quite different from another arrangement of the same letters. Even adding a single letter to a word can change the meaning dramatically. Adding a single "r" to the word "fiend" changes it to "friend." The letter "r" is innocent enough, but what power it possesses in this context. The assemblies of letters we call words have no meaning by themselves. Their meaning is derived from our experiences and the

An example of an architectural element that is "pregnant with meaning" is the mansard roof. This double-sloped roof, usually including ornate dormers and cornices, was used so extensively in the seventeenth century in France by the architect François Mansart that it was named for him, albeit with a corrupted spelling. In the mid-1800s, during the period known as the Second Empire, use of this majestic roof was revived as Paris was transformed into a city of grand boulevards and grand buildings. These roofs also served a practical purpose of enlarging the useful space of the attics while controlling the height of the cornice line above the street. Today, mansard roofs are frequently used to shield rooftop mechanical equipment on common, flat-roofed buildings. The use of the once-majestic mansard roof has unfortunately devolved to mean "fast food restaurant."

Here is a simple illustration of a mansard roof. Look around your community and notice how many bastardized examples of this elegant architectural form you can find. If you are lucky enough to find an example of a good mansard roof, you will have found something worth preserving.

rich history of human existence, and therein lies their power. Ideas and emotions are conveyed through otherwise meaningless scratches on paper.

Architecture is a language, too. On the surface, the parts of a building must first serve a function, shielding us from the elements and keeping us safe. But as we look past necessary functionality, buildings frame our lives and even convey emotions. Architecture communicates moods. A building can be shy and restrained or it can be flamboyant and boisterous. Some architecture is whimsical, some is serious. Cathedrals are obvious examples of architecture that express devotion and inspire quiet contemplation. Over the history of our civilization, certain forms gain status and meaning. Arches define entrances and passageways. Spires reach up to the heavens. Pillars convey strength. Rhythms, patterns, and curves express the passage of time, energy, and excitement. A sheltering roof expresses protection and safety. Whether we are aware of it or not, architecture speaks to us in a very real way.

Eclectic architecture—that is, architecture derived from different styles—borrows details and elements laden with significance. A professor of mine would often refer to elements that are "pregnant with meaning." This is a nicely poetic way of saying that past uses of an element have left it with the baggage of its history. Think of a French chateau or a woodland cottage and the architectural characteristics that distinguish these styles. Each is easily identified by certain stylistic trappings. Arched topped windows set in an aging stone or stucco wall and the heavy timber door with hand-wrought

hardware express the strength and security of the classic French chateau. Diamond-paned windows and steeply-pitched hip roofs remind us of paintings we have admired by French masters. By contrast, the steeply-pitched gable roof with the low eave line of the woodland cottage does not so much express strength but rather shelter and warmth.

Modern architecture, particularly the so-called International Style, sought to use elements that were free of meaning. The machine aesthetic was king. The Bauhaus, the influential German school of modern architecture, was trying to create a new language. Despite their purist efforts, it was not possible to create an architectural language totally free of past reference and any underlying meaning. Instead, the elements the modernists used spoke with a cold and inhuman voice to many people. Instead of connecting us to the people who had used these elements in the past and actually created the building parts, we were instead connected to the factories and machines that stamped and milled the steel and glass of modern architecture. I think the recent resurgence of the craftsman style is a clear indication that most of us prefer the warmth and human vocabulary of architectural elements that speak of the people who created them and do not glorify the machines our modern lives depend upon.

Architectural Grammar

If architecture is a language, what, then, are the corresponding parts of speech?

Rooms are our nouns. They are the building blocks of the design. These are the places where people linger and live their lives. We eat and sleep in rooms. We work in rooms. Each room must appropriately surround and respond to the activity it defines. Rooms for one or two people need to be proportioned to the individual. Rooms that serve larger groups must be scaled accordingly.

Doorways, windows, and passageways are the verbs. They define the action of moving about the house. Doorways connect one room to another just as verbs connect nouns in a sentence. Each house must complete an architectural sentence consisting of nouns and verbs, rooms and doorways and halls. Some doorways are wide and convey a lot of action between rooms. Others are subtle and smaller, expressing quiet movement.

The details of a space are the adjectives. They define and characterize the spaces. The style and details of doors and windows are the adverbs, modifying and enhancing the action between the rooms. Archways cut into a thick wall between rooms express the separateness of the rooms and the formality of the act of passage from one room to another. Sometimes doorways become so large they completely obliterate the edges of the room. When this happens, the verb expresses so much action that the two rooms, or nouns, merge and flow into one another. Full glass walls have the same effect in blurring the line between inside and outside, letting the definition of the space spill out to an outdoor space. Remember that your outdoor spaces are rooms, too.

Sometimes, there is a direct link between spoken language and the three-dimensional language of architecture. Take, for example, the word "paradise." It is derived from the Persian word for "walled garden." In the hot and arid climate of Persia, now Iran, water is scarce, and the hot dry desert is brutal. A walled garden provides shelter and refuge from the wind and usually has a central water source with water flowing in all four directions of the compass. Flowers thrive in this oasis of space that has been carved out of the boundless space of the desert by protective walls. In this case, the language of architecture, the feeling of these gardens and the pleasant emotions they convey, has evolved to become a word in our English language that conveys the same concept.

Special features and accents are the interjections, the "ah!" or "oh!," as it were, of the architectural sentence. Highlights, such as windows that frame views and fireplaces, add this kind of liveliness. One of the most interesting things you can do is introduce something unexpected to the design. Turning a corner and finding a cascade of natural light falling across the floor or a Zen window that offers a peek out at a manicured garden can enliven our experience of a space and simply delight us.

Composed together into architectural sentences, the rooms (nouns), doors and windows (verbs), details (adjectives and adverbs), and the special features and accents (interjections) become the prose of the architecture. Unfortunately, just like in writing, some sentences are doomed to be pulp fiction. *Your* Perfect House can be better than that. It should be destined to become great literature.

*The character of this Bali-style house in Hawaii is compelling.
Notice how the mass of the house reflects the traditional individual
bale or pavilions that are the essence of traditional Balinese
architecture. The mahogany and glass doors can fully retract into
the pockets in the walls, allowing the interior and exterior living
spaces to flow together seamlessly. When completed, the light gray
structure in the center will be clad with dark basalt stone with
water flowing through it and cascading into the swimming pool.*

Lesson Two

MAKING THE HOUSE A HOME

"All architecture is shelter, all great architecture is the design of space that contains, cuddles, exalts, or stimulates the persons in that space."
–PHILIP JOHNSON

We have seen that a good design must have an organizing concept. But even with a good concept, a house can have all the right finishes, the best materials, the finest appliances, everything can be as perfect as it can be—and yet, the house still doesn't feel right. Why doesn't it feel like *home*?

If you asked me to give you a short answer to the question, "What will make a house be *my* perfect house?" I would have to say this: Everything should just seem to be in the right place. Unfortunately, the word "seem" is pretty vague. So it follows that the characteristics that will create *Your* Perfect House are subjective, and the concepts are sometimes difficult to grasp. These are the immeasurable, unquantifiable aspects of architectural design.

These issues relate to emotions and to other sorts of perceptions that can't be described in feet and inches. It's a little harder to get your arms around the concepts we're going to talk about in this lesson, which may be the reason many books about designing homes do not even attempt to discuss them. But they are vital for you to be aware of so you can be a full partner with your architect in the design of *Your* Perfect House.

Let's discuss some basic architectural principles, and I'll try to show you how architects attempt to incorporate these principles into their designs. When all of these principles and concepts are added together, the house created by employing them will convey a wonderful, intangible, hard-to-describe feeling that it is truly a home.

Sequential Progressions—Our Minds Seek Order

As we saw earlier, human beings love to make sense of things. That's just our nature. Our minds, from childhood on, are always trying to find order and reason in the world around us. This desire for order results in a dislike of sudden changes and abrupt transitions. We don't like to go from silence directly to eardrum-shattering noise. We can't stand turning on a bright light when our eyes have adjusted to the darkness. There has to be a gradual transition, a segue from one thing to another. It's the same when we enter a house. We are most comfortable if the journey from the public spaces outside the front door progresses through a thoughtfully designed sequence of increasingly more private spaces,

eventually ending at the most private spaces. This sounds more complicated than it needs to be. Essentially, we are not comfortable stepping through the front door and directly into the living room. We dislike having the door to the master bedroom be located in the foyer.

Compare that public feeling you might have when standing outside your front door with the extremely private sensation you experience sitting in your master bedroom. These are totally different types of spaces, even though we might only traverse forty or fifty feet—sometimes even less—from the front step to the master bedroom. Yet, within that distance, we've made a substantial change, sort of a quantum leap, in the way we feel about our environment. We have made a transition from the most public to the most private space in the home.

A well-designed house offers a clear and comfortable sequential progression from public spaces to private. There should be no abrupt shift from public to private. The staircase itself represents another demarcation between relatively public and private spaces. Think about where it should fit and how public or private you feel it should be. Do you want to "connect" your foyer with the bedrooms? I have many clients who prefer a less public placement for their stairs.

If you prefer to think of things in numerical terms, you may want to assign percentages of "publicness" and "privateness" to the spaces in your program. For example, the covered porch outside the front door might be 10 percent private, 90 percent public. A stranger can step onto the porch to ring the

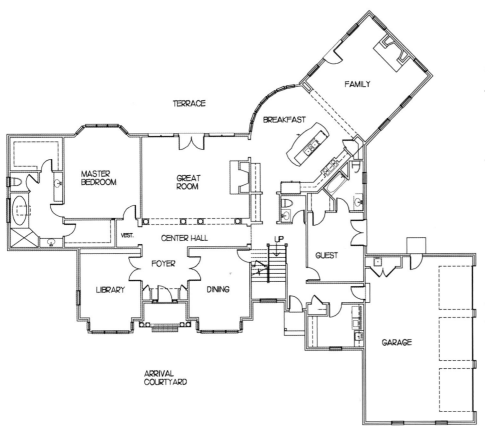

Two formal rooms, the dining room and the library, symmetrically flank a formal foyer in the "public" portion of this plan. As one moves through the house toward the informal rooms where the family actually "lives," the formality of the plan dissolves, even to the point of a quirky angle that responds to the direction of the view into the woods behind the house.

Note how the addition of a small vestibule between the central hall and the master bedroom provides one more step in the gradual transition from the public nature of the foyer and the very private nature of the master bedroom. Many house plans omit this gracious element in the name of reducing square footage. The actual cost is often a jarringly abrupt clash of public spaces to private spaces.

doorbell without an invitation. The study or library in your house might be considered 70 percent private and 30 percent public. You may choose to invite only your family and close friends into this room. After ranking the spaces, you'll have a good idea of the proper sequence they should have.

Designing Spaces

Architects don't simply design houses. We design spaces. The house is merely the enclosure and definition of those spaces, both inside and outside the house. We think in terms of spaces more than objects. I'll try to show you a little of the way architects think when they design spaces.

Let's start with the idea of an open field. An open field, of course, is a gigantic space. What defines this huge space? Horizontally, the distant hedgerows and surrounding trees; vertically, the clouds or blue sky. Obviously, this space is enormous. A human being would feel dwarfed standing in a field that seemed to go on forever. It may be attractive from an aesthetic point of view, but it's not the most comfortable of places for a human being. There's nowhere to hide. There's nowhere to feel secure. Architects would say the "scale" of the field does not match the "scale" of a person. It could be an exhilarating space to be in, especially on a beautiful spring day, but it would not be an appropriate place for us to live or to even have a picnic. We might feel a little too alone.

Now place a single tree in the middle of that gigantic space. All of a sudden, the space around that tree is different. The tree actually controls a certain distance around itself. It creates an invisible zone, a smaller space within the giant space of the field. Once you step within that zone, you will feel a sense of connectedness to the tree. You are no longer in an empty field. Instead, you define where you stand in relation to the tree and its overhanging branches, since you are in its "zone." Its shade provides a great place to spread out a blanket and have a picnic.

Let's now move from the gigantic field with a single tree to Washington, D.C. Think about the Washington Monument. The Washington Monument is surrounded by open land. When you turn the corner onto the National Mall and see the Washington Monument for the first time without any intervening buildings and begin to walk toward it, there will be a point at which you'll feel you are within the monument's "zone of influence." There will be some invisible but perceptible line of demarcation that, once crossed, places you within the space defined by the Washington Monument. Because the Washington Monument is so tall, the space it influences is considerably greater than the space defined by the tree in the meadow. It also will

not be as psychologically comfortable, either. Although the man-made monument controls and defines this space, it is still not a space on a human scale.

This same phenomenon of space being defined by an object, natural or man-made, carries over into the world of indoor spaces as well. We feel that same sense of minor discomfort if we are all alone in too big an indoor space. If we go to a nearly empty restaurant, we are more likely to sit in a booth, near a wall, within the "invisible zone" the booth creates than sit all by ourselves at a table out in the middle of the room. We'll probably sit somewhere in the vicinity of the few other people in the restaurant, but not right next to them. Most of us are just not comfortable with completely undefined open spaces,

If you were going on a picnic in this meadow, where would you place your picnic blanket? Probably somewhere near the tree would be my guess. The tree "defines" a space within its vicinity, a space that is of a comfortable scale for most people. Although being out in a broad and seemingly endless field might be exhilarating, it is not a place to linger and rest. Rooms and spaces in your house should acknowledge this principle of appropriate scale.

even in the cozy atmosphere of a nice restaurant. We derive a certain sense of comfort when we're close—but not necessarily too close—to another person or object.

It's not just people who feel this way. Have you ever noticed birds sitting on a telephone wire? They will space themselves at a certain distance from each other. You'll rarely see two birds sitting too close to each other. They have a sense of just how much "personal space" they need. We humans mirror this trait when we stand close to people. From culture to culture, the size of our comfort zone may vary, but everybody knows when they feel comfortable standing next to a person and when that other person is standing too close. We take offense, we might feel threatened, and we are uncomfortable

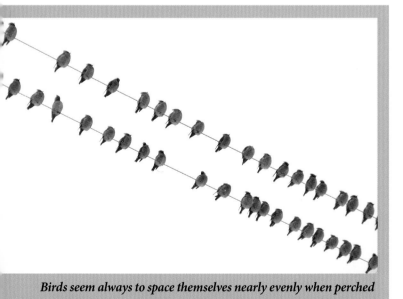

Birds seem always to space themselves nearly evenly when perched on a telephone wire. Might this be a response to a sense of personal space? Human beings do this, too. Do you find yourself leaving an empty chair between you and a stranger when you sit down in a waiting room or an airport? Most of us do. It's that sense of being too near or too far away that determines the size of comfortable spaces. It is not simply a matter of whether the furniture fits or not.

when someone enters our personal space, regardless of how we might define that space. We are constantly subconsciously defining ourselves in terms of how close or how far we are to a person or object in whose "zone of influence" we find ourselves.

How does all this relate to building a house? Everything that's true about a solitary tree in a field or the "zone of influence" that the Washington Monument creates or where a person sits in a restaurant also applies to the way spaces work in houses. Architects seek to create spaces that are physically comfortable for the kinds of uses to which they will be put. A dining room with too high a ceiling is uncomfortable. It just seems too vast for the human scale, especially when one is seated at a table. A master bedroom may look grand on paper because it is so huge, but even a super-king-sized bed can get dwarfed by too large a space, and the result is a room that is uncomfortable for sleeping.

The same thing is true when you're deciding where to place furniture within a room. If you put a sofa and two chairs in the center of a living room, everybody feels comfortable. But if you push each of those pieces of furniture just three feet farther apart, no one would want to sit and talk in that room. The comfort zone has lost its integrity because the subconscious bonds between people have been overly extended. The people in the room are no longer in the same "space."

When we design houses, we are actually creating spaces within those houses that will work for the people who will be living in them. This is what a good architect is trained to understand. This is what he should have a sixth sense about. What will the spaces feel like? What size is right? What shape and character is best?

Controlling Scale—Keeping It Human

A room is a stage for human activity. Rooms become important because of what happens within their boundaries. Because the rooms in a house are meant to contain human activities, they should necessarily be sized to match the intended use and therefore always maintain a human scale.

Many cultures use the human form to measure the layout and construction of their buildings. In Bali, builders use a unit of measurement called the *depa asta musti*. It is a measurement based on the home owner's body, derived from the distance from fingertip to fingertip of his horizontally outstretched arms (*depa*), plus the distance from his elbow to the tip of his middle finger (*hasta*), plus the width of his fist with the thumb extended (*musti*). These measurements are recorded on a bamboo pole that then serves as the yardstick for laying out the site and the house components. Japanese houses were laid out based on multiples of the tatami mat, the traditional woven mats used to cover the floor. These mats were used for sitting and sleeping. As such, they automatically related to the size of the people. These systems of measurement guarantee that a house will reflect a human scale.

Our English system does this to some degree, as well. Inches, feet, and yards are based on human fingers, feet, and paces. Over the years we have lost some perspective on the relevance of some of these units of measurement. Try to measure things around you and heighten your sensitivity to the sizes and scale of rooms and spaces that seem right or wrong.

Architects always want to create spaces that match the function for the users. Let's say that Joe down the street has a dining room that's 14 by 16 feet. Fred wants to build a house that will be "even better" than Joe's. Fred might say, "Hey, I don't have to have a 14-by-16-foot dining room. I can afford a room that's 20 by 24." After all, isn't bigger better? Not always, I say.

The problem is that Fred will end up with a very awkward, uncomfortable room in which guests won't enjoy dining. The furniture will be the wrong scale for the room; even a long table and large dining room chairs will appear too small. Think about hotels that place restaurants in their multi-story atriums. The space is soaring. There's no way guests will feel comfortable sitting at a table where the ceiling is a hundred feet above their heads. What do hotel owners do? They bring in ficus and palm trees in order to define the height of the space on a more human scale. They create a psychological ceiling. The trees define a space, and the space develops a better scale.

Bigger rooms may create a "Donald Trump" effect and may make a statement about the owner of the house, but they may not provide a sense of comfort or security for the people who actually live in that house. You may want to have a large room for entertaining, a great room/family room/living room, where you can entertain a group of your friends. But if you want to flip on the TV or read a book, you're not likely to head for such a huge room. It's easy to feel dwarfed by one's surroundings. Instead, you would more likely head to the library you created, which would probably be a smaller and more welcoming space for one or two people.

Think about it. What's the most popular room for people when they just want to hang out? It's often the kitchen, which is not nearly as large as the dining room or the living room and often is subdivided by an island or breakfast nook. But people tend to head for the coziest space in the house, wherever they can find it. Remember that cozy and intimate are positive words about a house. No one ever misconstrues them to mean, "They ran out of money and made that room too small."

The point is that when it comes to house design, sometimes the concept of "less is more" can be a truism.

How to "People" Spaces

When I was a student of architecture at the University of Virginia many years ago, a visiting architect and lecturer named Donlyn Lyndon gave a memorable lecture about how to "people" spaces. His talk may have been the most important thing I have ever heard about the psychology of architecture. He used the word "people" as a verb. To "people" a space, Mr. Lyndon said, is to make for a space comfortable for human habitation. His thesis was that we all perceive cues in spaces that let us know the space is meant for people.

The first concept Mr. Lyndon shared with us about "peopling" spaces is to introduce elements on a human scale—objects and features that relate to the physical size of human beings, thus making people feel comfortable in the space. These might include columns proportioned to relate to the scale of a person, mimicking the presence of other people, or garden walls that are the proper height to serve as benches, indicating that someone could sit there at any time, or windows subdivided into panes sized to the proportions of the human head and shoulders. When you want to create a human scale, you must avoid monumental forms and overwhelming heights. Massive sizing can create a grand impression, but such forms lack the suggestion of human habitation. They just don't feel like places where people live comfortably, and they do not convey the impression that human beings are anywhere nearby.

Another "peopling" feature is what Mr. Lyndon called "windows of appearance." These are windows of a scale and proportion that hint at the possibility that a person could appear behind them at any moment. These would be windows that are not so huge that they no longer match the "scale" of a human being. A famous Florentine architect of the fifteenth century, Leon Battista Alberti, said that a good measure of a window is that two people can have a conversation beside it. It's a shame we tend no longer to think of things in this anthropomorphic way.

Shutters can support this concept of potential human appearance. With shutters, there is the constant possibility that someone could appear and draw those shutters closed. After all, shutters don't operate automatically—they need a human hand to open and close them. Wherever a person is needed to operate something, it suggests subliminally that a person might be nearby, waiting to do something with that object. In the case of shutters, this suggestion persists even if they are not actually operational.

A third way to "people" spaces is to create places for planned and unplanned human interaction. Places for planned interaction might include a table and chairs arrangement or a seating group in a living room or on a deck. Unplanned places might include a crossing of paths, creating an area where you might accidentally encounter another person, or a balcony overlooking an attractive scene where someone might linger to enjoy the view. By contrast, think about an open terrace or a patio with no walls or plantings other than grass and no furniture. What's missing? Is there any clue that anyone will ever use that terrace? No. It is barren, and it is not a "peopled" space. It would feel more like that endless, treeless field I spoke of at the beginning of this

The size of this window, as well as of the panes of glass and especially the shutters, because they need a human being to operate them, make this a "window of appearance." It is easy to imagine someone appearing behind the glass.

A Juliet balcony need not be ornate to convey the "peopling" message. Imagine how much less human interaction would be implied if this bedroom had a pair of windows instead of the French doors with the Juliet balcony.

lesson. Now, imagine the addition of some plants surrounding that open terrace or patio. Let's say some of those plants are five feet tall. Add a stone wall about seat height along one edge. Next, place a group of chairs in the middle of the patio. Can you see how much more comfortable this terrace has become? It's not just that there is now a place to sit. The character of this space changes because there are cues that imply human occupancy.

You can readily imagine yourself sitting in one of those chairs or on top of the stone wall. Other people might join you, since there are seats for them, as well. The "people-sized" plants keep you company in a sense, since they resemble people in scale. This terrace has now become a "peopled" space, and it is therefore a much nicer place to be.

Mr. Lyndon then added a fourth method of "peopling" spaces: the inclusion of materials that indicate a human hand contributed to their creation. Hardwood floors, tiles, carved wooden details, hammered metal door handles, and fieldstone walls all need the hands of people—artisans—in their creation. The sense that a person has worked on a given item makes us feel the presence of that person. In quasi-psychological terms, you might say that the aura or essence of the craftsperson is still part of his or her creation. Whatever the reason, it's true that we feel less alone in the presence of materials that have been shaped by a human hand.

Have you ever wondered why people go to craft fairs and fall in love with hand-painted, hand-formed, even irregularly shaped items? In

A custom-designed and hand-built kitchen cabinet is not only beautiful, but it also connects us to the people who built it. The cabinets are built with rift-sawn white oak, and the flooring is cumaru, a wood also known as Brazilian teak. Rift-sawn oak was chosen for both its quality of being authentic to the contemporary craftsman style of the house and cabinetry and also for the compatibility of the grain with that of the cumaru.

Antique, hand-hewn oak beams accent the ceiling of this kitchen, defining the space and also linking this new house with the past.

home design, tiles are a great example of this tendency. Why do many of us love handmade tiles more than those that are crisp, clean, machine-formed, and perfectly cut? It's because we feel a subliminal connection to the person who created the handmade tiles, even when that person is unknown to us. That connection with another human being makes the handmade tiles feel more appealing, and the space where they have been installed feels better to us as well.

We have a basic instinct to make our lives easier, so it seems counterintuitive to include items in our homes that require maintenance. But many so-called maintenance-free materials fall short in terms of aesthetics, not so much because they're unpleasant to look at or touch but because if an item is never going to need human attention again, it somehow feels inhuman to us. By contrast, materials that have to be painted or have been recently cleaned communicate that someone has been there recently—and someone will be back again to take care of them later.

In short, "peopling" spaces is really just the use of materials and elements to indicate that a space has been occupied by people in the past and will be occupied in the future. It is a matter of tailoring the space we create to the human scale.

At the University of Virginia, the columns that line the colonnade and define Thomas Jefferson's famous "lawn" are on a human scale, each about the width of a human torso. Granted, they are taller than a person, as they help hold up the roofs of the buildings, but their width helps to relate them to a human frame and shape. If you've ever walked the colonnade, you know you never feel alone. Gently tapering shafts of plaster, about the same width as human beings, are your companions every step of the way.

If you would like a modern example of these principles, consider a shopping mall and try to remember walking through one in which all the stores are rented and one in which some or many are unoccupied. It just doesn't feel comfortable—it may even feel dangerous—to walk in a mall where the stores aren't all rented out and the display windows are empty. In one such semi-occupied mall, an enterprising storeowner convinced a mall operator to let him clean up the vacant stores near his occupied business and put mannequins in the windows, thus creating a sense of a human presence. People became more comfortable walking past the empty stores to get to his store. His business, not surprisingly, did much better.

That is why people cherish that "lived-in" look. They find themselves drawn to items that require

One of the many colonnades that connect the buildings of Thomas Jefferson's fabulous University of Virginia "academical village" provides an intimacy of human scale. Other humanizing features are the height of the edge of the water feature, which implies that people often sit in this place, the properly-sized balustrade that caps the colonnade, and the human-proportioned arch to the left, which reinforces the notion that this is a place for people.

maintenance or show the presence of a human hand in their manufacture. If you set out a newspaper, a chessboard, artworks, knickknacks, or family photos, you have "peopled" the space. Family photos, in particular, are more than just a reminder of what your family looks like. Those faces are now your companions in the room, even when you are otherwise alone.

Fieldstone fireplaces are especially attractive, because we have the strong awareness that someone put that beautiful fireplace together with his or her own hands. Even the size of the stones evokes a psychological connection with another human being because the stones are usually limited to those a person can lift and put into place. A stone wall built of massive stones that can only be moved by a machine might be impressive, but it will lose that handmade human quality.

Inlays and tile floors offer the same sensibility. Built-in kitchen cabinetry conveys the same comfortable feeling that communicates a human being created it. We want that sense of adjacency with other people. We gain the sensation that a level of care was taken in the object's creation. And care continues to be taken in the object's upkeep. Again, it's all about a human presence. The biggest objection to modern architecture, I think, is that it's too cold and machine-like. The best compliment we can give any item is to say it's handmade or handcrafted. Why do we like "less perfect" better than perfect? Because "less perfect" connects more readily with other people.

Sapele, a wood species reminiscent of mahogany, is inlaid in a white oak floor. When placing inlays, plan ahead so that they do not end up covered over by furniture or rugs. Open rooms, such as foyers and hallways, are good places for inlays.

What makes a house "feel right"? It's the sense that the spaces and the objects within those spaces are right-sized, appropriate for the uses to which they will be put, and on a human scale. It's a house for people. That's the secret of making a house feel inviting, both to its inhabitants and to their guests. That's the secret of making a house a *home.*

Certain shapes have become so embedded in our culture that they carry with them recollections that bind us together.
—CHARLES MOORE AND DONLYN LYNDON

MAKING "ROOMS" IN AN OPEN PLAN

For centuries, houses consisted of individual, well-defined rooms. Life was formal. Guests were entertained in the parlor. The kitchen was hidden. Dining rooms were enclosed and separated from the kitchen. In the sixties and seventies, all that began to change. Open living grew in popularity. Formal living rooms effectively became showrooms for the good furniture and gradually disappeared from newer house designs. Dining rooms were only used for Thanksgiving and Christmas. Family life migrated to family rooms, and gradually family rooms became great rooms that were open to the kitchen and breakfast room. Now, even the formal dining room is giving way to a more multi-purpose dining area that can serve both casual family meals and host dinner parties with friends.

This wide open living serves the needs of the modern family, but recently I've seen a yearning among my clients for some architectural and emotional definition to these rooms while still maintaining the open "communication" between the spaces. The question arises: How can you define the "rooms" while still preserving an open concept? Here are a few tricks you can employ to do just that.

1. Change ceiling heights and shapes. For example, you might maintain a flat ceiling in the kitchen so there is a top to the cabinetry and you have a place to install recessed lights for good illumination in a space that needs it most. Then create a shaped ceiling in the dining area. This will create a centering focal point above the table and give the space definition. Next, you might put a tray ceiling in the great room. These ceiling shapes are effectively "drawing lines in space" and imply edges that cause our minds to perceive the limits of the space without the use of actual walls.

2. This effect can be further enhanced by placing columns at the transition point between the spaces. The columns would be spaced far apart, nearly to the side walls. A dropped beam might be placed above the columns. The effect is to imply the end of one space and the beginning of the other while maintaining nearly all of the openness. The columns are also an opportunity to add detail to the architecture.

3. At the transition point between rooms, an eight to ten inch wide floor board of a darker wood species could be installed to further separate the spaces.

In fact, all of these tactics are essentially "drawing lines" in the otherwise wide open spaces. But psychologically, you will be separating the spaces while leaving them physically open to each other.

On a very steep site, an arrival courtyard was created to welcome guests. The well landscaped courtyard behind the brick wall provides a near view from within the house, thus maintaining privacy when visitors arrive. This difficult site was worth the effort to capture the long-distance view from every room in the house. The horizon line is just visible above the ridge of the house.

Lesson Three

UNIFYING THE DESIGN

"But Mom, I am one of the greatest architects of all times, I'm the founder of modern architecture, I can't do a traditional house for y…. Aouch! Okay, okay."
—ATTRIBUTED TO LE CORBUSIER

We've seen that when everything fits together in an orderly way, a house feels right. That special feeling of things being appropriate and "in place" makes a house truly a home. Let's discuss some important and useful organizing devices, strategies, and methods architects use to create a sense of unity in a home design. These concepts, tools, and techniques help the architect achieve the overall goal of making your house feel right and making things seem to be located exactly where they belong. Some of this discussion may seem a bit esoteric. Much of it falls into the topic architects refer to as "architectural theory." You might want to think of it as some of the magic you feel in good architecture.

The Axis

The axis is the classic and most widely used concept in organizing a house design or any other building for that matter. An axis is basically a centerline. In a house, a primary axis might be an unseen dividing line down the middle that balances one room on one side of the line with a matching room on the other. There is a symmetry or an implied symmetry to the axis. The human body is organized in an essentially symmetrical way around—or "about," as architects like to say—a central, vertical axis. We have a right eye matched or balanced with a left eye on the opposite side of the axis. When we have a single feature, such as the nose, it lies on this axis and is itself symmetrical in form. In the case of limbs and other paired features, one on the right side of the body is balanced by one on the left. Have you ever wondered how odd we would look if both of our arms were on one side of our chest? Lopsided and off-balance are not terms meant as compliments. Our sense of order clearly prefers balance around a central axis. I suppose that's why a flounder looks so odd with both eyes placed on the same side of its head.

The same principle holds true for houses. The easiest way to design a house and to achieve an organizational balance is through the use of strict symmetry around a center axis. We are comfortable when we walk into a house and see a room on the left with a companion matching room on the right. They balance each other out and thus provide a sense of order.

An axis line might begin at the front door, continue through the foyer or entryway, and then proceed onward to a room centered on that axis. That axis might end in a large window looking out to the back of the house and the view beyond. Everything relates to this central axis, just like the central axis of a human face. Even the view is brought into the organization along this axis line. Each of the spaces and elements along the axis is like a bead strung on a necklace. There is a purposeful connection between each of them. The axis unifies the house, which is to say it gives the house a sense of unity and clarity that is instantly recognizable to everyone who experiences the house.

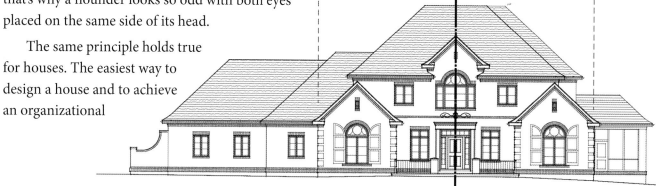

This house utilizes a strong, central axis to compose a formal elevation for the primary mass of the house. Portions of the house that are beyond the formal, symmetrical center can be shaped as necessary for the function without compromising the strength of the symmetry.

Architects utilize axes repeatedly in building design. The central axis may be the primary backbone of the design, but you may turn a corner in a house and find a new axis or centerline defining the center of a crossing hallway. More rooms and elements might be placed neatly on either side of that line in a psychologically orderly pattern. The cabinets and appliances might be arranged around a central axis in the kitchen with the kitchen sink and a window defining the centerline. Look around your current house and you will begin to see one axis after another.

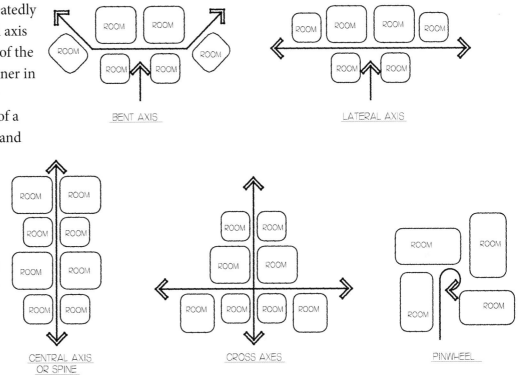

An organizing concept is critical to the success of a floor plan. These five, Central Spine, Cross Axis, Pinwheel, Bent Axis, and Lateral Axis, are just some of the many concepts that can lend order and composition to your house.

Utilizing axes is really not done to make the house more efficient. Axes are used to organize the parts of the house and thus make the house feel right. It's worth mentioning here that efficiency isn't always the primary goal of an architect. The desire for efficiency is often directly related to the budget. There are often good, sound reasons to let a design become less efficient. For example, in a larger house with a larger budget, you may want to "splurge" and enjoy a little extra separation between the master bedroom and the rest of the house. In doing so, you might choose to expand a hallway that leads to the bedroom enough so that there is room for some furniture in it or to fit a window on one wall. It might become a small "room" instead of simply a corridor. The lighting in the space could change from brighter to darker to brighter to darker as you walk along it. This improves the design of the house, changing the nature of the trip to and from the master bedroom suite to a richer, more dramatic experience, and that is a positive from an aesthetic point of view. The house is not more efficient, because it's likely you've added square footage, exterior surface size to the building, and a window

Arched openings, thick walls, side windows that provide pools of light, and a staircase as a focal point in the distance help this long, axial corridor become much more than just a hallway. The owners' magnificent art collection completes the transformation of a mere corridor into a grand gallery.

to create this more interesting space—and these other things were added without a practical, utilitarian purpose. But you love the effect.

Is it worth it? That is always the question for all of the decisions you will make as you design *Your Perfect House*. You are really the only person who can answer that question. Your architect and builder can help you, but many of these decisions come down to value judgments where you need to balance your needs and desires with your budget. Maximum efficiency isn't the be-all and end-all when you're designing a house.

The only time inefficiency can become a real problem is when the design loses its cohesiveness, when things become disjointed and seemingly out of place. The "giant economy-sized" floor plan isn't always best, even if you can afford it. When it feels as though it takes too long to walk from the kitchen to the dining room or between other rooms that should have been closely connected, the psychological connection is lost, and the design fails. The house loses its proper scale and proportion and becomes less human. It's not a people place any longer. There is no reason this has to happen, though. Even in exceptionally large houses, the spaces and relationships of spaces must maintain the qualities that make a house a home.

By creating alcoves to the sides and providing plenty of wall space for artwork, what could have been simply a hallway leading to the master bedroom has become a delightful nightly journey through an art gallery. The distant door to the left of the sculpture is the master bedroom door.

Although this house is quite large, the sense of appropriate human scale is maintained by keeping the rooms well proportioned and providing windows on two walls in most rooms.

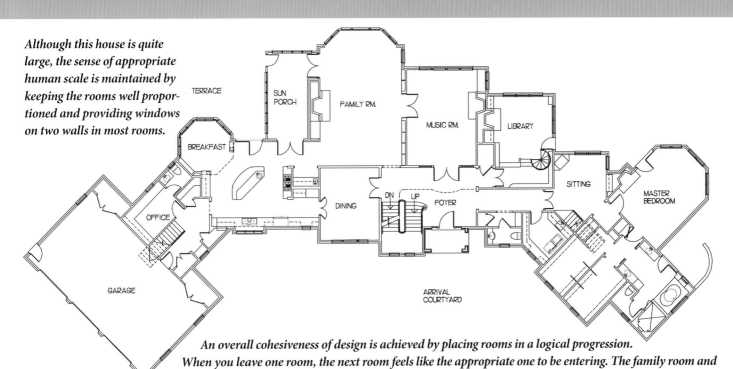

TERRACE

SUN PORCH

FAMILY RM.

MUSIC RM.

LIBRARY

BREAKFAST

OFFICE

DINING

DN   UP

FOYER

SITTING

MASTER BEDROOM

GARAGE

ARRIVAL COURTYARD

An overall cohesiveness of design is achieved by placing rooms in a logical progression. When you leave one room, the next room feels like the appropriate one to be entering. The family room and music room fireplaces align on the same axis, thus tying the rooms together despite the separation by French doors. A high degree of privacy is gained by separating the master bedroom suite with a transition hallway.

Symmetry and Composition

We spoke earlier about the usefulness of creating an axis or a central spine for the house. The fact is symmetry can cause a design to become static and less interesting. And it can become a crutch. I often joke that architects should love it when the client demands a symmetrical design because they only have to design half a house! Design one side and then photocopy that side in mirror image, and you have the other side. Symmetry has its place. It adds a sense of grandeur and formality to a building. It has served an important purpose in the past in the design of monumental buildings and will do so in the future. But symmetry is not the only way to create balance and harmony. Let me suggest to you that asymmetry—not having everything on one side be the mirror image of things on the other side of the axis—may actually be more

This house is not symmetrical, but it is composed. Notice how much more active your eyes are when viewing the façade. This principle is the essence of composition in paintings as well as in many examples of splendid architecture.

appealing to the eye. If you think about it, there really is no great painting, no acclaimed masterpiece that is perfectly symmetrical.

Even the *Mona Lisa* is asymmetrical! Why didn't Leonardo da Vinci paint her looking straight ahead, right at the viewer, like a mug shot? Because it would have been cold and static. Da Vinci knew that our eye would get "stuck" and not involuntarily move through the painting. Instead, Mona Lisa is slightly turned, making one side of her face a little more prominent than the other. The scene is dynamic and alive. Without the effect of the slight imbalance, the *Mona Lisa* would be just a picture of a girl. With the composition, utilizing asymmetry, it is a masterpiece.

Great pieces of art are all about balance as opposed to perfection and symmetry. Two small objects might balance one large object. A line that draws your eye in one direction might offset a feature that catches your eye elsewhere. My point here is that we should seek a good composition and not get stuck on symmetry. When we are thinking about house design, we want to think more about balance than about making sure everything is in lockstep symmetry across a given axis. Good composition offers so much more.

This front elevation does not depend on symmetry for composition. The asymmetry encourages the eye to move more, creating a sense of vitality and interest. The composition is achieved by balancing the visual weight of each side. This creates a dynamic yet orderly appearance. Note that the two flanking wings angle forward, something that an elevation view like this cannot show effectively.

The Golden Mean

It's almost impossible to discuss composition in architecture without referring to the golden mean, also called the golden section. Readers of Dan Brown's mega-bestseller *The Da Vinci Code* may recall the description of that formula in the book. As a brief refresher, the golden mean is the classic organizing and proportioning method or formula for art and architecture. Its theory tells us that human beings are most pleased when things are in a proportion of 1 to 1.618. In other words, if a window is one unit wide, it should be 1.618 units tall in order to be the most appealing to human eyes. The golden mean was used prominently in Greek and Roman architecture and is just as useful in today's world. Indeed, the same ratio that was applied to the design of the Parthenon is likely to aid your architect in the design of your new home.

The golden mean offers a comfortable proportion with which to work, but it's not the only comfortable proportion, so you don't have to feel locked into it. The intriguing thing about the golden mean, about placing things at this scale, is that it just about always works. Consider it a safety net for proportions.

A bit of architectural trivia: A classic and pervasive curved shape used to this day in crown moldings, wood trims, and other architectural details is the "ogee" curve. The "ogee" is a direct derivative of the golden mean. This curve originates with the Greeks and shows up in the columns we place on our front porches, crown moldings we place in our living rooms, and even the curves that are shaped into the aluminum gutters outside our houses. Who knew that ancient Greek classical design would eventually create aluminum gutters?

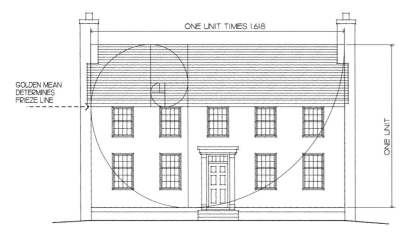

GEORGIAN STYLE HOUSE WITH FRONT ELEVATION BASED ON PROPORTIONS OF THE GOLDEN MEAN

DIAGRAM OF THE PROPORTIONS OF THE GOLDEN MEAN

The golden mean or golden section is the basis for many of the proportions used in classical architecture. It is found in formal residential styles like Georgian, Adam style, Italianate, and Greek Revival. Notice how the proportions are used to place the frieze board, thus marking the top of the wall and the bottom of the roof. The nautilus, curving volute (spiral) created by these proportions is intrinsically appealing to the eye.

A veranda across the entire front of this house adds one more layer in the transition from outdoors to indoors. The pale blue ceiling color is traditional in the homes of the south-eastern United States. It is derived from the Gullah culture and others of African origin who settled in the low country of the Carolinas and Georgia. Known as "haint" blue, a corruption of the word "haunt," it is said to ward off evil spirits, ghosts, or "haunts." Regardless of its alleged mystical powers, it also provides a soft reflected light to the interior of the house.

53

Breaking the Pattern for a Reason

The regularity of the day-night cycle provides a structure for the variability of the weather from day to day. We sense this constant despite the inconsistency of the climate. Once a pattern is understood, variations can bring joy without creating anxiety.

I mentioned that asymmetry adds a touch of intrigue and excitement to the design of the house. The acclaimed Swiss modernist architect Le Corbusier was a master at establishing a strict and rigid pattern and then breaking it, but always for a good reason. In his famous Villa Savoye, he laid out his modernistic cube on top of a grid of columns called *pilotis*. Then, he purposely moved one of those columns to place the staircase where he wanted it to be. Breaking that pattern draws the eye and increases the importance of that staircase. Everything else must comply with the grid, but the staircase is even more important than the grid, so the grid must give way to the staircase.

I'm not suggesting that you want a modernist box on stilt-like columns, like Le Corbusier would have designed as *Your* Perfect House. However, the effect of establishing a pattern and then purposely violating that pattern to signify importance is a tool that can be used with great effect. For instance, in the traditional Georgian or Palladian style house design, there is a central rectangular mass or box, which is the main part of the house. On either side of that might be two wings, other portions of the house looking almost like separate buildings. These wings are connected to the main body of the house by connecting structures called hyphens. The front door would naturally sit in the center of the whole arrangement, straddling the center axis.

In one house I designed in this style, I didn't need all the floor area that one of the wings of this classic arrangement would yield. So I eliminated one side wing, making the house the size the program dictated. To deal with the imbalance, I placed the front door purposely off-center. When the house became asymmetrical, the importance of having the front door in the center of the central mass was reduced. It actually made more sense to move the front door slightly off center. The result was that the front door now seemed appropriately placed with other elements and its arguably quirky, off-center location reinforced its overall importance. You want to be careful, though. Break the pattern only with powerful and important items. Avoid arbitrary anomalies or else the basic pattern will not be understood, and the impact will be lost.

Angles and Curves

Just about all the elements in buildings are rectangles and straight lines. After all, nearly all of the materials we use for construction are made that way. Plywood is rectangular, lumber is straight. Squares and rectangles are easy to fit together without wasted space in leftover corners. Consider adding angles and curves to spice things up and draw attention where you want it. When you add an angle or a curve, you're adding a dynamic characteristic to the design. As you view that special shape, you will think, "Why is that there? What's the reason for that?"

This semi-circular breakfast room is a perfect place to enjoy a meal or read the Sunday paper. It provides a 180-degree view of the garden, allowing one to sit essentially "outdoors" while maintaining the warmth and comfort of the indoors. Throughout the day, while the sun moves across the sky, patterns of light play across the furniture and floor.

Let one room join another at an angle to open up the intersection between the two. If you have an "L" shaped plan, see if you can bend the angle from 90 degrees out to 135 degrees, making the courtyard larger and less confined. It's fun to look at examples of interesting uses of angles and curves in houses and analyze what effect, both positive and negative, has been created. Of course, not all angles and curves improve a design. If you have a preponder-ance of angles and curves, you might lose the effective contrast that makes these features interesting in the first place. Instead, the angles and curves become part of the basic vocabulary of the design rather than the exception. The result could simply be a chaotic collection of odd shapes and angles without the critical organizing concepts we discussed earlier. A little seasoning is good. Too much and you'll spoil the recipe.

Changes in Height, Light, and Scale

It's often effective and dramatic to vary the height of the rooms in a house. One of the most famous architects in history—and arguably *the* most influential—the Italian architect Andrea Palladio utilized contrasting scales and ceiling heights like the virtuoso he was. He skillfully led you through low ceiling spaces that squeeze down the scale before he treated you to the explosion of wonderfully tall rotundas and great halls. He knew if he let you simply step from outdoors directly into his grand space that space could not compete with the vastness of the limitless space of the outdoors. Instead, he controlled your point of reference. He made sure you had first experienced the small-scaled space of the vestibule and then used the contrast as you entered the large space to make the greatness of the high ceiling and large features even more powerful.

A section view of the Villa Rotonda illustrates how the smaller spaces of the vestibule contrast dramatically with the soaring heights of the rotunda.

Plan view of the Villa Rotonda. This building can be approached from all sides, thus the four formal entrances.

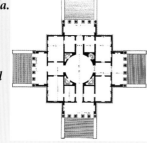

Similarly, changes in natural light—variability in brightness—can be used to an advantage as you design your home. Consider where pools of natural light pouring into your house might add to the feel of a room. It's a great treat to find natural light penetrating deep into a building in places where it is unexpected.

Changes in scale can be quite effective and should be thought through, as well. For example, your front foyer might have a large curving staircase, the purpose of which is to look monumental. When we are in the presence of elements like these, we feel somewhat smaller. After all, we use our own human size to "measure" the size or scale of the world around us. It follows that when we walk into the library beyond the grand stairs, we might sense the contrast because the scale is tighter and smaller. The parts or architectural elements of this room might be closer to our human size, and the room will possess a scale that is less than the scale of the grand foyer.

Always pay attention to issues of scale, as I've discussed earlier. Many mistakes are made here, resulting in rooms and spaces that feel uncomfortable. You might never ever really know why. As a simple example, you wouldn't want to locate a massive fireplace in a small, intimate library. It would dominate the room. Similarly, a two-story-high family room would require that large fireplace, because a small one would look out of scale. Take care to assess each feature in each room and ask yourself and your architect whether the scale is right.

This large bay window (right), stretching from floor to ceiling on two floors, extends the interior space outwards, while also providing panoramic views. The divided lites in the windows are large enough not to interrupt the view, yet they aid in maintaining a humanistic scale to the room within.

Changes in Materials

The very materials we use to build your house will send subliminal messages about the nature of the spaces we design. For example, a foyer might feature a marble or stone floor. Again, in the foyer we are making a transition from public to private. A marble floor makes for a formal welcoming area, a transition from outdoor space to indoor space. But we don't feel like lingering too long in a room with a marble floor. It is not a tactile material. It says "durability." It is cool and hard to the touch. It reflects sound. It is appropriate to a greeting space where feet might be wet and people are taking off their coats.

When we wish to sit and read a good book, we feel a yearning for a more intimate, private space. Here we want something comforting, something warm and soft, something quiet. So we go to a living room or a library where the warm wooden floor with a rug will provide a dramatic contrast to the stark marble entryway. The change in flooring will make that room feel as though it is a place where you want to stick around for a while. The materials play a key role in conveying this message.

Large blocks of marble give this foyer an appealing presence. Marble and other hard surfaces are perfect for spaces like this where people do not sit and linger. They signal a space where people move through, a concept reinforced further by the visually active diagonal pattern. Through the archway to the left the flooring changes to hardwood with a rug. That is where the softer furniture is located. It is a space for sitting, conversing, or reading. Keep in mind that even the finishes contribute to the message each space will send.

The Joy of Focal Points

Can you think of a hallway that's dark and depressing and that you hate walking through because it feels like being in a bad mood? We all have had this experience. Please avoid this in *Your* Perfect House. There are remedies. Hallways don't have to be this way.

How about adding a window or a work of art that's beautifully lit or a niche with a sculpture in it? If you place this kind of design element at the end of the hallway, then, when you first step into the hallway, your eye and your consciousness will be transported to this attraction at the far end of the hall. You will no longer be aware of walking those twenty feet. Your "awareness" will already be at your destination while your feet might be said to be catching up with your consciousness. In a sense, the hallway no longer exists. It becomes merely the presentation of the special feature. The lighting here is critical, and natural light or a view to outdoors is always best.

It's wonderful to tie in attractive focal points and little surprises around corners, in hallways or other spaces. Ask yourself again and again, "When I step in here, what do I see? Where is my attention drawn?" You'll see opportunities, and your architect should know what to do with them. These are the kinds of things that should be thought through and evaluated. These are the things that separate a house that is just shelter from a house that is *Your* Perfect House.

Special details, such as the wood inlay of this library desk, add delight and interest. The cabinetry is built of sapele. A dark stripe of ebony surrounds a veneer of sapele pomele. The grain of sapele pomele is uniquely rippled, evoking the look of leather or crushed velvet.

Just Say No to Avocado

A simple word of caution here. Try to separate passing fads from good, solid, timeless design. Styles come and go, but the principles of good design persist and transcend style. The qualities we have been discussing, such as composition, progressions of spaces, use of an axis, and "peopling" spaces, are all critical to making any house of any style live properly. These qualities and characteristics are the foundation of all styles, and they contribute to a quality of timelessness.

Often, when clients think about employing a nontraditional approach to home design, they worry that the house will look dated or inappropriate as the years pass. They want to make sure that their house

An interesting play of light shining through an arched top window, out of sight to the left, provides an ever-changing highlight that draws the eye through the arched opening to the foyer beyond.

Drawing on classical proportions, this cast limestone entry façade give this house verticality and an "Old World" dignity not often found in newly built houses.

design is not simply a passing fad but will look wonderful forever. Of course, there's nothing wrong with employing classical, tried-and-true proportion, no matter what the style or vocabulary of the house may be. The key is to think of a house like a classic car or a timeless fashion design. You can look back on the designs we refer to as "timeless," such as a Jaguar coupe from the sixties or a Mercedes convertible from the seventies, and you know you're looking at a classic. The proportions are still right, the lines move the eye, and they convey the same feelings they did when they were new. Even though these designs echo a place in history, the quality comes through. It's the same thing with a house. A well-designed house is like a well-designed car; the particular "look" of its design may recall an era, but the house will never really go out of style. Right now there is a great deal of interest in craftsman-style houses. The "look" is still appealing even though the handcrafting that created the style has faded away.

Nostalgia is a strong and valid emotion. Just be careful of confusing fads for style.

Don't Be a Slave to Examples

Often, I will propose a solution to a design problem, and the client will say, "But I don't know anybody whose house looks like that." By now you've done your homework and chosen your architect carefully. If you have a relationship of trust and positive rapport with your architect, this is the time to trust. A solution you might not have seen before may be the best way to go. A good architect creates things; he doesn't just copy things. Take advantage of his ability to create.

Here's an example from my own experience. I designed a house in Hawaii in the Balinese style. In Bali the traditional house is actually a collection of disconnected pavilions that are grouped together into a "compound." The warm climate precludes the need for total enclosure. The individual pavilions usually have thatched or *sirap* (ironwood) shingled roofs with one separate roof over each separate, disconnected pavilion or *bale*. And these pavilions usually don't have air conditioning. This is a charming concept, this assembly of individual pavilions, but there are some practical, western considerations that we had to merge with the authentic Balinese concept of "house." First, we needed to make the house become one connected space so the owners can lock the doors when they aren't home. Security is an issue even in a paradise like Hawaii. Second, a thatched or *sirap* roof in Hawaii over each unconnected space isn't practical—it would be eaten up by the elements in no time. Third, we wanted to allow the residents to go from pavilion to pavilion even when the

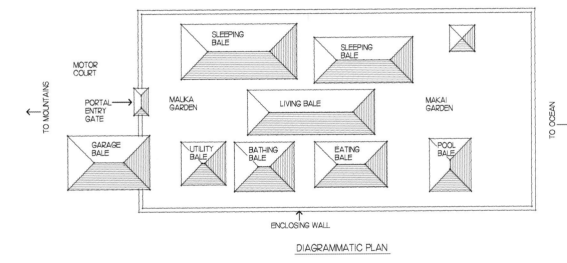

DIAGRAMMATIC PLAN

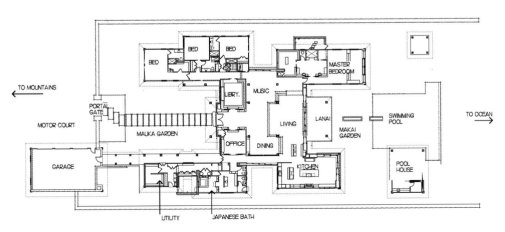

SCHEMATIC FLOOR PLAN

A typical Bali house is composed of detached **bale** (pronounced ba-lay). A **bale** is a simple pavilion-shaped structure, often covered with a thatched roof. Each **bale** has a unique and individual function. These pavilions are situated within an enclosing wall. Entry to the compound is through an ornate, wooden doorway within a roofed, stone, or brick framing structure.

In this project built in Hawaii, we wanted to preserve the concept of the individual **bale** arrangement, shown in this diagram, but everyday practicalities also had to be considered. Primarily, we needed to be able to lock the house for security, and we did not want to have to walk in the rain from **bale** to **bale**. The **bales** had to be connected to form one house.

The diagrammatic plan at the top shows the simplified concept of the room arrangement. The schematic plan beneath it shows the actual floor plan that was created based on the Balinese concept.

rains come. And finally, there has to be a way to provide central air conditioning. This is Hawaii, after all, and it can get hot and humid.

There simply is no house we could find that could serve as an example for the solution we needed to employ here. Even the so-called Bali-style houses being built in Hawaii were really nothing more than western houses with some Bali details slapped on. We wanted more. We wanted to capture the spirit of Balinese architecture and not simply the affectations and decorations of the Bali-style. What I tried to do was understand the overall design concept that my client wanted. What was unique to Bali? What made Bali-style different from Asian, Polynesian, or Hawaiian styles? It was my job to preserve these principles and combine them with the necessary, functional demands my client needed and wanted. Ultimately, everything had to be appropriate for the design. Remember what I have said is the hallmark of good design: Everything should seem right and appropriate.

*Although this is actually a single structure, there is the appearance of several **bale**, or pavilions, embracing the front garden and capturing the feel and scale of Bali.*

In this case, instead of designing a traditional western box-type house, I preserved the geometry of the traditional Balinese house. The living spaces occupied the central pavilion. The kitchen and eating functions were placed in another pavilion. The master bedroom suite was in still another pavilion. Ultimately, eight pavilions were created, each with its own simple, hipped roof to preserve the same feeling that is so important in a traditional Balinese house. Other "linking" roofs were then designed to connect the separate pavilions, uniting the group into one total building. Even when linked this way, the individual quality of each pavilion was retained, thus giving the house the appearance of being several buildings at once, with the connecting roofs being designed to be less obvious. The home still "feels" like a Balinese house, but it provides for privacy and allows the homeowner to lock the door.

This design cost the client more because it has significantly more exterior surface area in order to accomplish these goals. But the extra investment was worth it to the client because she got the house of her dreams.

As you might imagine, I think it's best to find an architect who can look at things from a different viewpoint. Find one who can place himself in the context of the style and the period of the type of house you want. One of the happiest moments in my career was when a client told me the local historical society in his small Pennsylvania town had knocked on his door to tell him they wanted to list his house on the Registry of Historical Buildings. They wanted to know how old the house was. From the look of the house, the historical society figured that it must have been at least 260 years old. It was located in a development of two-acre lots in which all the houses fronted the street. On this lot, however, a little stream angled across the property, so I designed the house to relate to the stream, not the street. A meandering gravel drive completed the effect of making the house look as though it had been there years before the development had been built around it.

Additionally, the client agreed to have made, at slight additional expense, special reproduction windows, historically correct details, and foundation vent grilles with vertical bars or dowels, all of which match the features of houses built in that era. The authentic details did not stop at the exterior. We placed a door three steps up from the bottom of the staircase in what would ordinarily be considered an awkward position. Beyond the door, the staircase continued to the second floor. Many early American houses were designed in this manner to prevent the heat from the first-floor fireplaces from migrating upstairs. In another interesting touch, we arranged the windows in a seemingly haphazard pattern, because a miller's house or a farmer's house in the pre-Revolutionary Delaware River Valley would have no formal window pattern. Windows were placed where they were needed, responding to internal needs and not a superimposed concept of how the exterior façade should look.

Nearly a clone of the historic John Chad house (ca. 1725) in Chadds Ford, Pennsylvania, this house "fooled" the local historical society when members guessed its age.

Imagine the historical society's surprise when the homeowner informed it that the house was only eighteen months old. That was a really fun moment for me—we hadn't set out to embarrass the historical society, which does a great job of preserving our architectural treasures. But their confusion is proof that the sum total of many seemingly minor details and design elements had combined to give the house the appearance of authenticity. Together, these features created the ambiance we were seeking.

Other architects might criticize this house by saying that there is nothing particularly authentic about it and that an architect today shouldn't be replicating buildings from past eras. I say, why not? Why should we have to listen to somebody else's rules? Truly good design transcends contemporary style. There is also freedom within any style to be inventive and even whimsical. Don't let the fear of doing something you have never seen before become a straitjacket that constrains your design.

Two other houses that presented similar intriguing design challenges come to mind. In Connecticut a client had me create a 3,500-square-foot addition onto a 300-year-old house.

The side and rear of our "John Chad" house (left) are new creations and not at all like the side and back of the original. In emulation of the architectural style, we placed windows in odd but appropriate locations, thus maintaining the integrity of that style. I am particularly fond of the placement of the attic window, necessarily offset to miss the brick chimney, and the tiny springhouse window in the basement.

One wing of that particular house, the part the owners fancifully called the "new addition," was more than two hundred years old. This house, once owned and lived in by the famous American artist Eric Sloane, was charming and beautiful, but it really was something of a "dollhouse," as my clients called it. The front door was only six feet tall, there was no bedroom that even resembled a modern-day master bedroom, and it lacked the bathroom conveniences we now expect. My clients had always maintained the integrity of the original house admirably, even retaining the true, non-electrical chandelier in the dining room. What they needed was an addition that preserved what they cherished but met the needs of space and convenience for a contemporary family.

The challenge for me was not to ruin the house, which is located on a beautiful piece of property, with an overwhelming new design. The additions I designed are placed so that they stand back from the original main house. The garage, an intrinsically bulky element, is practically buried, so it doesn't compete with the view of the 300-year-old main house and the 200-year-old "new" addition. The main part of the house has retained its prominence, preserving the look and feel of the classic house it is, even though it now contains the additional square footage necessary to make an old house into a modern home.

The central red portion of this house is the original building. I did not add the skylights. That was done by the famous American artist and preservationist, Eric Sloane. The larger red portion is what the owners refer to as the "new addition" since it was added merely a couple of hundred years ago! The red portion to the far right is the new living room. The shortest red portion to the left is another new addition, and the large gray structure, partially sunken into the ground, is the new garage with a complete master bedroom suite upstairs. These newest structures were carefully scaled and placed to diminish their bulk and prominence so as to preserve the integrity of the original house.

Along similar lines, a client in Maryland told me, "When you're done, I don't want anybody even to know that you've been here." I decided his comment didn't mean he didn't like me. I took it to mean he wanted the addition to his charming house to look like it had always been there. As with the other projects, the analysis necessary here was to decide what made the house unique. What gave the house the character its owners felt but couldn't actually verbalize? The most prominent design feature was a veranda, a roofed porch that wrapped around the entire house. It was the thread that tied the other rambling rooflines together. I made that the primary focus of the addition. We extended the veranda so that it wrapped all the way around the house, including the new part, and all the new roofs we added matched the proportions of the existing roofs on the original house. The design was so successful that the house appeared in a special edition of *Better Homes and Gardens*. It proves the point I made earlier: The greater the challenge for the architect, the more interesting the ultimate result will be.

But My Builder Says He Can't Do That

Everyone on your construction team has a role to play. Your builder may be exceptionally skilled and knowledgeable in construction matters, but his role is not necessarily answering those "what if" questions. Your architect is the person who deals in concepts and possibilities. Your builder is the person who turns those concepts into physical reality. As such, your builder will be focused on getting your house built right, on budget, and on time. If you ask the builder to do something that is different from the way he normally does things, he might initially object by saying that he "can't" do it or by telling you it is a bad idea. His answer could mean that what you've asked for might actually be impossible, or it could mean that your builder doesn't really "want" to do it. He might object because it's something he hasn't done before and is unsure about how to do it or because he feels his subcontractors might object. He might be worried about warranting the work, or what you asked for might add time and complexity to the project. This can be the case even when you tell the builder, "Just do it and bill me for the additional time."

I work with many fine builders who say, "Just tell me what to build." They really don't want to be placed in the design role. That is the role of your architect. Yes, your architect deals with the nuts and bolts of construction, understands structural design, and knows a lot about building materials and techniques. But he also sees the world through the eyes of an artist. He deals with issues like, "What makes this place so charming? What will the natural light be in this space? What's the best height-to-width ratio for this room? How do I preserve these elements and their character as I improve function?" The builder, on the other hand, worries about the quality of the workmanship, scheduling the work, and the costs of construction.

Sometimes your architect might see an innovative way to make a desired result happen. When he works with your builder in a solution-finding mode,

The cupola atop the roof ridge throws natural light deep within the kitchen below. It also adds an interesting feature to the roofline.

some very pleasing and unique results can occur. These types of discussions often get the entire construction team engaged and emotionally invested in the work. Good ideas crop up, sometimes from the subcontractors, the builder, or the architect. I have seen many cases where something that looked to be impossibly hard to do turned out to be a compelling feature in a house. I also have learned a lot from the people who are actually doing the work, things I never would have learned from books.

Here's an example. Brick masons love to do straight brick walls. They generally charge by the square foot, and straight walls go up quickly. This is where the profit is. You finish the work, you get paid, and you go home. Along comes the architect with all his "brilliant" ideas. "We could make this more interesting if we took a couple of courses of brick and had them project out slightly and then created a nice shadow line. Or we might have a pressed-in, recessed basket weave pattern at a forty-five degree angle." The brick mason looks at the architect as if he has two heads and thinks, "How many bricks will I have to cut for that basket weave?"

But they talk about it a while, along with the builder. The mason offers a suggestion based on the size of the bricks he is laying and improves the pattern. He is starting to see this new feature as something more interesting to build than a plain, straight wall. The builder suggests a colored mortar in the new brick pattern area to distinguish it from the rest of the wall. The architect likes the idea and agrees. At the end of the day, the brick mason is happy that he built something a bit different and interesting, the builder takes pictures of the wall for his new brochure, the architect wants copies of the photos for his portfolio, and the homeowners have a signature feature for their home.

The best way to get great work done on your home, of course, is to visit the building site and compliment the workers. Don't get in their way, don't suggest changes, don't grandstand, and don't quarterback. Just compliment them and thank them for their hard work. We all like to be appreciated, and we all like to gain gratification from our hard work.

This contemporary house was placed at a forty-five degree angle to the view-line. Large corner glass windows in the great room provide an exciting and unexpected view from within. The angled bay windows to the left and right are arranged to capture the view for the breakfast room and master bedroom.

INTO THE DEPTHS OF DESIGN

"The architect who combines in his being the powers of vision, of imagination, of intellect, of sympathy with human need and the power to interpret them in a language vernacular and time—is he who shall create poems in stone."

—LOUIS SULLIVAN

An interesting aspect of human psychology is that we tend to like things more and find them more appealing if everything about those things is not obvious the first time we experience them. This is certainly true in music. For example, we might hear a song on the radio for the first time that catches our interest and decide we like it. Then the next time we hear it, we hear a lyric we didn't catch the first time, or we might notice what the piano or drums are doing in the background. A special harmony emerges that we missed before. We hear more and more and understand more and more with each listening. Sometimes, the longer it takes for a work of art to reveal all of its subtleties to us, the more fond of that thing—whether it's music, art, dance, or architecture—we become.

Art, literature, and music that have this quality are called "multivalent." It has several levels of meaning. It can be understood on several levels. The more you dig into it, the more you see and understand. This is a hallmark of finer art, music, literature, and architecture.

Well-designed houses are, of course, architecture. Multivalence is a quality we should expect in them, too. The first thing we notice about any house is the overall design and the look and general characteristics of each room, hallway, stairway, and other spaces inside and outside the house. As time goes on and we have a chance to experience the house more

times, however, we begin to notice some of the small details that escaped our attention when we were merely experiencing the "big picture." These wonderful details might be the elegant wood joinery, the distinctive cabinetry, or the design that has been inlaid into the floors. It's easy to see that some of these types of details might have escaped our notice the first time around. There was simply too much to see. We couldn't take it all in at once, and now we can see the details. But if the design is good, there will be many more subtle realizations, such as a growing appreciation of how the house flows from room to room or the special quality a room takes on

A half-round breakfast room encloses a space that allows people to enjoy the garden while remaining in heated and air conditioned comfort. The covered veranda controls the amount of sunlight that can pour into the living spaces on the south side of this house.

when a group of people occupy it. A sitting area, such as a terrace off of a master bedroom, might seem to possess some added and indescribable calming effect when you sit there watching the sun set at the end of a hectic day.

These experiences of delayed aesthetic "gratification" and a growing understanding of the building design make us feel even better about the house. I sometimes get letters, calls, or emails from clients who have just noticed something special about their homes six months or a year after they've moved in, and they want to say how much that detail or quality, which is often something we thought through and discussed, has added to their enjoyment of and delight in their new homes. They tell me how happy they are that we spent the time and had the foresight to make the design better than it had to be. Naturally, I really like those days.

Sometimes the things we notice have a lot to do with the time of day we're experiencing a room. Spaces change from morning to evening and with the seasons of the year. It may take a few months before all the subtleties show up in a given house design. For example, you might be in your favorite spot in a house on a summer day and notice the way the indirect light pours through the windows while the intense direct sunlight is shaded by a purposefully placed overhang. Then one Sunday morning, you get up early, you amble into that same room and sit in your same favorite comfortable chair. But now it's winter, and the sun is lower in the sky. As you sit there reading a book, you feel the sun warming you up as it comes from a shallower angle that misses the overhang. You hadn't really expected or noticed this before, but you love it. Maybe you remember your architect telling you why he was designing the rooflines in this particular way, and now you're glad he did.

"God Is in the Details"

The famous architect Ludwig Mies van der Rohe made that statement, and it is absolutely true. There is a spirituality of quality detectable when you are in the presence of carefully performed design and labor. When the work around you in your home offers evidence of a high level of care on the part of the builders and craftsmen, you experience an elevation in your sensation of the quality of the entire space, not just the specific materials that were used and the skill with which the work was done. The more carefully the work is performed, the better we feel about the spaces we inhabit.

One way to offer a sense of quality and unity of design is to repeat a given detail throughout a house. It's very much like a musical theme performed and then followed by variations. For example, you might have an affection for a diamond shape, a stylized sea turtle, a dogwood flower, or some other shape. Maybe there's something with some family significance, or you might have some other shape you simply like. Think about using this thing as a subtle theme that threads and repeats through the design, reappearing in unexpected places. What if you walk in the front door and you see that diamond detail inlaid in the floor, maybe in a different species of wood? Later, you walk into the kitchen and see the diamond shape repeated in the glass doors, but here it might be smaller. Then you notice that in the living room, over the mantelpiece on the "mantel breast," diamond appliqués or on-lays (details carved and applied on top of the primary wood frame) are used again. Someone would have to be very observant to notice all the repetitions of the diamond motif the first time he or she is in the house, but eventually that person will. The presence of that repeated theme throughout the house will give it a sense of unity and completeness that a mass-produced house can never offer.

You can achieve the same feeling of unity with colors. Ideally, we don't want to have a jarring change of colors as we move from room to room. A basic palette of color or a signature material could be this same kind of unifying element rather than a shape. The marble tiles in the foyer might be made of the same material that surrounds the hearth in the living room. Small pieces of the very same stone might be used as accent pieces in the tile floor of a sunroom or kitchen. A material that when used as an entire floor might be very formal could become a sophisticated accent in a less formal location when a less formal tile surrounds it.

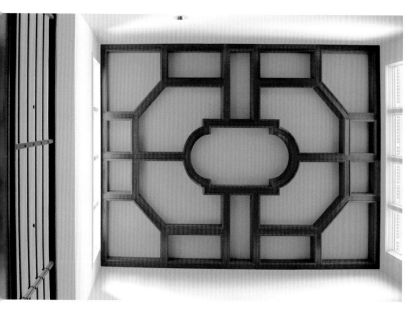

Walk into the two-story center hall of this house and look up. Surprise! The ceiling is adorned with a wonderful pattern of natural beams. The central, oblong shape is repeated throughout the house, albeit in different sizes. It recurs in the front door raised panels, wood details in the kitchen cabinets, and details in the mantel.

PINEAPPLES IN OLD VIRGINIA

Have you ever noticed pineapples carved into the pediment above a front door in a Colonial or Georgian house? Have you wondered what pineapples could possibly have to do with early American or English life?

This particular icon had come to be the symbol of the highest level of hospitality. In early centuries, fruit could not survive the long journey from the tropics, so people had to grow their pineapples in their own greenhouses. A pineapple plant must grow for two years to produce one fruit; then, the plant dies. Because the fruit was so hard to grow, only the most highly honored guests were served pineapple at dinner. Architectural ornament has meaning, and the "meaningful" pineapple was transformed into an ornament to grace the entrance of the home, signifying that all who passed through the doorway were indeed highly honored guests.

Elegant sapele woodwork with sapele pomele veneers creates a grand but clean and contemporary appointment in this house.

Details used elsewhere in the house are repeated in the mantel design.

Thick Walls, Solid Home

One of the hallmarks of the great houses of the past is the sense that they were solidly built. A house built of brick or stone was deemed a better house than one built of wood framing. Stone walls are thick whereas wood walls are thin. Thick walls give classic houses a sense of security, stability, quality, and beauty. Most new houses today have thin walls, which are less costly to build. They give up the aesthetic of the thick-walled, substantially-built houses of the past. But it's entirely possible for you to introduce the feel of thick walls into the design of your new home and thus provide a delightful sense of solid construction, care, and thoughtful workmanship.

A typical wood-framed wall is normally built with two-inch by four-inch wood studs. This is called a two-by-four wall, and it is plenty strong enough to support the floor and roof above, but a wall built like this is only 4½ inches thick when finished. If there is no doorway through a two-by-four wall, you might never notice this thinness. If this is the thickness of the wall between the foyer and the dining room, however, visually it might feel flimsy. In an old stone house, this wall might have been more than a foot thick. Why not make your wall that thick and not just the minimum width that is necessary? I do this all the time, and it imparts a sense of true solidity. It's not hard, and it's not really all that expensive, either, to build thicker walls. Doing this uses up some square footage, but this extra space can be put to good use. You could have recessed bookcases or display cabinets on one side of the wall. The doorway opening could have raised panels in the door jamb and oversized casing (trim) around it, adding to the importance of this passageway. These kinds of details provide that nostalgic sense of security, craftsmanship, and care on the part of the architect and builder of the home.

Thick walls with paneled jambs give this house a substantial feeling and make a statement about the transition from room to room.

Adding thicker walls doesn't mean that you have to have a traditional house. A contemporary house with thicker walls, combined with very clean lines and an unfussy feel, can lead to a wonderfully handsome result that still gives you a sense of security. Nearly everyone responds favorably to a house that has the weight of quality and doesn't look pre-fabricated or temporary.

I said earlier that a well-designed home presents everything exactly where it should be. The level of detail I'm talking about here, in which you find wonderful surprises months or even a full year after you've moved into your new home, completes the job. There's really nothing better than sitting in your house and discovering something special about it long after you have moved in. It provides a pleasing gratification for the long and sometimes arduous journey from the initial thought of building a house to the final reward of living in that house.

Provide Something Unexpected

When you're designing *Your* Perfect House, don't get stuck in a rigid mindset. It's okay to have some fun. Eccentricity can add a pleasing tension. You might want to create some spaces in your house where your guest might turn a corner and say, "Look at that!" It could be the placement of a piece of art or a move from dark to light or some other unexpected pleasure. It often happens that these elements are the last things to be added to the overall design for the house. I suppose these kinds of things are sort of like dessert in that way. For example, recent clients asked me to see if I could find a place for a meditation

Thick wall openings are taken a step further in this elaborate woodworking. Notice how the wide opening with a free-standing column defines the dining room without closing it off from the great room.

room. They wanted a cozy place that enjoyed the fabulous view their mountainside property provided. They did not want this quiet space to be obvious. On the contrary, they wanted it to be secret. The house was already under construction with the roof already completed, but it turned out that there would be some space in the attic over the master bath and closet area that could be put to a far more interesting use.

By "lifting" a small portion of the roof and adding a couple of triangular windows, I created for my clients a meditation loft—a space upstairs, above their private bed and bath areas, with an upholstered bench, pillows, and, not least of all, a forty-mile view. This space would have otherwise been unusable attic space. Instead, the loft adds a very special feel to the house. Intriguingly, it's not that easily accessible. You have to take a little journey to get to it. The staircase is not where you might expect it, and it's not readily accessible from anywhere else in the house. You might think the inaccessibility of the meditation loft would make it less attractive or desirable. Actually, the opposite is true. Because it takes a little bit of effort to get there, once you've reached it, you really feel you have arrived somewhere special.

And, indeed, you have. It's the same instinct that dictates why so many of us travel long distances to take vacations when there are perfectly good vacation destinations within a short drive of our homes. We like taking vacations to faraway places simply because those places are not easily accessible. This way, we get to tell ourselves and others, "It was worth the trip." Designing such "vacation spaces" into your home doesn't require much in the way of extra expense, but it provides lasting benefits to you and to everyone who visits the house.

Other surprises you might include could be much less extravagant. Maybe it's a tiny Zen window that gives a glimpse of a garden. Maybe it's a splash of color at the end of an ordinary hallway. Maybe it's a secret passageway. Who among us hasn't wanted one of those?

This structure we call the portal gate separates the motor court from the front garden at this house in Hawaii. Guests park their cars with no view of the front door of the house. They then step through the portal gate, finally seeing the house entrance ahead, but they still must make a journey across the stepping stones through this water garden. In true Bali style, "arrival" becomes a major event.

The Importance of Nostalgia

When you are planning your house, one of the most important questions to ask yourself is this: "Of all the places you've ever been—your house growing up, other houses you've visited, places you have dreamed of—what was the most wonderful and memorable space you can recall?" It might have been a cozy room in your grandparents' house. It might have been the private terrace of a hotel room that opened onto the Caribbean. It could be the day-dream of a fantasy private spa or the warmth of a gigantic stone fireplace. It might not be possible to recreate in precise terms the layout or design of the room from your grandparents' house, and it may not be possible to have the Caribbean lapping at your

When descending this three-story staircase, you are treated to an unexpected but intriguing view down through the open stairwell.

My client specifically wanted a narrow, enclosed porch reminiscent of the kind she enjoyed as a child. This one is designed to appear as if added on to the exterior of an existing house, despite the fact that it was built along with the original construction. This nostalgic element is clearly a signature feature of this wonderful house.

feet if you live, say, in the middle of Iowa, but it is possible to recreate the comforts and the serenity of those spaces in your new house.

The item about which you feel nostalgic may not even be a space or a room. It may be the design of an object in the home, such as the glass doorknobs in your grandmother's apartment or the pushbutton light switches in your great-grandfather's house. Today, thoughtful designers have created pushbutton light switches that meet electrical safety codes so

Who doesn't like window seats? Nothing conveys cozy comfort and human presence better than a windowed alcove with a cushioned seat to curl up upon with a good book. Notice how the owners wrapped the Toile de Jouy wall covering into the space, even carrying it up the sloping portions of the ceiling.

Another client requested an old-fashioned, wood-framed, glass storm door just like the ones she remembered from her family home. She said that in the wintertime she loved how her family would open the solid front door and let the sunlight pour through the glass into the front hall.

they are no longer fire hazards. The mantra of the sixties applies fully here: If it feels good, do it.

The design element that you like the most may also have to do with the ceiling of a space, such as a groin vault ceiling, a smaller version of the type of ceiling you might find in a cathedral. The acoustics are quite lovely in that sort of space. If that's what you love, tell your architect, and tell him right away.

I would suggest the notion that wherever you eat most of your meals is the most important place in your house. It might be the dinner table or it might be the breakfast table, depending on the pattern of your family. When you are considering the design of your eating spaces, think back to the kitchens you remember from your childhood or have fantasized about, and be sure to ask your architect to incorporate those design elements that make you feel the most at home. After all, this is going to be *Your Perfect House*.

Zones of Retreat

When I was studying architecture, my thesis project was the design of a psychiatric hospital. I felt drawn to the idea of creating a psychiatric hospital because I did my undergraduate work in psychology and had always been interested in what makes our minds work and how our minds relate to the spaces that surround us, what architects call the "built environment." One of the things I learned while studying psychology was that everyone, not just someone with a mental illness, needs a place where they feel safe. A place like this is where we hide when things get too stressful. It's our place to shield ourselves from the demands of daily life. I call it our "zone of retreat." This was critical to the design of the psychiatric hospital because mentally ill people are more sensitized to stress and have a stronger reaction to their environments than do those of us who are considered mentally stable. But stable or not, we all need zones of retreat—areas where we can close the door behind us and feel completely safe.

This concept translates into home design when you think about the idea of creating a home with places where each individual can say, "This is my space. This is my private zone. I don't have to feel vulnerable or even accessible when I'm in my private zone." Too often, houses are designed without such personal, private spaces or rooms that are appropriately sized and scaled for the convenience of one individual. All of us need a place where we can go and shut the door. For me, it's my home office. For someone else, it might be a study, a library, a meditation room, or some other uniquely private space.

This handsome paneled library is the inner sanctum for this avid reader. He starts his mornings here with coffee and the newspaper and ends his day with a good book. In the arrangement of the floor plan, this library was positioned close to the master bedroom, a private zone, rather than adjacent to the living room, a more public zone, because of its primary purpose as a "zone of retreat."

A retreat area doesn't even have to be an entire room. Sometimes you can dedicate part of a larger room to such purposes. For example, a nice window seat can serve as a retreat even within a much larger room. A window seat gives you the sense, when you're sitting in it reading a book or just relaxing, that you are out of the bigger space. Whatever the nature of the space that makes the most sense for you, be sure to discuss this concept with your architect, so that your home provides you with just such a zone of retreat, a zone of privacy, all your own.

Ideally, your home should provide spaces of graduated size, so you can have a room where one person can interact comfortably with one other, a slightly larger room where two people can interact with two others, and then four, then eight, and, should you be in the habit of entertaining larger groups, even more people. It's best not to have all your rooms the same size. Otherwise, the usefulness of each space would be redundant. You need to have a choice of how much interaction and how many people are appropriate for a space at any given time.

The point of all this is to think through these issues in advance so you don't end up with a situation where you have to adapt yourself to your house instead of the other way around. Don't just think of rooms in terms of "uses." Think in terms of interactions and perceptions. You never want the question of how and where human interaction will take place to be an afterthought.

Flow

A house should flow like a mountain stream. Walking paths, the hallways between rooms, and the paths within rooms are like a current. They are the flow of the water. Rooms and spaces are where the waters pool and eddy, resting quietly until it is time to move on. Hallways and paths of travel, like the movement of the stream, connect, whereas rooms, like the pools along the stream, collect.

It's not so much about how your feet move from one place to another within your house; it has to do with the way your mind or psyche moves from space to space. We often hear people say things like, "I like the way this house flows." I believe this kind of comment describes the sense of a house and not just the physical efficiency of the plan. Good flow means that the rooms and spaces have a unity and psychological "connectedness" that feels like everything is in the right order. Remember, that is the quality I have said earlier is the hallmark of good design.

We have already talked about this subjective element of design. A house with good flow has no abrupt transitions. Public places do not crash into private spaces. Outdoor spaces transition smoothly to interior spaces. Things seem ordered. There is an overriding and consistent style and feel. There is a subtle expectation of the next event, and transitions are comfortable.

Gestalt psychology says that the whole is *different* from the sum of its parts. This is often misquoted as "the whole is *greater* than the sum of its parts." The analogy often used to explain the concept is a brick wall. A brick has one identity.

When combined with other bricks to form a wall, it is not merely a collection of individual bricks. Instead, it is a brick wall, something distinctly different from just a stack of the bricks that are its parts. Your house design, flow, or overall feeling of unity and appropriateness of the design is the "whole," and it is different from the sum of all of the qualities of each space. I would suggest you pause occasionally as the design of your house progresses and take stock in where the design is going. Try to get a feel for the Gestalt that is the overall impression of the house. Try to see it as a unified whole. Ask yourself, "How will this house feel?" This is a bigger question than asking, "Are the rooms the right size?"

Light

Light, as both a contrast and a focal point, is a critically important organizing concept when it comes to designing houses. When pools of daylight stream into a room or hallway, the light itself changes the character of the space. When you walk down a hallway, your eyes are naturally attracted to the next pool of light you see. It is important to consider light as a design element that is no less important than the shapes and sizes of rooms.

As you look through the plan your architect has created, ask yourself and your architect, "Where will sunlight spill into the house?" Identify the sunny spots, the shady spots, and the dark spots in the house to make sure you have sunlight in all the right places. A valuable concept worth noting is that people are most comfortable in rooms that have windows on two sides. When light comes into a room from two different directions, the room will be naturally lit for a longer part of the day. The room will also "connect" more effectively with the outdoors because you can look out from the room in two different directions. These rooms simply feel better. The psychological feel of the room is improved. There are times when other considerations in a design may carry a greater importance, making it impossible to put windows on two walls of every room, but wherever you have the opportunity to do so, you should include this feature.

Rooms that have windows on two walls, like this bedroom, are not only brighter without added electric lights, but they also simply feel better.

Sometimes the second source of daylight can be achieved by introducing natural light into the center of the house. In my own house I have a couple of skylights placed above an interior staircase. Even though the skylights are way up on the roof of a two-story house, cheery daylight filters down, illuminating the central hall on both floors.

Artificial light can fill in where natural light does not enter the picture. The types of artificial light are subtle and varied and can be used to maximum advantage by a method known as "layering." In a dining room, for example, it's possible to have four or even five different kinds of light. First, you probably have a chandelier (magnificent or modest) over the dinner table. If so, the light fixture itself becomes the focal point of the room while also providing illumination. Since a chandelier may still leave dark spots on the dining room table, you'll look to a second form of artificial light, recessed lights in the ceiling, to throw "infill" lighting onto the table top, particularly near the ends where the light from the chandelier cannot reach.

A third kind of lighting in the dining room might be additional recessed lighting at the room's perimeter, shining on the buffet or on artwork on the walls. As a fourth type of lighting, you might have wall sconces, which are light fixtures attached to the walls. Sconces are often more decorative than functional, but they do contribute to the overall play of light in the room. Finally, you can put in a fifth artificial light source operating in harmony with the previous four. Concealed or cove lighting around the trim close to the ceiling and maybe in a raised tray

section of the ceiling can give the room a warm glow. Now you have one room with five different and complementary methods of providing light and each light source potentially controlled by dimmer switches to allow you to adjust the intensity.

At a dinner party, when the guests arrive, the room may be lit up with all five different kinds of light contributing to the sense of beauty and drama. During the meal, the host and hostess might choose to turn down the indirect lighting and turn off the sconces. Now the light becomes more focused on the dining room table and more dramatic as everyone sits down to eat.

Such changes in lighting levels can be accomplished easily today with the automated lighting control systems now available. These systems can reset all lighting to a programmed preset level. Each setting is called a scene. Lights are dimmed or brightened at a gradual rate. For example, if you hit the button that says "Dining," it will reset the lights, gradually, to the levels you had previously programmed, as though your dining room were a stage set for dramatic activity. There is cost involved, but in a high-end house this is certainly something to be considered.

Whether you opt for five different kinds of lighting in the dining room and a fancy control system or normal lighting with switches and dimmers, the point is to make sure you are considering how a room will be lit as you design the house. A single central light in the ceiling might not always support your other design concepts for a room.

"Layered" lighting gives you full control of the mood of a room. In this dining room, there are five layers. In lieu of a traditional chandelier, recessed lights illuminate the table. Cove lights tucked above the molding edging the tray ceiling add a soft light and ambiance. Downlights on the perimeter of the room light the bowed window area and sculpture. Wall sconces flanking the artwork add sparkle and style. Finally, the large painting that anchors the end of the room is lit by an accent spotlight.

The same thing is true in the bedroom. Today's "smart house" systems can provide for lighting opportunities that were unimaginable in the recent past. Automated systems that seemed like fanciful "house of the future" concepts are now possible. One example I know of is set up so that after a certain time of night, if someone steps out of bed, a pressure-sensitive pad hidden under the carpet will sense the footstep, and lights will gradually turn on to create a lighted path with just enough illumination to guide an individual to the bathroom but not enough so as to disturb someone else sleeping in the bedroom. On the way back from the bathroom, a person once again steps next to the bed to get back under the covers. That second step on the pressure-sensitive pad under the carpet will turn off the lights. This same kind of system can allow you to "call" your house from your cell phone as you approach in your car and tell your house to set the lights to "welcoming" and also turn on the gas logs in your fireplace. The system can allow you to answer the doorbell from your cell phone even if you're halfway across the country. I suppose that eventually you can have your robotic dog fetch you your slippers and afternoon newspaper and wait by the door.

You'll also want to consider how your house will look at night. Where do you want outside lights to go? Do you want landscape lighting that sets a mood by showing off your house from the street? Do you want floodlights on your house? Or do you want more of a sense of privacy? Lighting throughout the house serves many other functions as well. You can show off books on shelves. You can create good reading light in areas where you expect to be reading a book or watching TV.

The Third Dimension

I have consciously omitted much discussion of style and what *Your* Perfect House will or should look like. Style is very personal. There are really no commandments. As your plan develops, your architect will produce the massing and overall shapes. This might require moving some portion of the plan around until it and the exterior appearance agree. This is that balance between priorities we discussed earlier. Much of the shape of the house will be determined by where the second floor rooms are placed. Just as the design of the plan is like working a puzzle, the design

of the overall house is like working a three-dimensional puzzle.

Some people find that thinking in three dimensions is impossibly challenging. If you have trouble visualizing, ask your architect to prepare three-dimensional sketches or models to help. It is critical that you understand your design before starting construction. Changes to the drawings are easy and inexpensive to make. Changes to the actual building are costly.

Here are just a few general rules for making the exterior of the house look good.

1. Strive for an overall composition.

2. Don't let one side of the house be significantly taller or more dominant than the other.

3. Keep the proportions of windows the same. In other words, don't mix windows that are vertical rectangles with windows that are horizontal rectangles.

4. Remember that the materials you use have visual weight and need to be balanced.

5. Avoid the temptation to include every great idea you ever had into one house. This can lead to the "crazy quilt" syndrome, and the design will lose integrity.

6. Provide emphasis at the primary focus of the building. Usually this is the front door, where taller elements are best located, with secondary, supportive elements flanking the central emphasis.

7. Stay consistent with the scale of the building elements. Mixing finely-textured materials with large scales and coarser elements is problematic.

8. Look at the design from near, mid-range, and far away. Examine the composition of the overall design from each viewing distance.

Ultimately, drawings and models will only take you part way toward understanding the final appearance and feel of your house. At some point you will have to make a "leap of faith" and trust that all of your planning and hard work, along with your architect's experience and skills, have conspired to create a house that is better than you or your architect could have ever designed without each other.

This house draws inspiration from the work of the great English architect, Sir Edwin Lutyens. Lutyens was an architect ahead of his time. He was an innovator and one of the first "modernists." Although many of his designs look traditional to our eye in today's world, his clean lines, simplified details, and strong forms were a departure from the elaborately ornate designs of his time.

Lesson Five

WHAT WILL YOUR HOUSE BE?

"There will never be great architects or great architecture without great patrons."

—SIR EDWIN LUTYENS

Designing *Your* Perfect House is a process. Any good design involves the consideration of many criteria and, ultimately, the resolution of these criteria in a way that maximizes each factor without sacrificing any. You won't find a set formula for accomplishing this objective, but if you come to appreciate and understand the process, you will ultimately reach your goal. This process is the means by which you will discover what *Your* Perfect House will be.

The best way to start thinking about your house is to decide what your priorities are. Some people want a house with great "curb appeal"—i.e., it looks wonderful from the street and makes a powerful statement about the owners. Other people value their privacy and expressly shun "curb appeal" in order to create the sense of seclusion that a home built farther away from the street affords. One family might want to live nestled in the woods with trees shading the house while another wants open spaces and a distant view. Some live casually and prefer an open floor plan where rooms flow together. Others desire the formality of a traditional layout with distinctly defined rooms.

Some people want their homes to be as ecologically responsible and energy efficient as possible, especially in these days of unpredictable heating and energy costs and a heightened awareness of our environmental responsibility. Others may place a higher priority on open views and seek the feeling that they're practically sitting outdoors when they're in the house. Although glass is not as energy efficient as an insulated wall, creating a greater interface with nature has a high value and may necessitate certain compromises in energy efficiency or have other design implications. The right design for you will strike a balance between opposing issues like these.

Some people want to enjoy dramatic, soaring spaces in their homes; however, such spaces might come at the expense of additional rooms that could have been built into the same volume of space on the second floor. It is possible that the space you see as dramatic for your house may strike others as too tall, echoing, and cold for their house. Once again, the question becomes, what's most important to you? What will be your objectives? What should *Your Perfect House* be?

Tall rooms need not be uncomfortable and inhospitable. In this example the room is somewhat less than two stories and topped by a dramatic, coffered ceiling. The ceiling design and the pattern of the large bank of windows break down the scale of the room to one that invites human activity. While looking at this photo, imagine if the ceiling were a few feet higher and flat and the windows were large, blank, uninterrupted panes of glass. The result would be an austere, cold space.

A harsh fact of life is that every edifice ever constructed, with the possible exception of Bill Gates's house, has had a budget attached to it. People building their own houses are willing to spend a certain amount of money, but usually they're not willing to spend every penny they have. Since cost does act as a ceiling on what can be accomplished, everyone who wants to build a house has to make choices, and it is no surprise that everyone is going to make different choices. All of this means that the best house for you is the one that takes all of your criteria and desires, including budget, and manages to maximize all of them without forsaking or ignoring any of them.

The basic rule of thumb in thinking about your new house is that anything you do affects, alters, or possibly limits something else. For example, if we put an extra window in a kitchen, we are taking up wall space that might otherwise have been used for a cabinet or an appliance. Another constraint might be the site itself. There's only so much room in any given plot of land upon which to create *Your* Perfect House. The canvas is only so big. The crucial objective of your architect is to design a home in which everything complements everything else so that you, the client, get as much as possible out of the space available functionally, aesthetically, and emotionally.

Another typical tradeoff in house design might involve the windows. Everybody loves the idea of having a brightly lit and cheery home. If, however, you have too many windows, you may wind up with too much heat or uncomfortably bright sunlight at different times of the day. Lots of windows might create too much glare or may not provide enough wall space for displaying your art collection. Design of a house, like so many other things, comes down to establishing priorities and making choices. We try adding a little more of this and a little less of that until we find the right proportions.

Another comment about the "B" word—"budget." Perhaps the most basic criterion for perfection is simply keeping the house "on budget." No matter the size of the budget, for a design to be good it should always be an efficient use of the available funds. We are familiar with dealing with this issue when we buy other things, like cars for example. A Lexus is a terrific car, and it may be the perfect one for you, but it requires a sizeable budget. If your budget is not that large, a Toyota Camry might be your perfect car. Both cars are very well built, comfortable and offer a number of options you will also have to decide upon. Selecting one of these cars over the other or any of the options, such as leather seats or the super sound system, would not be a mistake. It would simply be a matter of choosing the right vehicle, the one that meets all of your criteria, including budget. Your house is no different. The only difference is that with your house, these types of decisions are considerably more numerous. Just as we do when we buy a new car, we have to factor in how much money we are willing to spend in order to create the kind of home that will suit us best.

Why Build a House?

When people hear I'm an architect, some ask, "Why would I ever want to build a house? Isn't that a lot of trouble to go through? Why wouldn't I just want to buy a house that's already built?"

It's a great question, and it's worth spending a moment or two to consider. Essentially, when you design and build a house, you get to adjust the house to fit your needs and desires instead of having to adjust yourself to fit an existing house. It's a little like going to the clothing store and having a suit custom made for you instead of buying a suit coat off the rack that *almost* fits. Yes, the custom-made suit costs more, but you feel so good when you wear it. It fits perfectly, it looks great, and you find yourself walking taller and being happier just because you're wearing that beautiful suit.

Similarly, a house should "fit" you. It should fit your needs, your desires, your lifestyle, your aesthetic sense, the needs of your family, your aspirations—everything about you. When you design a house just for

This client sought a clean, unfussy style. This contemporary craftsman house reflects that desire.

you, the house becomes a reflection of who you are and what your life is all about, which allows you to maximize your enjoyment of life.

My clients are often people who have a very strongly developed aesthetic sense. They appreciate beauty, they appreciate art, and they appreciate the finer things in life. Designing a house is an opportunity for them to become a co-creator of a very special work of art, a work of art in which they and their families will live, a work of art that will become a legacy for future generations. These individuals know what they want in life, and they're not afraid to put in the time and effort it takes to make great things happen. This is just as true in their professional and business lives as it is true in their marriages and families. They want to achieve the best, and they succeed in doing so. Often, their new house has been a dream for a long time. It is, in a sense, the culmination of years of hard work and planning.

When you design and build your own house, you get to achieve greatness in a new sphere—the sphere of architecture. Architecture is called the greatest of all of the fine arts because it combines the creativity of sculpture, art, and design with the functionality of science, engineering, and invention. It is something to be savored. The journey to creating *Your* Perfect House should be just as enjoyable as the act of living in that house once it's built.

Obviously, a lot can go wrong when an individual starts to build a house. We've all heard what I call "horror stories" about construction projects, costly delays, mistakes, budget overruns, and the like. Be reassured that these types of things do not have to occur. The more you know about how to plan a house, how to choose and work with an architect, a builder, and the other members of your team, and the more you know about architecture in general, the more likely it is that things will go smoothly from start to finish.

A formal house is fronted by a circular arrival courtyard, lending an air of elegance the owners favored. The interesting transom windows were "borrowed" from similar windows found in one of the client's inspiration images.

HOW TO MAKE A BEDROOM DISAPPEAR

Listen to the conversations at cocktail parties in new developments and you'll hear lots of horror stories about construction. Every story-teller has a tale to top the last one. Here's the most amazing one I have ever heard. Worst of all, it's true!

A couple purchased a lot, hired a builder on a design/build basis, had the house designed, and construction started. The husband and wife lived out of state and were unable to monitor construction as it went along. They were building their home for their retirement. As the construction progressed, mistakes were made in the framing, and the builder apparently found his own remedies. Amazingly, one entire bedroom was forgotten, and the three-bedroom house turned into a two-bedroom house!

How did this happen? The victim—excuse me, I mean the homeowner—told me the builder framed the roof wrong and the third bedroom had to become a loft because the new configuration of the room would not meet the building code ceiling height requirements for bedrooms. Later, the builder discovered that he had not planned on enough space for the heating and air conditioning units, so he put them in the bedroom-now-loft, and the loft was transformed into a mechanical room. Presto! The third bedroom has completely vanished right before your eyes! Houdini would have been proud.

Problems most often arise from a lack of communication. The client may be thinking one thing while the architect or the builder is thinking something else. Honest misunderstandings and issues that never get thoroughly discussed can turn into trouble down the road. Even simple language misunderstandings can create problems. If your architect or builder uses terms and jargon you don't understand, ask him to explain matters in plain English.

Building a sample wall where wall materials, roofing materials, and even paint colors can be evaluated onsite and in larger sizes allows a much better sense of things than small paint chips and tiny materials samples can ever provide. Consider painting out larger portions of interior walls with possible colors before making final choices, too.

Poor planning or a lack of planning can create pitfalls that could easily have been avoided. The most important part of proper planning is to get the right members on your team—the right architect, the right builder, the right landscape architect, the right interior designer, the right subcontractors, and so on. We'll discuss some ways to find, evaluate, select, and work with all of the individuals so you can communicate your desires to them and ensure that they get you exactly what you want.

A common problem develops when you and your architect have one picture of your house in mind and the builder has another. But the differences between those pictures are never discussed.

Let's say you were thinking about high-end, custom-made kitchen cabinets, but after the house construction has started, you find out your builder had budgeted low-cost units into the contract. This might have happened because he knew your concerns about the "bottom line" and was also worried that, if the total cost of the house came out too high, you might back out of the project—or maybe it was just the result of foolish optimism. To keep the

ALLOWANCES

There will undoubtedly be several items you will not have selected by the time you sign a contract with your builder. This is normal. There is just too much to decide, and delaying the start of construction to allow time to pick out the appliances, plumbing fixtures, or tile is not practical. Most projects start with allowances included in the contract.

An allowance is an amount of money devoted to the cost of items that are not yet selected. Some examples of these would be kitchen appliances, plumbing fixtures, light fixtures, door hardware, tile, etc. The costs of things like these can vary greatly. A low-end refrigerator might

cost less than $1,000 whereas a top-of-the line refrigerator might cost $6,000 or more. Until you actually pick out the exact refrigerator, your builder will have no way to assign a precise value to this item on his cost sheet. Instead, he will include an allowance.

Through conversations with your architect, dollar amounts for each unselected category will be established. The sum of these estimates becomes your "budget" when it comes time to make actual selections. Allowances should be as realistic as possible. You don't want to have unpleasant surprises later. If you are likely to pick items that are at the top of the price scale, adjust your

allowances accordingly. On the other hand, if you feel you will be cost conscious in your selection, keep the allowances lower to maintain an accurate total project cost and to prevent an excessive markup from the builder.

If you ultimately spend more on the allowance items, this difference will increase the contract amount you will owe the builder. He will issue a change order to adjust the contract. If you are fortunate and disciplined enough to select everything you want and have room left in your allowance budgets, this change order will be a negative number, and the contract amount will be reduced accordingly.

numbers looking good, he trimmed money out of the "allowance" he had budgeted for cabinets. You discover this only when he takes you not to the high-end cabinet designer but to the home building center out on the highway and shows you cabinets that don't match your vision for *Your* Perfect House. This kind of thing can happen even when your builder is truly looking out for your best interests if a misunderstanding arises about the desired level of quality.

What if the builder neglected some basic design issues in the very beginning? He might have chosen a poor site for you or not thought through drainage issues or situated the house too high or too low or failed to have the house facing the right way, thereby sacrificing a great view. Perhaps the house was situated too close to the street in order to save a few dollars on a driveway, but now the usefulness of the driveway is compromised because there's just not enough room for your car to turn comfortably into the garage. Unfortunately, you'll feel that compromise every time you drive up to your home, after it's too late to do anything about it.

Perhaps the plan that was chosen shaved a small amount of space from each room in order to save money—but with disastrous unintended results. There might not be space in the dining room for the antique linen chest you had planned to put there. Or when you put the extra leaf into the dining room table, some of your guests wind up sitting in the hall. Or the bedrooms may be uncomfortably small for the size and amount of furniture they have to contain. Or it may be awkward and unwieldy to get the groceries from the garage to the kitchen. Or your

rooms are the right sizes, but for some unknown reason they aren't as comfortable as you had hoped they would be. You get the idea. There are lots and lots of opportunities for miscommunication and oversights.

In one expensive house I recently visited in a high-end neighborhood, the powder room had been placed immediately adjacent to the dining room, most likely in an attempt to save a little bit of money or because of sheer lack of planning and forethought. As a result, any time anyone uses the powder room, all of the sounds—and I mean *all* of the sounds—echo, most uncongenially, into the dining room. To save their guests from embarrassment, the owners of the house have actually had to ask their guests not to use that powder room while dinner is being served, and instead their guests have to go upstairs to use one of the family's bathrooms. Obviously, this was not the best possible design. I think the number one problem most people discover after they have moved into their custom-built homes is that they experienced false economies and did not have anyone to help them weigh the ramifications, both good and bad, of each choice and decision they were making.

The bathroom is one area in which clients attempt to save a small amount of money. For some reason I don't fully understand, "Jack-and-Jill" bathrooms—a bathroom shared by two adjacent bedrooms—are very popular. They are thought to be an economizing feature. In my opinion, this is rarely a successful solution, because by the time children reach their adolescent years, privacy in the bathroom is at a great premium, to say the least. Later, after the kids move out and those bedrooms become guest rooms and your guests have to share a bathroom, the problem is even worse. It's easier to avoid that distressing problem down the road by creating two totally private bathrooms from the start. Often the cost is nearly the same as the Jack-and-Jill arrangement, and you don't create a maze of doors. You don't have to put *huge* bathrooms in your home—you just need to put in *enough* of them.

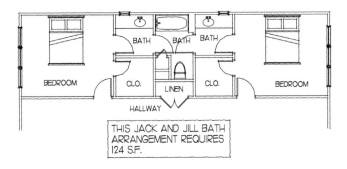

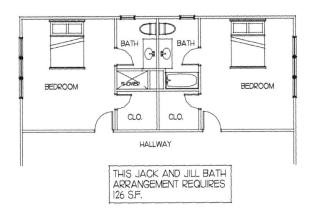

The top plan shows a typical Jack and Jill bathroom arrangement. The lower plan shows essentially the same space divided into two private bathrooms. Granted, the Jack and Jill bath yields an additional linen closet and saves the cost of an additional toilet and shower or bathtub. But the plan with two private baths saves two doors and provides invaluable privacy for the occupants.

Do I Need an Architect?

The reality in America is that the majority of new homes are not designed by architects. We are too often viewed as a luxury expense and, unfortunately, our value is not appreciated until too late. As such, many people select a builder and work out a design with him. Maybe the builder will have a draftsman on staff. Maybe he will hire an architect for you. Maybe he has a partner in a design/build firm who is an architect. If any of these scenarios matches how you are approaching the design of *Your Perfect House*, then this book can be of critical value to you. Ideally, it will serve as your "architect in a book" and help guide you through the process.

Naturally, being an architect, I think you should hire an architect. It is the easiest, simplest, and ultimately most cost-effective way of avoiding the problems we have just discussed, and the best way to put the concepts and principles of good design to work for you.

Essentially, the architect is the person who plans the house, and the builder is the person who executes the plans. The builder builds what the architect designs. An architect does not simply draw the drawings. He creates the design, determines how to build the design, and creates drawings that are essentially instructions to the builder, telling him how to build the house. You will want to choose your architect carefully. Choose an architect who listens, understands, and enhances your ideas and desires and then adds his own talents and experience to the design. This way the house will be a reflection of you.

Sometimes builders see themselves as the quarterbacks for the team. This is a natural tendency since they have many suppliers and subcontractors to coordinate and are ultimately responsible for the work of all of them. He may suggest that he hire an architect for you. Although this suggestion may be meant to make the process simpler for you, it can result in the architect ending up as just another subcontractor. I think your architect should be your point person, the individual who is completely responsive to you and completely responsible for making sure your desires are translated into the reality of the finished house. He should be the top person in your chain of command. Even if you pick the builder first, you should still wait to work with him until you have your architect on board. In my experience, most builders actually prefer this division of responsibilities because it relieves them of responsibilities they often have assumed by default, and they know that the entire process will go more smoothly if the architect worries about the design and the builder worries about the construction. Everyone is doing what he is trained to do.

Architects are the "glue" that holds whole projects together. We have to deal with all of the aspects of the house and not just one. Many days I might have conversations with my clients about things like how certain rooms will feel, how the staircase will look from the foyer, or how the house will look from the street, and then, an hour later, I'll have conversations with the builder about what size anchor bolts should be used in the foundation or whether the window sizes comply with the building code egress requirements. Every project has these two distinct sides, the aesthetic, subjective side and the objective, functional side. And one side always influences the other. Your architect is the person who unites and maximizes both halves to create a complete, beautiful, and technically sound building.

I think it's a good idea to avoid letting the builder hire the architect for you as a subcontractor to him. When that happens, the architect's loyalty flows primarily to the builder. That's who pays him, and he is going to be responsible to the builder, not to you. That doesn't do you any good. Many times when the builder hires the architect, the architect never even meets or talks with the client and never determines exactly what the client wants. Worse, an architect hired by a builder is less likely to speak up if he sees something amiss in the plans or at the site. He doesn't want to make trouble for his real client, the builder.

This is not to say that the builder shouldn't recommend an architect to you. There is a lot to be said for finding a builder and architect who have had good experiences working with each other. They can even have a business relationship, such as being partners in a design/build company. You can benefit from this past experience. Even with a builder's recommendation, the contractual arrangement should be between you and the architect and not be an agreement that runs through the contractor.

When you build a house, you need an advocate. You need someone whose integrity is not compromised because he is beholden to the builder, and you want to avoid situations where the architect or the builder is asserting his authority for no particular purpose. There's no room for grandstanding when it comes to creating *Your* Perfect House.

SIX WAYS AN ARCHITECT HELPS YOU

1. *The architect is the quarterback of the team and the owner's advocate.* You'll be dealing with a host of new faces as your house comes off the drawing board and onto the plot of land you've selected. There will be the builder and all of his contractors and subcontractors. There are the other designers who may be involved: the landscape architect, the interior designer, and so on. And then you've got all those friendly faces from your city or town government who will be poking around and wanting to know exactly what's happening on your property, making sure that everything is in line with your community's building codes and standards. It can be a confusing and bewildering world, and there is no substitute for having someone on your team who understands the process thoroughly, knows exactly what you want, and can and will fight for you.

2. *Your architect can foresee things that you and the builder may not be able to see coming.* Most individuals who build houses won't be building more than one or two in a lifetime, so it's imperative to have someone on your side who has a wealth of experience with the sort of design and construction issues that will arise. Similarly, a builder is going to be limited by his own particular experience. He may be *capable* of building the type of house you want but not be *experienced* at building that particular kind of house. The architect will serve as the eyes and ears for the builder as well, recognizing potential issues that can be addressed at the outset, lest they cost tens or even hundreds of thousands of dollars to remedy down the road.

3. *Your architect unifies the design.* You could think of a house as a jigsaw puzzle—all of the spaces inside and outside the house represent different pieces of that jigsaw puzzle. How will the rooms fit together to get the right flow of spaces? How are you going to get the groceries from the garage to the kitchen? Where will dinner guests go to the bathroom? Where will your children take off their backpacks when they come home from school without cluttering the living areas set aside for adults? How will I get all of these considerations to come together in a house that looks like the house in my mind's eye? There has got to be someone who sees "the big picture" and can make sure all the puzzle pieces fit together in the most perfect way for you. That person has to unify the aesthetics of the house, figuring out how it looks and feels while being mindful of the "nuts and bolts" of actual construction.

4. *Architects offer the kind of technical experience their clients need.* How will the house get built in the most aesthetically pleasing manner? How can we build "green" and maintain the aesthetics? How can the house be built without breaking the budget? How can the house be made as practical as possible? How can we keep the rain out? What makes a house livable, and what makes a house feel uncomfortable or intimidating? These are questions to which your architect will have the answers.

5. *You get a wider view.* Accomplished architects have years of experience turning their clients' dreams into reality, working with budgets, and overcoming obstacles. All of that expertise will serve you from the moment you begin to think about your new home and long after you've moved in.

6. *Architects deal with how buildings feel to the people who live in them.* Beyond the pragmatic issues of size of rooms, quality of construction, and cost of construction, an architect deals with the intangible aspects of feel, appropriateness, scale, and aesthetics.

In some states it's possible to hire individuals who are "house designers." The house designer can serve the same role the architect plays but with one caveat: House designers do not have to undergo the rigorous sort of training and testing architects need in order to become professionally certified and legally licensed in their profession. Moreover, architects are personally liable for their actions, because they're licensed by the individual state or states in which they practice. House designers, on the other hand, can incorporate and therefore shield themselves from legal responsibility in the event that things don't go right. If you choose to work with a house designer, be sure that a licensed structural engineer reviews and seals the plans.

Choosing the Right Architect

I've been practicing architecture for over thirty years and have come to realize that many people choose an architect by looking through an architect's portfolio until they see a house that approximates what they have in mind. That architect will be the architect they hire. For example, if the client is thinking about building a craftsman-style bungalow, he will look for an architect who has already designed a craftsman-style bungalow. This method of selection emphasizes a "focused" experience. Although I agree that experience in designing a particular style of house may be helpful, there is another kind of experience and talent that will help you more.

I think the wiser criterion should be, "Did this architect help each client achieve his or her dream house?" Many competent architects may not have designed the particular type of house you have in mind. But that doesn't mean they're wrong for your project. It just means they have plenty of experience satisfying the desires of other clients and therefore can most likely satisfy yours as well. The key is not whether architects have already built houses like the one you have in mind. The key is whether they build houses that have truly satisfied their past clients and whether they have made the experience pleasant and rewarding.

When you are interviewing your architect, don't be afraid to ask whether he is the one who will actually be doing the work. Some architects, especially those with larger offices, will pass the project to the "back room" junior designers. Essentially, the role of these architects is to bring in the business and perhaps maintain some sort of control over the design process. But are they going to be fully involved with your house? Who will be the real designer of your house? Who will carry through with the design? With whom will you actually be communicating on a day-to-day basis? These are very fair questions for you to ask. Be sure you interview the person who will actually be designing your house.

You don't necessarily need an architect with a large office. The larger the office, the less likely it is the architect whose name is on the door is going to be the individual who will actually design your house. He is less likely to go out to the site with you, monitor the builder and the contractors, and generally serve as your point person or advocate. Please don't let a small office dismay you—a small office can be just right for most residential projects, and your money for architectural fees will go further.

Should you consider the young-and-eager, less experienced architect or the seasoned veteran who has been practicing a while? The only thing I can say is that I used to think experience was overrated…until I got some. Maybe Mark Twain said it best: "Good decisions come from good experience. Good experience comes from bad decisions."

MOLASSES

Ever hear of the Great Boston Molasses Flood? Although "molasses" and "disaster" aren't usually found in the same sentence, there once was such a tragic event. Back on January 15, 1919, in Boston, Massachusetts, a 2.3 million gallon molasses tank, 50 feet tall and 90 feet in diameter, burst and flooded the surrounding area, killing 21 people and injuring 150 more. The gigantic tank was built of half-inch steel plates riveted together. The tank was filled with molasses, the sweetener of the time. No provisions had been made in the design of the tank for potential fermentation and temperature expansion within the molasses. When some unusually hot weather moved in, the molasses began to expand until the tank could no longer contain the enormous pressures that were building up inside. The steel shell gave way in a gigantic explosion. Molasses burst outward, sending a fifteen-foot-high tidal wave of sticky, deadly goop flooding the streets and trapping victims in neighboring buildings. The explosion created a huge vacuum, and when air rushed back to fill the vacuum, buildings that had withstood the initial blast collapsed.

Some time earlier, the tank's owner, U.S. Industrial Alcohol, had been warned of structural weaknesses. The company's response was to paint the tank brown to make it harder to see the brown molasses seeping from the expanding seams between the steel plates. Within hours of the explosion, company lawyers were on the scene, falsely blaming others for the tank's failure.

Later investigations found that the tank rupture was caused by inferior construction, cheating on the specifications of the steel tank walls, and no oversight by the design professionals to see that the work was "up to spec." The disaster caused the implementation of building codes and started the requirements for architects and engineers to sign and seal their plans. Accountability in construction was born.

Remember, a registered architect has passed stringent professional examinations and, unlike a home designer, he assumes responsibility and liability for the building plans he prepares. Among other protections, he can assure you that you are also safe from the perils of molasses!

The Wright Way

Many people have an image of architects that is shaped by the temperament—and, yes, ego—of one of the greatest architects of recent times, Frank Lloyd Wright. Wright was a pioneer. He redefined how we think of a house. But, he was not a client-oriented architect. Wright had little concern for what was right for his clients and great concern for what he wanted to design for his own architectural agenda. For this reason, I would suggest that Frank Lloyd Wright, by my definition, never designed anyone's *perfect* house; instead, he designed the houses he wanted to design, and his clients had to love the result. If they didn't, he was not shy about pointing out their low intellect and inability to understand "great" architecture.

Many stories surround Wright's legend, but despite his difficult personality, Wright was critically important to architecture. He created a true paradigm shift. For generations, the Georgian house was the American concept of "house"—the gold standard of house design. Wright was one of the first to say, "Why should I keep things the way they have always been? What should the American house of the twentieth century be?" He definitely kept the traditional sense of hearth and home, making the fireplace the anchoring center of his houses. He saw the qualities of security and shelter the hearth provided, both physically and emotionally. But other traditional aspects of eastern homes didn't work on the prairie that was his canvas. He rejected the notion of individual, clearly-defined rooms and pioneered the "open plan" that we find, at least in the family-room-kitchen-breakfast-room arrangements,

in many homes of today. He emphasized in his designs the horizontal lines that dominate the prairie. He made use of newly-available materials, such as large panes of glass. For centuries, big pieces of glass were expensive and hard to make. Wright saw how he could use big window openings to connect the indoor spaces with the outdoor spaces. He wanted to take advantage of the natural beauty of the land surrounding the homes he built. He used walls to extend out into the land, anchoring the house on its site. He combined the large openings with extensive overhangs of the roof to preserve the comfort of a sheltering home while letting the spaces flow outward.

A classic story about Frank Lloyd Wright that illustrates his unique personality involves Herbert "Hib" Johnson, CEO of Johnson Wax. Wright had designed a fabulous house for Johnson, replete with an intricate, long skylight that ran the length of the ceiling above the dining table. Johnson was entertaining guests at dinner when a rain storm cropped up. As most of Wright's skylights often did, this one began to leak. In Wright's defense, skylights were not "off the shelf" items back then, and these were built on-site, as well as the technology of the day permitted. Johnson telephoned Wright. The conversation went something like this:

"Hello," Wright said, answering the phone.

"Lloyd, this is Hib," Johnson said. "I'm sitting at my dining room table entertaining distinguished guests from around the world and your damned skylight is leaking on my bald head! What are you going to do about it?"

"Hib," Wright answered, "I suggest you move your chair." And hung up.

Wright believed the entire house should be "of" the land rather than "on" the land. A house shouldn't be imported and plopped down on a piece of property with no regard for the nature of that property. Instead, to Wright's mind, a house should be responsive to the land in terms of both shape and choice of materials. For example, Wright considered it inappropriate to place a red brick house on brown dirt. He would insist that the stone for the fireplace and walls be dug up from the property on which the house was built. This way, his houses would "grow up out of the ground" instead of being superimposed randomly on pieces of land.

Much of Wright's thinking has been incorporated into today's buildings. But again, an iconoclastic individualist, experimenter, and pioneer like Wright was far more interested in creating what I would call his *perfect architecture* and not his clients' *perfect houses*. His happiest clients were those who shared his views and wished to be the owners of a work of art by the grand master. For all his visionary ways, Wright was pretty nearsighted when it came to meeting the specific desires and concerns of a client and that client's house.

What does all this architectural history mean for you? It means you don't have to treat your architect

Frank Lloyd Wright's famous Falling Water is an icon of modern residential architecture.

like Frank Lloyd Wright. And your architect shouldn't be treating you the way Frank Lloyd Wright treated his clients. Your architect needs to be responsive to your concerns. All of us hope to get everything right the first time, and your architect may experience a slight sense of disappointment that his first draft didn't solve all your needs and desires completely. But if your architect is a responsible professional, he will be more than happy to make the changes you suggest, as long as they make sense from a design standpoint.

At the other end of the spectrum, some architects take the desire to please a client a little too far and become obsequious "hired pencils." They'll draw it up your way just to collect the check. You don't want a "hired pencil" any more than you want a Frank Lloyd Wright wannabe. You want somebody in the middle, someone who will be responsive to your thoughts and will share with you how it's possible to translate those thoughts into reality but will also tell you when it's not appropriate to do so.

Once you're communicating effectively with your architect, the two of you can embark on the exciting process of making *Your* Perfect House feel like home.

102

TWENTY QUESTIONS TO ASK A PROSPECTIVE ARCHITECT

1. How will you discover what my perfect house will be? Please explain your process.

2. How many projects do you have going at once?

3. Will you design my house yourself, will someone else on your staff design it, or will a team design my house? Can I meet the other architects who will be working on my house?

4. Do you work in one particular style or do you work in a range of styles?

5. Can you tell me your design philosophy?

6. Can you show me some of your past work?

7. What kinds of drawings or models will you prepare? Will you use computer imaging? Will you build cardboard models?

8. What percentage of your office's work is custom residential?

9. Are you a registered architect in the state where the project is being built?

10. What type of contract do you use? Is it a "percentage fee," "hourly fee," "fixed sum fee," or some other format?

11. How long will the design and construction documents take? How long until we get bids from builders?

12. What would you estimate the approximate cost of construction to be, based on your usual projects? Or based on the description I have given you of the types of appointments and finishes I will want in the house?

13. How accurate have your construction cost estimates been in the past?

14. How will the costs of design changes be handled?

15. When can you realistically start my project?

16. How long have you been in business?

17. Can you provide me with a list of references and a list of all the projects you have done within the past five years?

18. How will you work with my builder?

19. Are any other consultants included in your fee, such as a structural engineer, landscape architect, or interior designer?

20. If we were to stop this project before construction, how would our contract be terminated? What would be my financial obligation?

Interior Designer and Landscape Architect

The other two individuals who may play a part in the design of your home are a landscape architect and an interior designer. Your architect will advise you whether a landscape architect is necessary and to what degree. This does not just depend on the size of the area surrounding your house. Often, something like a narrow city lot can benefit most from the talents of a good landscape architect. What matters more than the size of the lot is what you would like your property to be. You can generally count on your architect to give you names of landscape architects with whom he has had successful projects in the past. If your property is challenging, such as steeply sloping land, or has unique features that offer interesting opportunities, the communications between your architect and landscape architect are even more critical. If your property is not large or difficult, or if your plans for the outdoors are not overly complex, or if you have landscape experience and specific ideas for your land, it may well be that the landscape contractor, the contractor who actually installs the plants, can come up with a plan for your property without the advice of a landscape architect by simply working with you and your architect.

An interior designer can be valuable to your project. Select your interior designer using the same criteria you would use for selecting your architect. Some designers work from their preferred palette. Others work with what you have and who you are.

Just ask yourself whether you want your house to be the interior designer's "signature" or *Your* Perfect House? Also, don't select someone who will ride roughshod over your architect's work. You don't want competing consultants engaged in a "turf war." Try to find someone who is compatible with the approach you and your architect have toward the design of the house.

The interior designer's amount of involvement is for you to decide.

Do you want an interior designer simply to select the colors and finishes, or do you want that person to make most of the decisions about how the inside of your house will look by also focusing on the questions of built-ins, window treatments, and the like? I think it's usually best to have the house substantially designed *before* you bring in the interior designer. This helps you avoid the headache of having two people competing to design your home. The interior designer can comment on aspects of the design, and refinements can be made after the overall concepts are well established.

You should have some direct contact with the landscape architect and the interior designer because there will be aesthetic considerations in their work and decisions for you to make. Your preferences guide their work. These individuals may or may not be part of the contract with the architect. In any event, the architect should coordinate communication with them to avoid confusing the process. Remember, communication is what's needed to steer clear of those "horror stories" we discussed earlier.

The line between architectural design and interior design is indistinct. Interior features, such as fireplace mantels and crown moldings, have a significant impact on the style and feel of a room. These details become signature features and set the tone for other choices. Often, the design of these items is the result of a collaboration between the architect and the interior designer.

The structural engineer is the individual who calculates beam sizes, designs foundations, addresses other technical matters, and basically makes sure that the building is structurally sound. Normally, the architect will design the entire building with a strategy in mind for the structure. Then the structural engineer will complete the framing plan and calculations without compromising the aesthetics of the rooms. The structural engineer might say things to the architect like, "This column should be bigger" or "I need a brace there." Generally, the client never meets the structural engineer. The architect hires the structural engineer as his consultant, and often the structural engineer's fees are included in the architect's fees.

Design/Build

I stressed in the previous lesson that having an architect gives you an advocate, someone looking out for your best interests as you build your house. Many times, clients come to me and say, "I've heard about something called design/build. Wouldn't that be a good way for me to save money?"

The answer is "yes and no." It all depends on the particular design/build company. Design/build is essentially one-stop shopping for a house. The concept is undeniably appealing and can be effective and simpler. The most attractive aspect of a design/build arrangement is that you make only one agreement—with the design/build company. You don't need a separate architect, an interior designer, a landscape designer, or anybody else. In the most basic version of design/build, which I'll call pseudo-design/build, you go to a builder and select from his house plans that are "ready to go." Some people find this arrangement to be great because they don't have to spend the time it takes to design a house, get those plans approved, get a builder on board, and so on. The builder says, "I've got all that covered. Architects are expensive, and they make your house cost more, too. My wife will help you with the colors, and Joe, my landscaper, can sketch something up for the plantings. Let's keep it simple and easy." What you certainly don't get is a true custom house. This is simply a stock house that has not been built yet. You have the opportunity to make selections of finishes and possibly a few nominal changes, but little else can be customized.

In truth, this kind of pseudo-design/build offers only the *illusion* of control. If you don't have some-one directing the builder, then the builder, not you, is the person who is really in charge of creating your house. Will the builder get you exactly what you want? Can you count on that happening? These are legitimate worries. There are no guarantees. What if you want to do something the builder has never done before? What if you want to do something that's going to take the builder a little more time or cost him a little more money or that he doesn't feel like figuring out how to do? Realistically, what do you think the odds are of getting a builder to pull away from the tried-and-true approach that he has used so many times in the past? It may be tried-and-true, and it may get great results, but those great results are from the builder's point of view, not necessarily from yours.

If your builder has standardized plans from which he can build your house, they will succeed only if you don't require modifications, added detail, and specialty work. Even if you like the plans, you will find yourself adapting to the house instead of customizing the design to meet your needs. If it happens that the house the builder happens to have in mind for you—and for many of his other design/build clients—matches up perfectly with the house you envisioned, then you're in luck. But if you want something that in any way deviates from this stock plan, you won't be completely happy.

If the house of your dreams does not match up neatly with what the builder has to offer, this kind of design/build arrangement is probably not for you. It may well work for other people, in the same way that a suit right off the rack will pretty much fit a lot of people, although it may not fit anyone precisely.

There is another type of design/build that can provide you with a truly custom-designed house and the convenience of a single contract. There are many good, professional design/build companies that have an architect as one of the partners, have architects on staff, or have a long-term arrangement with an independent architect. Many good architects who love to design houses have taken their businesses this direction in order to find more projects and have more control over the ultimate outcome without compromising their professional integrity.

These design/build companies usually will offer a two-part contract. Part one is the design services, similar to the design services offered by an independent architect. You work with him in the traditional manner and develop a custom design for your house. Cost estimates for the construction are provided along the way with a final quote coming at the completion of the design and construction drawings. If you terminate the contract along the way, you are obligated for the cost of the design services.

Part two is a contract for the actual construction of the house. Once this phase is started, everything proceeds in a similar fashion to a traditional construction contract except that the architect is working for the builder and is not independently hired by you.

In many cases, this type of arrangement can give you the true custom design you want and give you much of the design control that comes from having an architect work for you. Like many things in life, this arrangement is only as good as the people behind it. Check out the architect's references and talk to past clients. Remember, in this type of arrangement, you are depending on the architect to be your advocate even though he is allied with the builder. If he is a member of the American Institute of Architects, he has adopted a code of ethics that can give you some comfort. Ask about his state registration to be sure he is really an architect or a registered house designer and not merely "implying" or allowing you to presume that he is. Because design/build lacks the checks and balances that exist in a traditional owner-architect-builder relationship, a design/build arrangement requires a measure of trust.

Site Unseen

Which comes first, the site for the house or the plan for the house? I advise my clients to choose the site first. This allows you to design a house to fit the land. You wouldn't buy a rug and then figure out what room it fits in later on, right? I believe a house should "grow" from its site and not look like it has been imported and plopped down haphazardly. If you have already selected your architect, bring him along to offer his opinion on the sites you are considering. He may well see things about a site, both positive and negative, that you may not see. The site you have in mind might not be appropriate for the house you desire. How many times have we seen houses placed awkwardly on a slope when the house design would clearly have been more comfortable on a flat site? Developments of tract houses are fertile ground for examples of poor assimilation of the house

This oceanfront house makes the most of its incredible site.

design to the site. These mismatches of house to site are akin to wearing a tuxedo with tennis shoes.

I know of one project where a very nice house was designed to sit on a steeply sloping site. Extensive outdoor spaces were planned on several raised decks. The house ended up over budget, the decks were cut, and all of the elevated outdoor spaces the homeowner wanted in the first place were lost. Had this house been planned for a more level lot, the outdoor spaces would have been less expensive and would have remained a part of the design. They also should have done a better job of forecasting the construction costs, but that is a topic we will discuss later in this book.

Once you've chosen your architect, your builder, and your site, you'll have a rough idea of the scope of the project. Together with them you can begin the exciting process of "dreamwork"—deciding and discovering just what kind of house you want, what its special features and qualities will be, and how your new house will reflect your tastes, desires, and dreams. You will already begin to see how *Your Perfect House* will embrace you and your family. Yes, the process can be fraught with pitfalls, but not if you know how to ask the right questions and how to choose the right people.

Because the front of this house faced a wonderful view, a terrace was designed in conjunction with the house's entrance. The result is a delightful garden that not only greets visitors, but also extends the interior spaces outward through the French doors opening from the dining room.

Lesson Six

MAKE PLANS BEFORE DRAWING PLANS

"Ah. To build, to build! That is the noblest of all the arts."
—HENRY WADSWORTH LONGFELLOW

Because it takes a lot of money and time to build a house, it is essential for you to keep control of the process to avoid spending more of either than is necessary. There are two critical components to keeping control. The first is to find the right team members, and the second is planning.

How You Really Live

The next major step in controlling the process is thinking through exactly the sort of lifestyle issues that drive your concept of *Your Perfect House*. Think about how you really live and not merely how you think you live. Some families want to have a big communal living space opening to a kitchen, where Mom can serve breakfast to the kids at the island. Some families even want to have computers right in the communal space so that the children can send messages to their friends or do homework while being supervised instead of being isolated in their bedrooms. Similarly, does Dad need a place to get away—a place where he can spread out his business papers, sit and read, or even smoke a cigar? These sorts of issues really drive the design of a house. By determining the critical variables and establishing your design criteria early on, you will avoid having to adjust the design of the house later to meet these needs.

Nostalgia, whether planned or subconscious, plays an important role in our tastes and desires. Some of my clients envision a big front porch just like Grandma's house had. Others want to capture a view or, conversely, have their houses tucked into trees just like places they have visited and found enchanting. They need their houses to become an extension or a manifestation of these wishes. Let yourself think back to your childhood and recall places you have been that have left a lasting impression on your memory. Ask yourself what memories of those places you would like to re-create—or, if these were not pleasant experiences, to avoid.

What other concepts might drive the house design for you? Do you want to have a big lodge room with a central fireplace? Don't limit yourself to only the big ideas. Details are important, too. Do you want to have glass cases for your collection of fine porcelains? You can control the process by thinking through in advance how you want to live, remembering elements from past homes that you especially liked or ones you want to avoid and then prioritizing each concept. Take notes about concepts that will make the house you build precisely right for you.

The best way to maintain control is to remain proactive rather than reactive. Stay ahead of the decision schedule so that if a panicked call comes in

Built-in display cases frame the doorway to the dining room. The glass shelves allow light to reach every corner of the display.

from the builder—"Should we do it this way or that?"—you already know what you want. If you and your architect have already thought through the impact of each decision, you will be avoiding time-consuming and money-consuming problems down the road.

Let's look at an example of this. Suppose a house is being designed to be built in a warm, southern climate and that, because of a view from a certain room, the client asks for lots of windows in a wall that is exposed to intense sunshine. It is likely the architect will not simply stick more windows in the wall, but instead he will point out the impact of that decision. Vast amounts of glass on the western wall will lead to the late afternoon sun pouring in mercilessly. The homeowner will end up having to install expensive blinds and keep them shut much of the time, giving him no view at all at the end of the day. The architect can help him think through the ramifications of this decision and others like it. In this case, the architect might use fewer windows that are selectively placed to capture the view and incorporate some sun-shading elements, such as a covered veranda, on the wall in question. Thus, the architect has gained control over the amount of light and heat that pours in without sacrificing the view.

The sheltering roof of this veranda helps control direct sunlight while allowing pleasant, reflected illumination to light the rooms beyond.

Another client might say, "I like big spaces—soaring spaces. It makes the house look important." As we mentioned in the first lesson, a potential problem is that a big space can feel hostile and echo like a gymnasium. Intriguingly, sound is an important part of how we feel about a space. When a room echoes, it feels cold and unwelcoming. The architect will be able to design a space that's impressive without making the occupants feel they're in a museum. Throughout the design process, your architect will help you see the ramifications of any decision before that decision is implemented, thus saving time, money, and heartache.

Critical Design Questions

Here are some questions you can ask yourself and some preliminary planning tasks you can perform to help you to organize your thinking.

1. What are the size and scope of the project?

2. Create a preliminary program and visit houses that are for sale to get an idea of the approximate square footage that can hold the rooms you want.

3. Do a preliminary cost assessment. Talk with builders. Compare sale prices (minus the lot value) of houses for sale to get a range of costs per square foot.

    A. Evaluate the range of prices for building lots and sites that may suit your requirements.

    B. Compare the overall cost with your budget.

    C. Have preliminary discussions with architects and builders to get opinions on costs and scope.

    D. Find a balance between your budget and your desires and needs.

4. Who is going to help me with this project?

5. Select an architect.

6. Select a builder.

7. Where will I build it?

    A. Select a building site.

    B. Consider site characteristics, opportunities, and restrictions.

    C. What covenants are there? Do they have an impact on building costs?

8. What will this house be?

    A. Make a list of rooms and spaces.

    B. Compile magazine clippings and notes.

    C. Write brief descriptions of the qualities and characteristics you want.

9. How will the house sit on the site?

    A. Compile site analysis, schematic floor plans set on the site, determine the approach to the house, and so forth.

    B. Evaluate several house placement options.

10. Where will the rooms be positioned?

    A. Do preliminary layouts.

    B. Evaluate several layouts and decide on basic concepts.

11. What will the house look like?

    A. The floor plan grows to three dimensions and becomes a house.

B. Investigate several alternatives.

C. Don't be afraid to reassess earlier decisions. You will "know" the house better and better as you go through the process. Don't latch on to early concepts so strongly that you are unable to see the shortcomings later on. Be agile in your thinking.

12. Is the design on budget?

A. Do preliminary cost estimates. You can use a prospective builder for this, or the architect may do it.

B. Determine what the lowest price the house can be without altering the program in some way.

C. Determine the highest price the house is likely to be unless you choose very expensive or exotic fixtures and finishes.

13. How will I get exactly what I want?

A. The architect completes the construction documents (drawings and specifications). These substantially detail the house.

B. Items not yet determined are included as allowances.

C. Owner reviews and approves the construction documents.

14. What is the actual cost going to be?

A. Construction documents are given to the builder(s) for pricing.

B. The builder(s) respond with either bids or solid estimates for a cost-plus contract.

15. What if the bids exceed my budget?

A. The architect and builder work together to establish a list of possible adjustments to the project and what the approximate savings of each would be.

B. The owner then decides which changes to accept, and the builder recalculates the project's cost with the changes.

C. The architect revises construction documents to reflect all changes. These revised documents become the contract documents between the owner and the builder.

16. How will I pay for this?

A. The owner decides on method of financing (such as construction loan and then a permanent mortgage, a construction loan that converts to a permanent mortgage when the house is complete, or cash and no financing).

B. The builder provides an estimate of a schedule of payments and monthly amounts.

C. The contract stipulates how and when each progress payment is to be made.

D. The contract stipulates how it will end—that is, when the final payment is to be made to the builder, when the builder is deemed to have completed the work, and what warranty the builder will provide to the owner.

17. When does the construction start?

A. When a contract is signed with the builder, the builder submits the architect's plans to the city or county building department for a building permit.

B. Once the permit is issued, construction can begin.

18. When do I decide on the items we include as allowances?

A. During the course of construction, the owner, architect, and often the interior designer continue to work on the allowance items, finalizing the designs and making selections so that these items can be given a final price. Until these decisions and selections have all been made, the price of allowance items is not fixed.

B. The builder should create a schedule of when he needs these things to be decided before they start to affect the construction progress.

Making a house "energy efficient" does not have to mean small, uninteresting rooms and spaces. This high-ceiling room is spacious and pleasant to be in, but, surprisingly, it is just one of several large rooms in a very large house that only costs about $100 a month to heat and cool.

"Green" Mansions

Recently, substantial increases in energy costs and a renewed awareness of our environmental responsibility have been quickly changing the way we think about our way of living and the methods and materials we use for construction. More and more, people are interested in building "green."

A "green" house, by the current definition, is a house that is both energy efficient and constructed with "environmentally-friendly" or sustainable materials. Our first impression of what a "green" house should look like might be something ultra-contemporary, industrial looking, or covered with solar panels and ugly materials. This does not have to be the case. It is completely possible to design and build an environmentally-responsible, energy-efficient house without giving up anything regarding aesthetics. Your "green" house can match your vision of your "dream" house. One example I can point to is a large French country style house in North Carolina I designed that costs only about $100 per month to heat and cool. There was never a thought of compromising the aesthetic, but there was a lot of planning for efficiency that happened right from the beginning. *Your* Perfect House can do the same thing.

Building "green" is both a matter of having a design strategy and selecting materials properly. An appropriate, integrated design is essential to creating an energy-efficient house. It is not merely a matter of slapping some solar panels onto a poorly sited, badly designed building. You need to plan the house as an entire system right from the beginning. Passive energy efficiency is created by properly positioning the building on the land. Mechanical energy efficiency requires adequate air duct sizes and proper equipment location. Both of these considerations are hard to address at some later date.

We will discuss the house on the land in detail in a later lesson, but for now, suffice it to say that the energy consumption of a house can be greatly reduced by properly positioning the house on its site. The direction the windows face, the lengths and positions of roof overhangs, and the way the building sits on the land relative to the sun and the weather are the key factors in making a building intrinsically energy efficient. This is the heart of passive solar design, and it is the single most important planning consideration for building "green."

The second planning consideration involves the mechanical system. A "standard" type of heating and air conditioning system depends on a fairly high velocity of airflow and a fairly small volume of air, which is why you can often hear the system so much when it comes on. This is also why you sometimes feel drafts. A better way to design a system is with large ductwork so you can provide each room with a larger volume of air that is moving more slowly. The comfort of the occupants is greatly increased, the efficiency of operation goes up, and the sound levels go down. Of course, to build a system like this requires adequate space for the larger ductwork, so early planning is critical if you want to avoid conflicts and compromises.

Using multiple HVAC (heating, ventilating, and air conditioning) units that handle separate portions or zones of the house has been the traditional way of designing mechanical systems. What works more efficiently is to have multiple units placed in series, along one main trunk line, that all serve the entire house. What happens is that when the temperatures outside are moderate and the system does not have to work very hard, only one smaller HVAC unit, with a smaller, more efficient compressor, comes on at a time. You are not cycling a big compressor on and off throughout the day. That repeated cycling is very energy inefficient because the startup of the unit causes a big power draw, and the charging up and cooling down of the unit are simply wasted heating or cooling that slips away from your house unused. On those days when the temperatures are more extreme, the second unit comes on to assist the first, and the proper amount of heating and cooling is provided. The "zoning" of the right amount of air to various portions of the house is achieved by means of automatic dampers that are activated by thermostats throughout the house.

There are other energy-saving measures that can occur behind the scenes. Proper insulation, including draft blocking to prevent convective loops of cold or warm air within walls and ceilings, will reduce heat loss in winter and heat gain in summer. I've found that in southern climates insulation and building tightness are often not seen as critical issues. This might be because in the north, in the wintertime, we can feel cold drafts indoors, and we want to eliminate them. But in the summer, we are not as aware of warm drafts, even though our air conditioner is working very hard and costing us money.

Attic ventilating fans and new products, like reflective-faced roof sheathing, do a great job of keeping an attic from overheating, thus reducing the work of the air conditioners. High-quality windows and doors, programmable thermostats, lighting controlled by dimmers, and compact fluorescent lighting will reduce your energy consumption.

An energy management system can reduce your electric bill and help reduce energy demand at peak times. This system monitors and controls what equipment can come on during certain hours of the day. It may block an electric water heater from starting until an air conditioner that is already running has completed its cycle. Most power companies allow residential customers to switch from the standard residential billing rate to a demand rate, which can be substantially lower if your peak usage is not high. When you change to a demand rate, you allow the power company to monitor your usage throughout the day, checking for peak demand. They will then bill you at a rate that is based on the highest peak they see. The energy management system suppresses peaks by controlling what is turned on, thus controlling your billing rate. You will not be using less electricity, but you will be using it at cheaper times, and you will be contributing to the overall "leveling" of electrical consumption in your community. This leads to less pollution being produced by the power generating plants.

An energy monitoring system can generally pay for itself through savings on your electric bill in about three years. Thereafter, you will be saving about one-third on the cost of your electricity and doing an environmental good deed.

Sustainable building materials are more and more available these days. "Sustainable" means the materials are manufactured in environmentally responsible ways. They may be made from recycled materials, such as tile or wallboard. Some are made from agricultural wastes, like wheat straw and rice hulls. Still others are made from rapidly renewable materials, such as bamboo or hemp. Wood products from managed forests and "engineered" wood products that make use of all of the parts of the tree can qualify as sustainable, as can salvaged and reused materials like brick, stone, or slate roof shingles taken from demolished buildings. Newly manufactured materials with long life cycles, like bricks and porcelain tiles, are sustainable in the sense that they do not have to be replaced, so that no future resources are required to manufacture replacements.

Plumbing fixtures that reduce water consumption, landscaping that requires less watering, storm water management and retention, and materials that limit toxic off-gassing all contribute to making a house "green." You can incorporate all of these things without changing the look of the house in any way. You might think of this as building a stealth "green" house. You will be building responsibly without making a show of it just to impress you friends and neighbors.

A wine cellar, when located in a basement space, can be energy efficient. Even the materials, such as this brick floor, are earth friendly.

Sidewalk Superintendents

There is one method of control that is actually *not* in your best interest. Sometimes people get so excited about building their own houses that they love to tour the job site, unaccompanied by their architect or builder and play the role of sidewalk superintendent. This is a dangerous and often expensive role to play. Here's an example. If the homeowner sees the tile contractor hard at work, he or she might say, very casually, "I think it would look even better if we turned that pattern on an angle."

The tile installer may assume that this is a command and not just conversation. After all, the homeowner is the customer, and we all know "the customer is always right." So, the tile contractor makes the change and sends a bill to the builder. The builder passes that bill along to the homeowner, who says, "Wait a minute. I didn't tell him to change this. I was just *talking* to the guy! I had no idea it would be so much more expensive to do it that way!" It's a little bit like scratching your head at an auction and inadvertently buying a $100,000 painting!

Keep in mind that what may seem like a friendly conversation with a subcontractor may actually result in a serious change in the cost of your home. It's never inconsequential when the homeowner tells a subcontractor to do something in a different manner without consulting the architect and builder. Ideally, the homeowner should talk to the architect, who will talk to the builder. The builder will then get an estimate from the subcontractor for the change. At that point, the homeowner and the architect can decide together whether the change and the cost of the change make sense. This is the best way to avoid costly misunderstandings.

It has been my experience that individuals who tend to go onto the job site and "suggest" changes to the subcontractor don't do it just once; they may do it ten or fifteen times before the bills start coming in. It's not difficult to add tens of thousands of dollars to the cost of a home simply by having a handful of "casual conversations" with the subs. My sage advice is this: If you want to maintain control over the cost of your house, don't talk to anybody but your architect and your builder, except to chat about the weather or last night's ballgame. Be sure your builder knows that no changes are ever authorized without a discussion about cost.

Architectural space is different from the void of the philosophers. Space is the architect's medium and its manipulation our most rewarding task.

—CHARLES MOORE AND DONLYN LYNDON

On the other hand, it's a great idea to go through your home site and compliment the workers. Home building is hard work. No one likes to be taken for granted, and everyone likes to have hard work appreciated. If you go onto the site and compliment the tradesmen, they'll appreciate it, and they'll end up doing an even better job for you. You'll also make them happy, and isn't it a worthwhile thing to make someone happy? Simply offer compliments, observe what's going on, and do not try to micromanage the process.

Controlling the process of designing and building *Your* Perfect House isn't as hard as it may appear. First, avoid the illusion of control that pseudo-design/build offers, because you can seldom get the customized house that fits you perfectly by going from someone else's prepackaged plans. Second, take full advantage of your architect's training, knowledge, and ability. Third, think through in advance as much as possible the rooms and spaces you need and how they should relate to each other as well as the special design elements and features you want your house to have. The more guidance you can provide your architect at the beginning of the process, the more thoroughly your architect can meet your expectations and needs.

Stay proactive rather than reactive with planning, planning, and more planning. Lay out the "program" for your house before actually laying out the house itself. The plan of the house should happen only after you have selected your site so that the design of *Your* Perfect House will relate to the land and maximize the land's potential.

YOU CAN'T PREDICT THE FUTURE

There is always the real possibility that your life will change. Other family members might need or want to live with you or your mobility might diminish. If anything like that happens, you would not want to be forced to move out of Your Perfect House. Fortunately, there are a few things you can include in your planning and design now to make alterations and additions easier later.

1. Position the house on the lot in a way that leaves room for an addition if you think you might need to expand the house in the future.

2. Plan how an addition might connect with the other rooms in a cohesive and logical way.

3. Design a spare closet on all floors large enough to be a future elevator shaft. These closets should be stacked up on each floor and be accessible from a hallway. Check elevator sizes and make the closets large enough. Then frame a "knock out" floor in these closets. For now you will have nice closet space. Later, if needed, you can easily install an elevator.

4. Install wood blocking behind the wall board for future grab bars.

5. Consider future accessibility with regard to doors, steps, and bathroom sizes.

This house denies its youthful age. The choices of material, the overall form and shape of the structure, and the attention to detail are critical to creating the right effect. But none of these things would be as successful if the house did not sit appropriately on its site. Notice how the form of this house "embraces" you by virtue of the angled wings. The shape of the house defines a large outdoor room that welcomes you when you drive up.

Lesson Seven

CHOOSING THE PERFECT SITE

"No house should ever be on a hill or on anything. It should be of the hill. Belonging to it. Hill and house should live together each the happier for the other."
—FRANK LLOYD WRIGHT

It's a good idea to have a basic concept of what kind of house you want before selecting a site because the type of house will dictate to some extent the nature of the site that makes the most sense for you. Do you want a house tucked in the woods? Do you want everything on one floor? Do you want to have a useful lower level with windows and doors? These are generalities, but they are important because these types of issues will influence the type of sites you might choose. But don't get too far along in the actual design process until you have selected the right site.

I feel it is critical to avoid imposing the house on the site. The building should be "responsive" to the site. As you consider various building sites, look at the shortcomings and opportunities that each one presents and consider how these factors will impact the design of the house. Issues like the orientation of the site, e.g., whether the house faces north or south, and the shape and the size of the lot have a great deal to do with the ultimate design of the house.

When I see houses I would consider unsuccessful, I have a strong feeling that they were built from ready-made plans—plans taken from a book or purchased and then pressed onto a building site. Even the most basic rectangular site in the most standardized subdivision imaginable has unique characteristics that need to be considered. Even if your site is exactly like every other site in the subdivision and maybe in the entire town, there may still be opportunities to make more of your property than the others have been able to do. The expedient and popular solution is not always the best solution.

The folly of shoehorning a house design onto a given plot of land is a little like going to the store, seeing a pretty dress on sale that doesn't fit you, and saying to yourself, "Maybe I can lose enough weight so I can wear it." You will be altering yourself to accommodate the dress, and, worse yet, it's unlikely that will happen. Just because it was purchased on sale doesn't mean it's a bargain if you can't use it. Our earlier exercise in planning helped you know basically what kind of house you want and what sort of features are most desirable to you.

When you start looking for land, there are a number of considerations to keep in mind that can impact the appropriateness of various sites. Let's look at some of the key concerns that run through my mind when I'm considering a building site for a client, which may help you judge whether a piece of property is right for you.

Too often, development houses are simply plopped down on the land without regard to the slope or orientation. In this example the sloping land would have allowed a livable lower level with full windows and possibly doors out to a rear patio or yard. Instead, an extra-high crawlspace was built, and an elevated deck provides the only outdoor space available from the rear of the house. All contact with the land has been cut off.

Zoning, Land Use Ordinances, and Covenants

The very first thing you need to do is research the zoning and land use ordinances that might apply to the property you are considering. The legal limit on the use of your land is called "zoning." The zoning designation determines whether your land can be used for residential, commercial, institutional, or other uses. These ordinances also restrict how large and tall a building can be, as well as how close it can be to the property line. Other regulations might apply, such as the distance a well or house must be located from the septic system, steep slope ordinances that prohibit construction, impervious surface limitations, clearing limits, etc. Many communities, especially oceanfront and beachside properties, have height restrictions to preserve sightlines to the view for everyone, and they may have restrictions on the shadows that one building can cast on a neighboring property. Community zoning codes often have height restrictions as well to keep a sense of harmony among the various homes in the neighborhood. Measuring starting points for height restrictions can sometimes be complicated. If you find yourself not understanding the government requirements, consult your architect or a civil engineer to be sure you know all the limitations from the beginning.

It is also important to check the zoning of any neighboring land. You would not want to build *Your* Perfect House next to a property zoned for an office or commercial use and find out in a few years that a parking lot is going to be your new neighbor.

Buying property within a planned community provides you with a great deal of protection from neighboring nuisances, but you need to familiarize yourself with the covenants and deed restrictions that will certainly come with the property and apply to you. These covenants may restrict the building materials you can use, the allowable roof pitch of your house, the trees you can cut down, and even fences or outdoor lighting you might want. Covenants and deed restrictions are the backbone of planned communities and create the harmony and high quality of the neighborhood, but if you start your project unaware of these regulations, finding out about them after you have your heart set on something that turns out not to be

It is critical that you make sure your site will have sewer and water for your house. Otherwise, your building lot is useless as a home site. Perc tests, short for percolation tests, are tests to see how fast water soaks or percolates into the ground. Septic systems are designed based on perc test results. Sandy soils soak up water quickly. Heavy, clay-type soils do not. If you are considering a property that is not connected to the public sewer system, be sure the property has passed an approved perc test and that a septic system has been or can be designed for that property. In locales where the soils do not percolate well, your septic system may have to be quite elaborate and expensive. Find this out early, since this kind of septic system can have a major impact on your budget. Also, if you cannot connect to a public water system, it is a good idea to have the well drilled early on so you are sure there is adequate water available. The cost of the well is dependant upon its depth. Again, the costs can add up, so find these things out as early as you can.

allowed will make those protective covenants seem onerous and harsh.

Planned communities often come with an Architectural Review Committee that reviews and either approves or rejects everyone's house plans. I would strongly suggest that you familiarize yourself with this process, possibly even making a preliminary submission if *Your* Perfect House will be "edgy" in any way so as to avoid unpleasant choices down the line.

Lot Size and Buildable Area

A major issue to consider is how big the lot should be. The early planning you have done should give you a sense of a required building area—that is, the amount of space you need in order to have everything fit on the land nicely. There has to be enough room for the garage and the driveway. There has to be enough space for all the different rooms you'll need. Most importantly, things have to fit together well. For example, even if things fit mathematically, i.e., the square footage adds up properly, you don't want to have to take a long walk around the garage to get to the front door of your house just to fit everything into the available space on the site. Plan some area for the connections between spaces, too. You'll need room for your outdoor "rooms" and outdoor activities. Don't forget space for gardens and play yards.

If you want a swimming pool, this is the time to think about it. A pool and its accompanying deck areas require about as much space as a two-car garage with its auto-maneuvering area in the drive-

way. Just like a garage and driveway, a pool needs to be built on a fairly level spot. Otherwise, you'll be faced with a large expense for retaining walls. Additionally, a swimming pool needs to be built in a private area. It needs to be gated or otherwise secured in keeping with the local building code so that it doesn't serve as a dangerous attraction for the children of the neighborhood. If you want a pool, it's wise to make that decision *before* you pick out your lot.

Architects use the term "footprint" to describe the way a building "sits" on a site. Strictly speaking, the footprint is the area that the house requires. The rooms on the main living level, the garage, and covered porches are all part of the footprint. But, in a practical sense, accessory areas, such as the swimming pool or any garden, terrace, or deck that you want to include, require space on the site, and they should be included, too. Everything must fit together within the buildable area of the lot.

Be aware that the total area of your property does not equal the buildable area. In most places, you're not permitted to build all the way to the lot line. Most communities have setback restrictions, which means you're required to keep a certain amount of distance from the edge of your house to the edge of the lot, thus affording you and your neighbor light, air, and a measure of privacy. Setback restrictions vary from community to community. Sometimes these are referred to as front yard, side yard, and rear yard restrictions. You may have heard the term "zero lot line." This is a building lot that has no side yard restriction, and at least one side of the house can be built directly on the property line.

Easements are another consideration. An easement is legal permission for the municipality, the gas company, or the water company to run pipes and wires under or over your private property. An easement grants the easement holder—generally municipalities and utility companies—the right to enter the property and actually dig up its pipes or wires, when necessary, to repair or replace them. Their easements will be recorded as part of your deed. You are not permitted to build any permanent structures in easement areas or within the property setbacks. You may think of your present property as going all the way out to the street. After all, you have to mow and maintain this area. But the truth is that most often your property line is set back from the curb or edge of the street. The area between the paved street and your actual property line is part of an easement called the "right of way." Power lines, sewer lines, and sidewalks are located within the right of way and are not actually on your property.

The net of all this is that the area within the property lines, minus the area of the setbacks and easements, is the legal buildable area. But it still may not be the practical buildable area. Other issues may restrict the useful area of the site. A site analysis should be done to determine the practical buildable area as well as the best location for the house and many other site-related issues that should be addressed. They can have a major impact on the design of the house.

Even if your property consists of many acres and is not simply a building lot in a subdivision, I believe a site analysis is critical. Although your house placement will not be limited by legal constraints, there are many other factors you should evaluate to determine the *best* location on the property for your house and the actual area available for the house. Woodlands, wetlands, watercourses, and steep slopes might restrict the buildable area of an otherwise large piece of property. In fact, these site features can present some of the best opportunities and should not be overlooked.

The adjacent drawing is a site analysis.

It looks a little more complicated than it actually is. It shows where sunlight strikes the house at morning, noon, and evening during summer and winter and indicates the site's slope, view lines,

Mid Summer Sunset

Slope Exceeds 20%

Mid Winter Sunset

SLOPE EXCEEDS 20%

SIDE STREET 60' R/W (PRIVATE)

Midday Sun

Primary Direction of Approach

POSSIBLE HOUSE LOCATION

Indicates Significant Tree

Mid Summer Sunrise

Mid Winter Sunrise

MAIN STREET 60' R/W (PRIVATE)

Viewline

setbacks, neighboring structures, and other features. The purpose of a site analysis is to indicate key facts and opportunities about the site and to represent them in a graphic way so that you and your architect can determine the likely location or locations of the house, key aspects of the topography, the nature of the descent or climb of slopes, how the house relates to the surrounding views, and how parts of the house fit onto the site.

Orientation

When I say a house is "oriented" in a particular direction, I mean that it has the majority of the windows and glass doors on the side of the house that faces that direction: north, south, east, or west. Orientation has everything to do with keeping the house warm in cold weather and cool when it's hot and doing so in the most energy-efficient way. Orientation also directly affects the amount of natural light that comes into the house.

The most useful tool you can take with you to a prospective site, in addition to a pad and pen, is a compass. It's easy to become disoriented when you're driving on a lot of twisting and turning roads in the country or in a planned subdivision. A compass will help you keep oriented and will also help you determine whether the site—and therefore the house—will face an ideal direction. The compass doesn't have to be some expensive high-tech gadget, either; the one I carry when I visit sites is my daughter's old Girl Scout compass. Expensive surveyors' tools are not required.

Another piece of relatively sophisticated but inexpensive hardware I suggest you do purchase is a hand-held sight level. This device, which looks a little bit like a small kaleidoscope but without all the pretty colors at the end, has a horizontal line in the middle of the view scope along with a bubble like the kind you find on a carpenter's level. When you tilt the instrument until you see the bubble move to the precise dead center of the line, you will know your view of the terrain is dead level.

The purpose of a site level is to determine preliminarily whether there's a slope to the land and approximately how much.

There is a basic optical illusion when you look at land. Often, we look at a slope with the unaided eye and think the slope is much more gradual than it really is. In fact, the ground actually falls away at a much steeper rate than the human eye can easily see. What we think is level can actually be sloping down more steeply than our eyes can perceive. Conversely, if we are looking uphill, what our eyes tell us is level is actually more uphill than we think. Sometimes my clients who go out to visit properties without a sight level will tell me, "We've got a level lot." I'll go out there with my trusty sight level and discover that if they built a house on that lot, they would actually have a walk-out basement! The unaided eye is great for a million other things but is not a good instrument for measuring gradients or slopes on pieces of property. I look at building sites all the time, and I still get fooled by this optical illusion.

Whether you build your house in a cold or warm climate, the side of the house that will end up with many windows is likely to be the rear of the house. The back of the house is generally where you'll have the rooms such as the kitchen and the family room where your family does the most living. And naturally, these will be the rooms that probably will face the outdoor living spaces, the yard, or the nicest views. For the sake of privacy, you also may want the back of the house to have some of the bedrooms, especially if your site is on a busy, noisy street or the house will be situated close to the road where headlights can shine in the windows at night. The ideal site for your house should allow the side of the house with the most windows to face in the most advantageous direction.

If you're building in a wintry climate, you will want your house designed to capture natural light, brightening and warming the rooms you use the most during daylight hours. Winters can be gloomy, and light deprivation can cause a wintertime depression. A properly oriented house can relieve these symptoms simply by allowing as much of the available daylight into the house as possible. As a general though not absolute rule, houses built in cold climates should have southern exposures. This simply means that the side of the house with the most windows should face south. Southern sun is the easiest to control, and properly designed roof overhangs can limit the amount of sun that shines into the house (called solar gain) in the warm months when the sun is high in the sky, thus reduc-

If your view is of the Pacific Ocean, every decision concerning the house design will naturally revolve around this compelling feature.

ing heat buildup. Then in the wintertime, when the sun is low in the sky, lots of sun can stream in beneath the overhang, warming the body and cheering the soul.

Proper orientation is the first and most important principle of passive solar design. Positioning your house thoughtfully will keep your heating bills down by allowing the solar energy of the sunshine to warm your rooms for free. Conversely, if you're building in the South, I would suggest thinking about a piece of property with northern exposure. In hot climates, heating the house in the winter is much less of a concern than cooling the house in the long, hot summers, so it makes sense to keep the majority of your windows away from the intense summer sun.

A house oriented toward the east is nice in any climate. The morning sun is often not overly hot and is a welcome sight in the kitchen or breakfast room of your home. In the spring and fall, the low angle of the eastern sun can be glaring, however. You may find a need for window shades to keep this under control. Deciduous trees—trees that lose their leaves in the winter—can help with this condition. Try to utilize any existing trees when positioning the house to help control the sun naturally.

The western sun is the hardest to control and can be the biggest problem of any orientation. Unfortunately, this hot, low, glaring sun occurs at the hottest part of the day. Window shades can help, but western sun will radiate on the walls of your house, overheating the entire building. Even extremely large overhangs offer little shade because of the nearly horizontal angle of the setting sun.

Please keep in mind that these are merely guidelines and suggestions, not commandments. There are advantages and drawbacks to any orientation of a house, and the trick is to determine the best placement for your particular home. You don't have to reject a site just because the house cannot be oriented in the "ideal" way. A terrific view, a beautiful stand of trees, the Pacific Ocean, or some other attraction can compensate for the disadvantages of a problematic orientation.

Howdy, Neighbor

It is not enough simply to consider how your house will look from the street. You need to think about how it will look from other vantage points. If your house is on a hill, how will it look from a distance? Are there particular vantage points from which people in other houses can see yours? Early in the design process, you need to identify these critical vantage points and add them to your site analysis.

Every point from which your house can be viewed can and should be controlled. I like to think in terms of how a building looks from the long-distance point of view, the mid-distance point of view, and the close-up point of view. There is probably a place at some distance down the street where your house will be seen long before you actually arrive there, a place where the entire house is visible. Think of this as the "postcard" shot of the house. The angle at which the house sits on the site, the shapes of the rooflines, the height of the house above the ground, and the surrounding landscaping all play a role in composing this picture. The larger details of the house will be particularly important. Features such as the massing (overall shape) of the house, colors, and the play of light and shadow influence this view.

The mid-distance view is that from which visitors park their cars and start walking toward the front door. At this distance much more detail is visible. Things like window shapes, the pattern of the stone, and the chimney are features that influence the mid-distance view. It is likely at this point of view you may no longer be able to see the entire house because you may be too close.

The close-up view is what you see as you approach the front door. Here the finer details play an important role. The texture of the materials, the window muntins (window grids), the door handle, and the front door itself can be seen. If you think of the presentation of your house in terms of these three distinct vantage points, you will be better able to decide what features are important and which are superfluous.

You may wish not to present your house from one of these vantage points. For instance, what if you want to shield your house from the distant view, creating a perceived or actual remoteness from the street? You might want to position your house behind a stand of trees or over a rise and around a bend in the driveway to orchestrate a journey to "find" it. If you do not have the benefit of distance for this purpose, you can still create a house that "turns its back" on the street by designing the massing and details of the house to be more subdued and reserved. A front courtyard that encloses the

true arrival point can aid in achieving this sense of distance from the street, adding another layer to the entry experience.

Think about what might eventually happen on the empty lots that are adjacent or near to your site. If you don't own something, you don't control it. Too often people are surprised and angered when their neighbors have the audacity to build a house on the lot next door and block out the view! Or worse—the rolling farm field you can see from your family room soon becomes a hundred new houses. The reality is that those other properties belong to someone, someone who has a legal right to develop that property, just as you have a right to build on your property.

To prevent this heartache, factor in the likelihood of the location, type, and size of house or houses that might be built on those pieces of empty land. That way you won't have your future neighbor peering into your backyard or vice versa. Recognize that all that pristine acreage might also be subdivided into building lots. Instead of a meadow or a potato field, you might end up with houses and more families surrounding you. It's not free parkland if it belongs to someone else who might sell it to a developer.

Ironically, the loudest protesters against development are often those individuals who have just moved into the neighborhood. I've heard this called the "I've got mine" or "last settler" syndrome. You can call it pulling in the drawbridge or pulling up the ladder, and it happens all too often. I live near an airport, and I was amazed when my neighbors in our relatively new development were outraged that the airport was planning to expand. They didn't want the noise. Most of us moved to this part of North Carolina expressly because of the growing economy. We chose our particular neighborhood at least partly because it was convenient to the airport. I asked one of my neighbors if when he moved in he actually thought the airport was going to stay the same size while everything else grew up around it. Did he really think he was going to be the last one to move in? That question was met with a blank stare.

Remember, you don't control what happens to another piece of land unless you own it, and the things you can't buy, like an airport, need to be considered along with everything else. One creative solution to this dilemma is to purchase a "view easement." I saw a beautiful villa in Indonesia that afforded a long-distance view across some rice fields. The house was critically dependant on this view. The villa's owner purchased a view easement. He had struck a deal with the rice farmer. He paid the farmer an annual fee to keep growing rice and not to sell the land to a developer. It was a classic win-win situation. The farmer saw an increase in his income, thus removing any pressure to sell the land for profit, and the villa owner maintained his view for a fraction of the cost of actually buying the large acreage.

If you find a piece of property that happens to abut a national park or a forest, that is an added value. You will get the visual use of that parkland or forest without having to buy it. This is the primary reason property adjacent to golf courses is more expensive than interior lots. It's not because people may especially like watching other amateurs play golf but because a golf course offers controlled open space with no immediate neighbors. It is a more attractive view out across a fairway than into someone else's backyard. Plus, you don't have to mow the grass. When developers are looking for an edge, a way to make a new development more attractive and have their building lots sell for higher prices, they often build a golf course. Oceans and lakes are attractive, too, for much the same reason—but it's a lot easier to build a golf course than an ocean.

Slope

The slope of the land is a major consideration when selecting a property. Is there a slope, and how much does it slope or fall? Which way does it fall? By "fall" I mean which direction would I walk to face downhill? Does the entire property slope, or is the slope in just a portion of the property?

Sloping lots can offer many wonderful opportunities, but if the slope is too severe, problems and added expenses arise. I've found that many people avoid sites that fall or slope downward from the road. The fear is that you will end up with what I call "a house in a hole." As you approach a house like this, you feel like you are driving onto the roof, and not much of the front of the house is visible. If the steep driveway ends abruptly at the house, you may feel like you are about to drive onto the roof or crash into the front door. One remedy for this can be to position the house farther from the road, if the site allows. In so doing, the house may actually end up even lower down from the road, but the added distance back away from the road can allow you to see more of the front walls of the house and less of the roof. This may require a fairly large lot with adequate depth from the road.

Certain kinds of features add a sense of verticality to a house and can aid in reducing the sense that a house is too low relative to the road. A front door assembly with a taller window above it or a two-story entryway can help make the house taller. A front facing gable at the second-story level increases height. Gables look taller than hipped roofs because there is more visible wall surface. Dormers break up the massiveness of the roof. Roofs offer a comforting, sheltering sensation when viewed from below the eave line. When you see a roof from above, we become disconnected from the people living within,

and the house seems less welcoming. When dealing with a downhill lot, anything you can do to present more wall surface, complete with windows and doors, and less roof surface to the approaching viewpoint will help to pull the house, visually, out of its hole.

A nearly impossible situation is a site that slopes steeply downward from the road and is shallow, preventing you from placing the house back from the street. I would recommend that you avoid such a property unless it offers benefits, such as a marvelous view from within the house. That sort of major asset might make the challenge and the likely compromise on the appearance from the street worth overcoming.

A site that slopes upward from the street, if not too steep, can make your house look majestic and offer some nice separation from the road. If an

This house suffers from the "house in a hole" syndrome. It was positioned too close to the road, thus creating the appearance of the house having "slipped over the edge." Additionally, the house lacks any verticality. A one-story front façade never has a chance to assert itself when the land drops away so abruptly.

impressive "curb appeal" is one of your objectives, you might want to look for a lot like this. But choose carefully. If the upslope is too steep or abrupt, the house may look as though it's perched on the side of a cliff. Although that can be a dramatic look in some people's eyes, it can be an uncomfortable feeling for others. A steep upslope can also provide a physical challenge in reaching the garage and the front door. Handicapped accessibility becomes nearly impossible. Consider where your guests might park and the hill they may have to climb. Consider also the hill you will have to climb to get your mail and newspaper.

I feel the most versatile slopes are "cross slopes." A cross slope is a slope that falls from left to right or from right to left as you stand on the street facing the property. If a house sits on a cross slope, the ground can usually be sculpted to achieve the precise effect you want to create. It allows you to plan some of the rooms on the main level of the house to be at ground level. These rooms might be the kitchen and family room, thereby allowing for easy access to patios, terraces, yards, and gardens. The garage could be at this same level, making automobile access, daily entry to the house, and the connection to the kitchen from the garage convenient by eliminating stairs to climb when you are carrying an armload of groceries. The front door is best located only a few steps above ground level. When the front door is unusually high above the natural ground level, the house will inevitably look awkward and will not seem to suit its site.

When working with a cross slope, consider placing a first-floor master bedroom on the side of the house where the slope has fallen away. With this arrangement, your master bedroom would be essentially on an upper floor relative to the ground, at a nice elevation above the property. Many people are uncomfortable with exterior doors that lead directly into the master bedroom and feel less safe in that situation. A sloping lot can easily solve this problem while still keeping the master bedroom suite on the main living level.

Another consideration with a sloping site is drainage. If a house sits at the bottom of a hill, drainage is going to be a challenge, although not necessarily an insurmountable one. Dealing with water is arguably the toughest problem a building site can present. It's expensive, time-consuming, and frustrating to get water to change its natural course. Water that drains downhill and then is blocked by your house will need to be diverted. Drainage swales, yard drains, and earthen berms may be necessary to resolve the issue. I have seen far too many houses positioned so that rainfall landing on the driveway runs directly to the garage doors. This creates a situation where the water from a cloudburst thunderstorm can flow up to and sometimes into the garage. If this water is diverted just in front of the door, puddles form and unsightly stains develop. In the wintertime, in northern climates, these puddles become dangerous patches of ice.

Don't buy a piece of property that collects water from neighboring properties unless there is adequate space on the site to divert this extra runoff properly. Surface runoff—the water on top of the ground—along with the subsurface flow—the water you can't

This house sits well below the level of the road, but because it has been positioned farther back, the front wall of the house is clearly visible. That attracts our eyes to the wall and not the roof. The two-story façade, the vertical features on the front, and the dormer windows that dot the roofline also enhance the height of the house and prevent the "house in a hole" syndrome.

see that runs between layers of subsurface soils and rocks—can combine to create expensive nightmares. The more water that flows into your property, the more cash is likely to flow out of your bank account. Be extremely wary of any property that has drainage issues. Try to figure out how much of the surrounding land is shedding its rainfall onto you property. A gentle rise on the neighboring land is fine, but if you're looking at a piece of property that is situated toward the bottom of a hill, thus gathering the runoff from the entire neighborhood, I would strongly suggest that you look elsewhere unless this site offers other substantial benefits, such as lush

vegetation or a "postcard" view. Be sure that the probable location for your house is not the lowest spot on the site. Water problems will be inevitable unless you bring a lot of fill dirt in and raise the level of this low spot. Water just will not run uphill.

Parts of a site may be unbuildable because the slope is too severe. This may not be simply the determination of your architect and builder. Many properties are regulated by zoning and planning ordinances that prohibit construction on slopes steeper than a maximum rate. These rules are created to prevent excessive soil erosion and to control flooding.

Views

Arguably, the most compelling aspect of any piece of property is the view. It could be an awe-inspiring view of the red rocks of Sedona or a peaceful view into a woodland glade. If your property has a view, spend some time considering how your house will relate to the view when it is positioned on the site. One thing often overlooked is the impact of the angle of the sun on the view. If you are considering a waterfront site, think about whether there might be sun glare from the water. If your house looks out on the ocean or a lake and the sun is setting into the water, you might have a wonderful sunset to share with your loved ones each evening—or you might have a level of glare and reflection off the water that is difficult to control. Still, sunset views are so compelling that you may very well choose to deal with the sun glare in order to gain the great sunsets.

South facing waterfront sites can receive glare at midday, but because the sun is high in the sky then, roof overhangs can control the solar heat gain effectively. Personally, I prefer a waterfront site that faces north when you have a water view because it eliminates or reduces the problem of glare and having the sun at your back illuminates the view so beautifully. East is the second best waterfront orientation, causing glare only in the cooler morning hours. Later in the day, when the sun has moved to the southern sky,

the objects within the view will be nicely lit.

Another issue to consider with site selection is the "direction of approach" to your new home. In most cases, you, your family, and your friends will always approach your house from one particular direction. It may be that the house lies on a cul-de-sac, in which case you will always approach the house from the same direction. Even in neighborhoods where streets do not end in cul-de-sacs, chances are you'll still approach the house from the same direction every time—the direction that takes you to and from the highway or some other primary street.

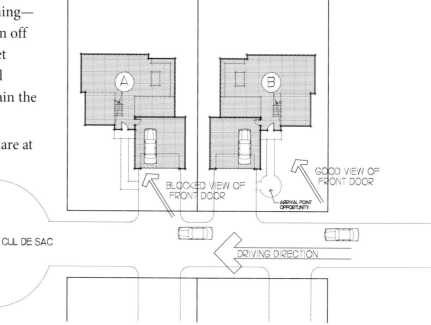

Pay attention to the orientation of your house, especially on narrow lots where the garage is prominent. If you will always be driving toward your house from the same direction, such as when living on a cul-de-sac street, don't let the garage block the view of the front door as you drive up, as illustrated by House A. Flip the house plan, if possible, as illustrated by House B. This will create a more pleasant arrival. Even in a narrow lot situation, a "point of arrival" can still be created by framing and presenting the house to the road or by creating a "place" in the landscaping at the bend in the walkway.

Too often, this issue is not addressed or even considered, but I feel it is a critically important factor in the design of your house. This is the important distant viewpoint you see when first encountering your house that we discussed earlier. As simple and obvious as it may seem, you should locate the garage so you see the front door of the house before you reach the garage. Otherwise, you'll have to look around your garage to see the front of your house every single time you approach your house. When an architect makes the simple decision to put the garage on the correct side of the house, a host of problems are solved very easily, but I am stunned at how often this basic principle is neglected.

Boulders, Trees, and Other Physical Features

A "conventional wisdom" myth says that big rocks or boulders on a building site create a serious problem. This is sometimes true, but in reality boulders usually can be handled without too much difficulty. Most can be rolled away, and very large boulders usually cost only about two or three thousand dollars to break up and move, and the rocks that remain can be great features in your landscaping. Depending on your budget, this may be an acceptable cost.

I did, however, say that this myth is sometimes true. On a recent

project, those "few boulders" that showed on the surface turned out to be the top of the mountain! Tens of thousands of dollars later, the rocks had been broken up and moved. These costs will not be absorbed by your builder. Every contract has a "rock clause." The land is yours, and you are responsible for all of the underground conditions, including rock, water, or buried washing machines. Don't laugh. I actually had this happen. Or skeletons! I had that happen, too. But that's a story for another time.

Another conventional wisdom myth is that you should dig test holes in order to find out whether there is rock underneath the property. The problem with test holes is that they tell you only what's in each test hole. There could be a massive boulder a foot away from the test hole, and you wouldn't know it was there until you dug the real hole for the house

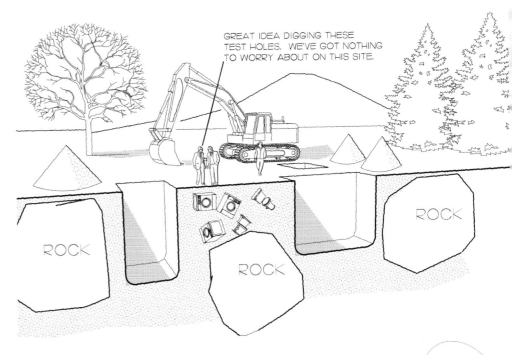

GREAT IDEA DIGGING THESE TEST HOLES. WE'VE GOT NOTHING TO WORRY ABOUT ON THIS SITE.

ROCK

ROCK

ROCK

foundation. I usually only recommend digging test holes if the geology of the area is known to have a shelf of rock and you want to know how deep the shelf lies or if there is a reason to worry about a high water table. Test holes usually don't give much information on underground water problems like springs either, unless you happen to dig directly on top of a spring.

If you are building in an area with questionable soils, such as low-lying areas or areas with expansive clay soils, please bring in a soils engineer to properly evaluate the soils and determine what type of footing is required. The same holds true if you are building in a seismically active area. Consult an engineer or architect.

Trees are a major site feature that can become an unexpected problem. We look for trees when we scout building sites. We fall in love with the foliage. The site looks "homey" from the start. More often than not, however, the big tree you liked so much when you first saw the property turns out to be located exactly where the house needs to go. This can cause no small amount of heartache, because it's painful to see a big, beautiful tree uprooted for the sake of building a house. Specimen trees should be accurately located on your site plan and subtracted from the practical buildable area in your site analysis. You should do the same with any other unique physical feature. Maybe there is an old stone wall or foundation from a demolished building that might become a focal feature in a wonderful garden. Maybe there is a depression in the land that could become a water feature or a bog garden.

In many new communities, where developers are trying to squeeze as many lots as possible out of the overall piece of property, there may be little or no regard for where trees are situated or for drainage issues. Because of this, a tree or drainage course could end up right in the middle of where you want to build a house. This is why you see so much clear-cutting of trees in tract home developments.

In well-planned communities, before subdividing, enlightened planners perform a site analysis of

We encountered rock on this site and positioned the house accordingly. The rocks were no longer a problem and actually formed the inspiration for this lovely water garden.

HOW TO SAVE TREES

Your trees are a valuable asset on your building site. With all due respect to your builder, don't leave the protection of your trees entirely up to him. This is a place where you need to pay attention. Improperly protected trees may look fine for a year or two, but unfortunately they will gradually die. You need to know what you can and cannot do near trees. As a rule, the worse the soils, the more sensitive the trees will be. If you are building in an area like where I live in North Carolina, it seems that all you have to do is look at a tree cross-eyed and it dies. Our soils are composed of heavy clay that compacts easily and does not hold water well.

During construction, the area beneath the limbs of any tree you wish to save must be blocked off from construction traffic. The outward extent of the limbs defines what is called the "drip line." It indicates the portion of the ground that the limbs and leaves of the tree shelter from rain.

The majority of the tree's feeder roots are located within the drip line. These roots are at or near the surface of the ground. If they're damaged, the tree will die. Vehicular traffic can damage these roots and compact the soil. Compaction is bad, as it prevents the feeder roots from getting oxygen. If soil is deposited on the feeder roots, even if only a couple of inches deep, the roots will be smothered and damaged. Don't bury the feeder roots! If more rainwater runoff is directed toward a tree than was flowing there prior to construction, the tree can drown. Roots need oxygen.

Contrary to popular belief, most trees do not have tap roots, i.e., roots that extend deep into the soil directly under a tree. Most roots spread horizontally from the trunk and don't penetrate the soil very far. The roots near the surface are the critical roots to be saved.

In order to save a tree, you must erect tree protection fencing beyond its drip line. The people building your house often want to park their trucks under trees to keep them in the shade. This protection fencing prevents that from happening. It's not a bad idea to begin feeding and mulching the roots of trees before the trauma of construction begins. Make sure they are adequately watered. All of these measures will help compensate for the loss of any feeder roots that extend out past the area you have protected. Poor soils, such as heavy clays, cause trees to extend feeder roots much farther than the drip line. Be aware of this and take added precautions.

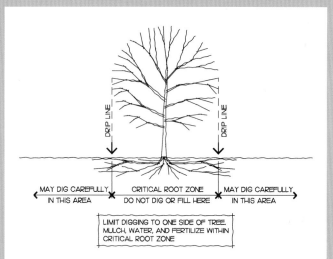

The area beneath the limbs of a tree is critical to the tree's survival. Tree protection fencing should be placed around the entire drip-zone to prevent vehicles from compacting the soil on the feeder roots that occupy this zone. No soil should be placed on the roots. Often, tree damage does not show for a year or two after the construction is completed. It is better to be overly cautious and not have to remove a good tree a few years later.

There are methods that let you place limited fill-in soil on top of feeder roots, cut through portions of the roots, and do other things while still saving a tree. The National Arbor Day Foundation has free information that tells how to do these things. It might also be a good idea to get the advice of a professional arborist.

the entire tract of land to determine where the natural drainage patterns are and to locate the significant wooded areas, specimen trees, and other natural features. Then the planners establish property lines along drainage courses, preventing natural runoff from flowing through the middle of a building lot, and they will work to place property lines in positions that eliminate the need to uproot specimen trees or bulldoze groves. The developer may even designate sensitive environmental areas as "common property," thus giving up valuable building lots he could have created. Often the building lots in communities like this will cost more, but they are worth it.

Noise and Wind

Other site-related issues may not be readily apparent when you initially visit the site. These might include noise and other inconveniences. Find out whether your new home is going to end up located under the takeoff or landing routes of a nearby airport or near a highway that may be widened in the future. Will you be dealing with rush hour or special event traffic? These aren't necessarily deal killers, but they are things you want to think about before plunking down any money for the land. Ask the neighbors what it's like to live under the flight path. It may not be as bad as you think. In fact, many fine developments are situated underneath the flight paths of regional or executive airports and don't suffer for it.

Prevailing winds can offer natural cooling, and the house should be designed to receive this natural air conditioning; however, too much wind can be a problem. I recently designed a house in Hawaii where wind is a major factor. The islands are blessed with persistent, cooling trade winds that blow more than ninety percent of the time. But when the wind

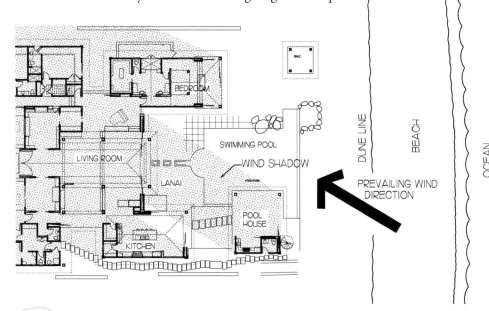

On a beachfront site, where the trade winds blow most of the time, portions of the structure were placed to buffer the wind. The shaded areas represent the wind shadows cast by the pool house and the house walls. On the ocean side of the pool house, sliding glass doors were installed to be pulled across and shield the space on days when the trade winds blow hard. The result is that the pool house is comfortable to use on nearly any day.

is strong, it can limit the enjoyment of lovely tropical outdoor living. I had to consider the wind's direction and think about how to place outdoor living spaces within "wind shadows" I could create through careful placement of building elements and land-scaping. The result was that even on the windiest days, at least some of the multi-paneled, sliding glass door units could remain open without everything in the house blowing away.

Problem Lots

The Chinese symbol for crisis is also the symbol for opportunity. And this concept applies to so-called "problem lots." It often happens that in any given subdivision there will be at least a few lots that don't conform to the basic expectations of architects, builders, and home buyers. These lots might be similar to the type we discussed earlier that may have many large rocks that will be expensive to move or have a large tree located right in the middle of the property. There may be drainage issues, or the slope may not be ideal from the point of view of placing a relatively standard house on the lot. You don't, however, automatically have to shy away from a problem lot. It can actually provide outstanding opportunities for houses that are truly unique and delightful. From an architect's point of view, problem lots can make for more interesting final designs. When a piece of property has restrictions of slope, special trees to work around, or rock outcroppings, an architect usually finds such a challenging site more interesting and exciting than a flat, plain-vanilla lot. Granted, working with difficult land is

Faced with an exceptionally steep lot, we created a delightfully private motor court, held securely between the house and brick garden walls. Beyond the motor court is a private walled garden. An overview photo of this courtyard can be seen on the first page of Lesson Three.

harder, but it is actually more fun and rewarding because the end result is usually far more dramatic and creative than a house on a standard lot will be.

Ironically, problem lots can possibly save you money. They get passed over by others who lack imagination, so they can often be purchased for tens of thousands of dollars less than neighboring "good" lots. Don't be afraid to negotiate a better price. These lots are sometimes extremely difficult for a developer to sell to a builder. In some cases, a builder may own the development and build all the houses. Other times, the developer may select builders to build the subdivision, either by selling lots to individuals who then must use a builder from the list of approved builders, or the developer arranges for a few builders to put up spec houses and then places those builders on the list of approved builders. Generally, when builders are building spec houses, they want to bypass challenging lots. So those lots are often left over and built on last. An opportunity may exist to make a pretty good deal by taking a problem lot off the hands of the developer if you're not worried about how to squeeze a standard house onto an unusual lot.

Keep in mind that problem lots can also cost you extra money. You're going to have to pay for good advice from your architect, your builder, and your engineer. The key is to know exactly what the problem is and how to solve it before you put your money down. Your goal should be to get enough of a discount on the lot price to compensate for the possible extra costs of building the house. In these cases good advice is essential. A problem lot is a little like finding an undervalued stock on Wall Street. Its value will rise in the hands of the individual who recognizes what it is truly worth.

Reading a Site Plan

A site plan is a drawing that shows the physical and legal aspects of a given piece of land. It's up to the architect, landscape architect, and engineer to create a site plan for you, but you, as the client, should make sure you understand it.

The site plan will show many of the things we have previously discussed. There will be property lines that define the perimeter or limits of the site. Again, in most of the United States, your property

stops short of the curb. The site plan will show where your property stops and the public right of way begins. The site plan is a graphic representation of the property. Your deed is a written representation of the property.

Setback requirements for the side, front, and rear yards will be shown as well as any easements. The site plan should also show the topography. Topography is the lay or slope of the land. It is shown with "contour lines" that represent the elevation of the land above sea level. Contour lines are often delineated in one-foot, five-foot, or ten-foot increments. If you have a contour line that is labeled as 100′, that means if you were to walk along the property following that line, you would be constantly at an elevation of 100′ above sea level. If you were to walk to another portion of the property that was delineated by the 90′ contour, you would have descended ten feet. One way to get a feel for the slope is simply to look at how close the contour lines are to each other. The closer they are, the steeper the slope.

A site plan may also denote any surface features, tree locations, and existing buildings or other constructions. I always recommend that a proper survey be done by a professional surveyor to be sure you have accurate information about the site to work from. This is critical to avoiding unpleasant surprises later on.

Once you go through the process of considering all the factors we've discussed in this lesson, the right building location on your site will all but announce itself. On a large piece of property, you might have several different ways to position a house. On a

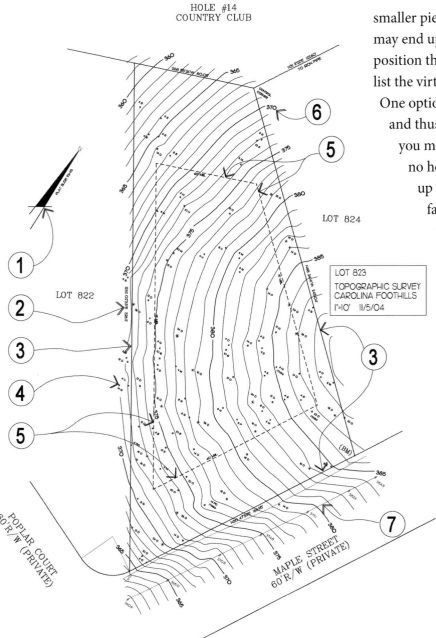

HOLE #14
COUNTRY CLUB

LOT 824

LOT 823
TOPOGRAPHIC SURVEY
CAROLINA FOOTHILLS
1"=10'   11/5/04

LOT 822

POPLAR COURT
60' R/W (PRIVATE)

MAPLE STREET
60' R/W (PRIVATE)

smaller piece or on a so-called "problem lot," you may end up with one way—one perfect way—to position the house. If you do have multiple options, list the virtues of each possibility before you decide. One option might take better advantage of the slope and thus afford better views. Another might offer you more privacy from your neighbors. Again, no house can be all things to all people—so it's up to you and your architect to decide what factors or amenities matter most to you and what you're willing to sacrifice in order to get the house that most closely resembles the perfect one of your dreams.

I have spent a lot of time discussing how to evaluate potential sites for *Your Perfect House* because this is arguably the most critical issue since the site can present so many opportunities and so many restrictions. Doing the proper homework in site selection will greatly improve your chances of success. Once you've chosen the site that best meets your needs, it's time to finish planning the house. Architects call this phase "programming," and it's the subject of our next lesson.

A typical property survey will have the following information: 1–A North Arrow indicating which direction is north; 2–Metes and Bounds or another property boundary definition indicating the length and direction of the property lines; 3–The Property Lines; 4–Significant trees or rock outcroppings; 5–Maximum Building Lines indicating the limit of where construction can occur; 6–Contour Lines and Elevations indicating the height of the ground above sea level; and 7–The line of the curb or the edge of the pavement of the street. Easements, existing buildings, culvert pipes, etc. may also be shown.

A rotunda breakfast room topped by an office of similar shape is reflected in the infinity-edged swimming pool. The roofed veranda, the built-in outdoor grill, and the screened gazebo to the right complete a restful, private oasis.

Lesson Eight

PROGRAMMING THE HOUSE

"The dialogue between client and architect is about as intimate as any conversation you can have, because when you are talking about building a house, you're talking about dreams."
–ROBERT A. M. STERN

Once you've selected a site—or possibly while you are selecting your site—you should refine the planning of the house. Known as "programming" in architectural terms, this is when you and your architect decide exactly what the house and its grounds will contain and what the characteristics of the house will be. Programming is the process of determining what rooms and spaces you want, what their characteristics will be, and how each room or space will interact with other rooms or spaces. Often, it is easiest to start with a simple list of the primary rooms and spaces. Then, refine the list as you become more immersed in the planning process. Ultimately, you will be creating one basic list of rooms with target sizes and another detailed list of each room with a paragraph or a series of notes about the characteristics of those rooms.

This is the time in the planning process when we begin to ask questions not so much about design but about the way you live, or the way you would like to live. There are too many possible questions to list here, but here are just a few samples:

- How old are your children?
- What rooms or spaces should be adjacent and communicate with each other?
- Which rooms or spaces should be separated from others?
- How often do you eat meals as a family?
- How often would you like to eat meals as a family?
- Should the kitchen overlook the playroom, so that you can cook a meal while keeping an eye on the children?
- Do two or more people work in the kitchen at the same time?
- Where will televisions be located? Will sound be an issue?
- Do you want your kids to be able to have computer bays in a children's work/play area that can be monitored from the kitchen? This is an increasingly popular alternative to having the kids be alone in their rooms doing homework, with or without their computers.
- Do you need work spaces, private offices, or project rooms?
- Do you need a music room?

Try to think through every aspect of your daily lives and jot down notes as you go. Think about the houses where you have lived in the past. What worked and what did not work for you? What have you wished you had? What could have been better?

After thinking through the living spaces, we come to the bedrooms. In the programming phase, you will decide how many bedrooms will be downstairs and how many upstairs, if you're planning on having an upstairs. Think about creating a buffer between the first-floor bedrooms, which are very private and quiet places, and the kitchen, a "public" and noisy space. If the transition between these two functions is too abrupt, there will be a harsh interface, and both areas will become uncomfortable. You don't want to have the smell of food or the sound of food preparation interfering with a good night's sleep, and you don't want to feel that the people in the kitchen are just a step away from your bed. If the house is fairly large, sheer distance may provide all the transition necessary, and you may find yourself considering a back staircase that leads from the bedroom area upstairs to the kitchen/family area downstairs.

What about the bathrooms? Does the master bedroom have separate "his-and-hers" vanity and sink areas? How much closet space do you want? Are the closets separate or joined? Are there other "specialty" spaces you need or want, such as a wood shop, a home theater, or an exercise room?

Be as thorough as you can, but accept the fact that you cannot sit down and think of everything off the top of your head. Consider this to be an open list. You can always add things later as they occur to you. Once you feel you have captured most of your ideas, it's time for you and your architect to write up the list of rooms and target sizes. From here, you will start to decide how one space will relate to another. For example, will the family room be open to the kitchen, or will it be separate? Will there be a separate living room and family room, or will they be connected as well? Which rooms should enjoy the view? Which rooms need to have access to the outdoors? Where should sunlight enter? Do you want morning light in your bedroom, or should it be as dark as possible? You may already have been making notes about these things as you were asking yourself all those questions about how you live.

A difficult question to answer is, "How big should the rooms be?" Most of us are not accustomed to thinking of our rooms in terms of feet and inches. We simply know, like Goldilocks, that they are too big, too small, or just right. Your architect, however, will need to convert those feelings into real dimensions. To help him and to give you some sort of yardstick for knowing what the right sizes should be, I would suggest you use your existing house as a baseline and tell your architect, "I want my new dining room to be five feet longer than my current dining room." Or, "Our master bedroom is pretty good right now, but I would sure like it to be a little wider so we don't have to squeeze by each other as we walk past the foot of the bed."

Another useful way of getting at the answer to the "How big…" question is to tell your architect what you would like the room or space to do. What function must it perform? For instance, a comment like, "I want to be able to seat sixteen people in my new dining room, but I don't know how big that needs to be," is extremely useful. Your architect can

then figure out the best size for the space, and you'll be sure it will serve your needs.

Putting Walls and Ceilings around Spaces

Many clients believe the design of a house begins with the design of the exterior. That's actually putting the cart before the horse. I like to start off with the program we just created.

Each space or room needs to be the correct and appropriate size for its function and "feel." That means it should not be too large or too small. Room design is not a case where bigger is better. For instance, a dining room should be big enough for its function, and the furniture should fit comfortably without crowding. On the other hand, you don't want to have an overly large dining room because you don't want your dining table and your guests to feel dwarfed by the space. It would lose its comfortable quality. To envision this, think of how your dining room set might look floating around in your great room. It would be noticeably awkward.

A huge master bedroom can be dramatic, but it may actually be cold, drafty, and not conducive to good sleep. Intimacy could be lost. Your living room needs to be large enough to hold the furniture but not so large it feels like a hotel lobby. It is a valuable exercise to revisit room sizes several times, asking yourself, "What's this space for? How much space does it truly need? How will this feel?"

Think through the function of each space and how much area each space needs to fulfill that function properly, both in a physical and psychological sense. The design of the house will put a "shell" around those spaces. This shell, or physical embodiment of the edges of the space, whether it consists of walls, columns, a shape in the ceiling above, or whatever will define the space. In architectural terms, we have "concretized" the space when we have created a physical and/or perceptual edge around it. We will have created a solid manifestation of the space we perceive. The magic of good architecture happens when we feel and sense that the physical definition of a space is appropriate and "fits" the space just right. It is your architect's job to define that space in physical terms and to manifest it in the built environment, carving it out of the endless space we discussed early in this book.

Look around you as you go through your day and take note of how spaces are defined. Four walls are an obvious way, but try to notice how a rug in the middle of a large room can define the space within a larger room. See how a special ceiling does the same job. Make yourself more aware of these effects.

Why Did They Ever Call It a Living Room?

Today, many of my clients eschew the traditional living room and family room in favor of having a study and a "great room." A study is a room where you might sit next to the fire, watch TV, or read the newspaper or a book when you don't want to be interrupted. A room like this might be comfortable for one to four people. Any more than that and it starts to feel crowded. If the room is large enough for more people, it will lose its quality of comfort when only a couple of people are in it. This is often the most comfortable place in the house. The great room is used for an assembly of friends, yours or your children's. It is a room that should be larger and able to embrace more people comfortably.

Traditional living rooms often suffer from the "museum factor" we discussed earlier. They tend to be in an area of the house where no one goes.

Rooms can be defined while still flowing together. Here a wide, trimmed opening punctuated by two Tuscan columns clearly marks where the dining room ends and the living room begins. The two arched openings define a stronger separation between the living room and the elegant foyer beyond.

Usually, they have only one way in and are not conducive to through traffic, so even when you are entertaining they become a dead-end for guests. Worst of all, they are the home of the "good furniture." You know the kind I mean. This is the furniture no one is supposed to sit on. People often feel too intimidated to sit in living rooms, even their own living rooms. These rooms often look as if they've been designed for a photo shoot by interior designers who really don't want anybody messing up their creations. Sometimes it seems that the only real purpose of a living room is to intimidate the boyfriend of your teenaged daughter when he picks her up for a date. Few people really make much use of their living room, which is why it makes sense to use that square footage elsewhere, like some place that might actually get some use.

It does not increase the cost of construction to think these issues through in advance and put things in the right places. In fact, this kind of thorough planning will save significant amounts of money by avoiding later costly changes during construction when it suddenly occurs to you that you should have done something another way.

Programming Equals Learning

While you develop your list of the rooms and spaces you desire in *Your* Perfect House, you will naturally be developing notes about the characteristics of those spaces. Here's where you can put your word processor to good use. I think it's a good idea to create an evolving list of the criteria, characteristics, and interrelationships of these spaces. It must be

"evolving" because, as I said earlier, it is impossible to sit down and think of everything you want or need. Your first effort will be a start; then, as you work through the process, more ideas will come to mind. When you visit other houses, see photos of rooms, or when you are simply going about your daily life, your mind will keep working, and you will find yourself adding things to the list. I think these later thoughts happen because the entire process of designing your house is actually educating you and sensitizing you to design issues you may not have paid much conscious attention to in the past. You will be "learning" what your house "wants" to be.

Begin the list with the names of the primary spaces. Then, beneath each room name, add the characteristics and criteria as you think of them. Make notes on even the most detail-oriented items, lest you forget them. These notes will later serve as a checklist for you and your architect. Don't worry about prioritizing the list just yet. We'll do that soon. The benefit of using a word processor for this task is that editing is very easy.

A Matter of Style

Thomas Jefferson said, "In matters of style, swim with the current; in matters of principle, stand like a rock." This is good advice. Style comes and goes with the times and is subject to our individual whims and tastes. Principles of good design endure. Good architectural design has a place in any style.

You, and you alone, should determine the style of *Your* Perfect House. Do you want it to look like a French farmhouse? An English manor? A contemporary, hillside retreat? Is it a Balinese-influenced house in Hawaii like the one I just finished? Is there an image in your mind's eye? Do you want the architect to interpret your wishes and create something unique? Is your style hard to express in words, but you'll know it when you see it? Whatever it may be, it should be yours, alone, and not simply a response to other people telling you what to do.

Now, I have to confess that I have a very hard time placing a style label on the houses I design. I leave the labels for others. I did make up one recently for clients named Carol and Rick. Their friends kept asking them what style their new house was. I suggested "Carolandrick," which I pronounced, "Car-o-lán-drick." It gave them a good answer for the question, and the questioner never wants to admit that he or she is unfamiliar with the "well-known" Carolandrick style.

Most of my houses tend to grow out of many influences. Much of the fun of what I do is creating houses that are not all the same. It's more challenging—and more rewarding—to avoid designing with the same "kit of parts," project after project. Many architects limit themselves to one style, and many openly disdain vernacular architecture or criticize new buildings done in a traditional style. This is unfortunate. I consider style to be simply one criterion of the program. After all, good food comes in many different styles, and it can all still be great cuisine. Why shouldn't great architecture come in many styles? There is a current trend toward creating what is called a "new old house," in which the detailing—and thus the charm—of a two-hundred-

Style is a matter of taste and personal preference. The style of Your Perfect House *should be unique to you and your family.*

year-old house is built right in from the beginning. We talked earlier about the value of nostalgia and the humanizing qualities of traditional design. Factors like these may drive the style of *Your* Perfect House.

Be aware, though, that labels and style names can be confusing. If you tell me that you want a house reminiscent of the Italian hill country, you may have a mental image of a refined, hillside villa that is dramatically different from the image of a rustic, agrarian building that may come to my mind. Remember what we discussed earlier. Communication failures are the cause of many problems in design and construction. Communicate as clearly as you can. To that end, I urge my clients to start clipping out pictures from magazines. An excellent interior designer I work with refers to these clippings as "inspiration images," a wonderful phrase. Inspiration images do not dictate exactly what the house will be, and we are not planning to copy the buildings and details that are shown in the pictures. The pictures simply communicate an idea or an impression. These images don't even have to be consistent with each other. They can show a wide variety of styles and details. Leave it to your architect to find the common threads among the images that inspire you. Inspiration images are truly pictures that are worth a thousand words.

It is just as useful to cut out pictures of things you don't like as it is to show the architect elements you do want in your house. The more visual information you can provide your architect, the easier it is for him to create *Your* Perfect House. You can even tell him things like, "I like the way the doorway opens up to the room beyond in this picture, but I don't like these windows alongside it. I like the windows in this other picture." Your job is to select the players, so to speak. If the architect is a good one, he'll get them to play as a team. Never be reluctant to discuss or show your architect things you like just

because you can't envision how they can become a part of the design. Leave it to him either to incorporate what you want or show you why it doesn't work.

Once you have some idea of the basic style of the house, it's time to enhance the program with a wish list of special features or characteristics that will make your home a unique and special place. Some examples of elements like these might be a sunken tub in the master bath with a glass door to a private garden, a meditation loft reached by a nearly secret passageway, a breakfast area that places you fully into the garden, a study with heavy wood paneling, or a massive stone fireplace that psychologically anchors the entire structure. I urge you to write out a list of what you want. Even small details should be written down when you think of them. It's nearly impossible to think of them later, and no detail should be forgotten.

Provide your architect with the most information possible about the way you want to live. Try to avoid vague statements and generalizations such as "I want my house to be traditional." What exactly does that convey? After all, there are a lot of different traditions in the world. One of my clients once said, "I want the library to look like a gentleman's smoking club, without the cigars." This description gave me a very clear indication of what he wanted: a very British feel, with wood paneling, rich colors, and elegant bookshelves. Whether you use photographs cut out from magazines or you paint word pictures for your architect, the more visual information you can provide, the better off you both will be.

This accomplished golfer has an extensive collection of golfing memorabilia, but he did not want to display it prominently in his paneled library. The spiral staircase descends into the room he calls the golf room, where only selected guests may visit.

We mentioned earlier the idea of nostalgia as a key driver in the process of designing a home. Now is the time to wax nostalgic and ask yourself what design elements from your childhood home, your grandparents' home, or even the home you have only dreamed of appeal to you. There is no need to know exactly where or when you saw something you always wanted. That doesn't matter. What matters is to get it into your program list. It's often hard to retrofit a design with these sorts of specific details later on.

After you've written down your wish list of design elements, you should categorize these desires in importance. I suggest putting them into three separate categories. In Category A place the elements that the house absolutely must contain. In other words, you're telling the architect it's not worth building the house without these elements. In Category B place the items in which some compromise may be acceptable, but you want the architect to find a way to make them happen. Category C is for items about which you'd say, "Don't compromise something else for this, but if it's possible, please find a way to include it."

Balancing and Maximizing Priorities

It is an inescapable fact that every issue in the design of a house will affect every other issue, at least to some degree. The most basic and fundamental trade-off is budget versus size and complexity. The bigger the house and the better the materials, the more money we are likely to spend. Reality says that it is not possible to get 100 percent of everything. The goal is to create a home design that satisfies 90 percent of all of your wishes without leaving any of the Category A items behind. That's a lot better than getting 100 percent of one criterion and only 20 percent of another. Focus first on Category A items, i.e., the "I wouldn't build the house without…" items. Later, you will work on the Category B, "Some compromise is okay…" items. Lesser priorities do not have to be fulfilled quite so thoroughly. Your architect will help you see how each issue influences the others. Trade-offs will need to be assessed. Sometimes the cost or trouble of certain things isn't worth it. Like everything else in this process, make these decisions with your eyes open.

The kitchen is arguably the place where the most key compromises have to be made when designing the house. More than any other room, a kitchen represents "competition" for wall space. If you put a window in a certain wall, you'll have less room for wall cabinets. If you want to make the kitchen more open to other rooms such as a breakfast room or a family room, you'll lose space for cabinets, appliances, and counters while possibly opening up an undesirable view of the dirty dishes. Many people prefer a wall oven and a separate cook top instead of a range under a stovetop, but a wall oven also eats up cabinet and counter space. It all comes down to the vital question of what you need versus what you want. For all of these questions there are some good, basic rules, but many of the decisions will come down to simply deciding how you want *Your* Perfect House to be.

Sometimes what you leave out is as important as what you include. Anytime you delete something superfluous from your plan that you don't truly need, you have more money in the budget for improving the quality of the rest of the space, such as better lighting and more durable and attractive finishes. It's a matter of trimming the fat. Give each space a thorough critique, and be sure it is valuable to you.

The purpose of this entire exercise is to give you and your architect the clearest possible picture of what you want your house to be. Having said that, I must remind you that the program for your house is not the same as the actual design. If I were to tell you that I'm going on vacation to Kapalua Plantation on the island of Maui, I would be telling you the design of my vacation. But if I tell you I'm going to somewhere with tropical weather, nice beaches, good restaurants, and a peaceful atmosphere, I would be telling you the program for the vacation I want. Left to be decided would be what ocean, what kind of room or hotel, and so forth. Regarding the design of your house, this is where we want to be right now. We only want the parameters, objectives, criteria, or whatever you care to call them. You want to describe what type of house you desire; the actual design comes later.

Up to this point, the "plan" for your house consists of a list of rooms and spaces you want along with general information about what the house might be like. Armed with this list, your architect can make an initial estimate of the overall square footage of the entire house before you get too attached to the idea of a particular floor plan.

You don't need an actual floor plan to start determining a likely cost per square foot for the kind of house you have envisioned. You can get a rough idea of that cost even as early as when you are doing your initial research of talking with builders and architects who have worked on similar types of homes. The "cost per square foot formula" is *not*, I repeat, *not* the method your builder will use to establish the actual cost of your house. These figures are determined after the builder has calculated every piece of the building, how many pieces of plywood, how many bricks, etc., added up those costs, added in the labor costs, added in his overhead and profit, and come up with a bottom line number. Then, most builders will go back and divide their calculated price by the number of square feet to see what the "cost per square foot" is. They can then compare this number with similar numbers for recent projects they have built to see where you stand relative to those.

A Reality Test

At about this point in the process, I apply a reality test to see whether I am heading in the right direction in terms of construction cost. I have gotten a ballpark estimate of the cost per square foot that I can expect for the type of house we are designing. I need to know how many square feet the house will have in order to get a cost total. I write another simple list of the rooms or spaces I have already included in the program, making sure to include closets, hallways, powder rooms, and every space I plan to have. Don't forget the staircase. It occupies floor area, too. I assign a hypothetical size to each room and calculate the square footage of each. Then I add up the square footages to get a sub-total. To that I add 15%. This added factor is to take into account the area that the walls will occupy. Remember, they are not made of paper. Three running feet of a typical wall occupies one square foot of floor area. Also, no matter how clever an architect is, there will inevitably be some inefficiency in the layout. Some rooms will need to be adjusted to fit the whole floor plan together, and hallways may turn out to be a bit longer. The 15%

ELEVATORS

I know it sounds extravagant to have an elevator in your house, but there are times when paying for one can save you money. For many, many years, most houses were designed with all the bedrooms on the second floor. This led to an efficient design since the total square footage of the rooms on the first floor is about the same as the total square footage required for the rooms on the second floor. A two-story box is about as efficient and inexpensive a house as you can build. Nowadays, however, many people want their master bedrooms and baths to be on the first floor. This means that about two-thirds of the square footage of the house will be located on the first floor and only one-third of the square footage will be on the second floor. The two floors don't "stack up" anymore. This reduces the efficiency by increasing the building footprint, increasing the foundation's size, and increasing the area of roofing needed.

If your reasoning for having your master bedroom on the first floor is because you want it to be handicapped accessible, if that ever is a need, or if you just don't like walking up and down stairs but otherwise you prefer or would tolerate a second-floor bedroom, think about planning in an elevator. Currently, a residential elevator costs between $25,000 and $30,000. The construction cost savings by having a floor plan that "stacks up" more efficiently could be $100,000 or so. This is a savings you might want to consider. Also, if you don't need the elevator now, it can easily be added later if you simply lay out the floor plan with closets on each floor that align vertically and are large enough for the future elevator.

factor accounts for much of this. Add it all together and you will have a realistic target square footage required to accommodate the rooms and spaces in your program. Then, I multiply the total square footage times the cost per square foot to get a grand total of construction cost.

What if this exercise shows that your program square footage is not matching your budget? It would be great if the programmed space is less than the budgeted space. Call me if that happens, since you would be the first person to do it. You would have a budget cushion to play with. Usually the opposite happens: The programmed space exceeds the budgeted space. In this case we would be trying to put the proverbial ten pounds into a five-pound bag. To accomplish that, you will need a magician, not an architect. The numbers have to come close to matching, so something will have to be adjusted. You will have to rethink your program or increase your budget. Most of the time, a little of both happens. One reaction many people have to this dilemma is to start getting unrealistically optimistic about what the house will actually cost to build. It isn't possible to develop a definitive cost based on the kind of planning we've discussed so far, but it's certainly feasible to come up with an accurate ballpark figure. Talk to

All rooms are not created equal. Some rooms are much more expensive than others. Kitchens contain expensive cabinetry, appliances, and countertops. Often there are more electric lights, power hook-ups, gas connections, and plumbing requirements, too. Bathrooms contain a lot of plumbing, tile work, and cabinets. The kitchen and bathrooms are likely to be the most expensive rooms in your house. Any rooms with specialty paneling and cabinetry, such as a library or rooms with lots of windows, will be expensive. Less expensive rooms are more simply finished and appointed, such as bedrooms, dining rooms, and living rooms. If these rooms were to be enlarged, the added cost would be less than the average cost per square foot for the overall house.

The least expensive rooms in your house will be rooms built within the roof structure, e.g., the attic, or in the basement. The framing of a roof creates an attic space that is going to be there whether you finish it off or not. Because it is necessary to create a roof with a slope, an attic is the by-product. The steeper the roof, the greater the volume of space created within. The same goes for a basement space. If your site or climate dictates that you build a basement, adding heat and air conditioning, an electrical system, drywall, paint, and a floor finish can often be done for a fraction of the average cost per square foot of the rest of the house.

One room in this category is the inappropriately named bonus room. That is the name often given to the space above the garage. "Bonus" makes it sound like it's free. Although finishing it off is not actually free, it is a pretty good bargain for the useful area you will gain.

The message here is to consider the sizes of the expensive rooms wisely. If you need more space, think about utilizing other unfinished areas.

your architect or builder about the costs of recent projects that might be similar in scope to yours. Don't dance around this issue. It is always a difficult conversation, but you will do yourself a favor by insisting on discussing it. There is no sense in buying a ticket if you're at the wrong ballpark. It may be bad news for your plans, but it is better to find out earlier, when you can do something about it, than to wait and have your dream house completely designed only to find out that it is hopelessly out of the reach of your budget.

No sensible architect will spend your money recklessly, but your architect does need to know exactly how much money you want to invest in order to create the house that is perfect for you. Don't keep your budget a secret from him. He is working toward your best interests, and he will also be frank with you about the cost of the house you have in mind. You need to be candid with your architect, and he needs to be realistic with you.

Before your house is designed and before the builder has calculated every part of your house and tallied up the cost, this "cost per square foot" method, despite its inaccuracies, is virtually the only means of guessing what a house might cost; therefore, it is often used. With so many variables from one house to another, it is hard to use this method with any satisfactory accuracy. Returning to my earlier car analogy, would you care to think of your car in terms of how much it costs per square foot? Of course not. You would first want to know what engine it had, what features and equipment it had, how good the engineering was, and things like that. At that point, comparing the cost per square foot

would become irrelevant. What would be more important is whether those characteristics are worth the price to you. The same thing holds true for your house. Unfortunately, until the house is completely designed and we know the equipment, finishes, and other factors, this "cost per square foot" method is the only tool available to us to estimate costs. So we all begrudgingly use it. Just please be sure to keep an understanding of how inaccurate it can be.

In addition to the fact that one house cannot be compared accurately with another unless they both have identical features, there are other variables to be understood. Builders can have different ways of computing square footage. Sometimes their purpose is to make their bid look lower and more appealing than those of their competitors. For example, some builders will include the areas of the garage and decks with the total square footage whereas others figure it at 50 percent—i.e., two square feet of deck equals one square foot of interior space. In these cases, the total cost of the house would be divided by a greater number of square feet, and the "cost per square foot" would be considerably lower. I prefer the "heated or air conditioned square footage" method. This is the most commonly used method. I count only the square footage within the outer surface of the exterior walls. I do not count the garage, decks, porches, or attic space. No matter what method you use, make sure you are comparing apples to apples when you're looking at different bids and different builders.

Even though outdoor spaces are not figured into the total square footage of the house, you need to program them in from the beginning. Think about

Outdoor living was a major consideration in the design of this tropical home. The sliding glass doors disappear completely into pockets in the walls, allowing the inside spaces to spill out to the ocean-facing lanai. The roof covers a portion of the lanai to protect against sudden tropical showers.

outdoor spaces as "rooms." Just as you know that you want a certain number of bedrooms, a certain kind of dining room, and other indoor spaces, similarly, outdoor rooms will have a size and character. Think them through and add those "outdoor rooms" to your basic concept of your new house. Many outdoor spaces need to have access to the kitchen or connect to other interior spaces. Include those relationships in the program. If you wait until the interior of the house has been planned before you start to think about where things will go on the outside, you might wind up without the right kind of outdoor space where you want it. Add this information to your program while you are thinking about how you live, how you entertain, or how you would like to live and entertain in your new home.

By now, you and your architect have a fairly clear picture of where your house is going to be placed on the site, its orientation, what rooms and what design elements it's going to contain, its approximate size, and about how much it's going to cost. In our next lesson, we will begin to determine how all the design elements you've chosen will come together.

Stone, brick, and stucco are skillfully composed to create an impressive yet friendly home, evocative of classic European mansions.

Lesson Nine

PUTTING PENCIL TO PAPER

"A man who could build a church, as some may say, by squinting at a sheet of paper."

—CHARLES DICKENS

When architects design houses, they usually begin with diagrams of the first floor. Most of the important elements of a house, from the food preparation and dining areas, to the living areas, the garage, and the outdoor living spaces that we discussed in the previous lesson are likely to be located on the first or main floor. This is the floor that usually contains the majority of the square footage. It's the engine that drives the train, so to speak. I rarely worry much about how the upper and lower floors will work out until I get the first floor right. It's usually relatively easy to get the second floor, which is primarily the location of the bedrooms, to fall into place. Similarly, if there's a basement or lower level in the house, it's easier to plan the basement once the first floor is to your liking. I won't ignore those spaces on the other floors entirely.

They are always in the back of my mind. The location, shape, and size of second-floor spaces has a great deal to do with the shape and massing of the house, which in turn has everything to do with what the house will ultimately look like. But at the first stages of designing the floor plan, these are not the most critical elements, and I let them simmer in my thinking for later use.

Tiny Bubbles

Working from the "program," the written description you created earlier of what you hope your house will be, your architect may draw simple "bubbles" that represent the various rooms. These will be sized in a way that relates to the target sizes in the program. He will then review where each of these rooms should be placed in relation to the others. He'll draw the bubbles again in an arrangement that addresses those relationships, with lines drawn between each of the bubbles to represent the connections that must be created between rooms. For example, he'll certainly want to place a line between the kitchen and the dining room and position them near each other since you will want to bring food and tableware conveniently from one room to the

other. The first bubble diagram is unlikely to resolve all of the relationships, so the architect will keep sketching revised diagrams until he ends up with one or more that satisfy the program criteria. Even though these crude bubble diagrams don't show it, the architect will undoubtedly already be anticipating the massing and shape each trial layout might entail.

Architects think graphically and spatially instead of verbally. They prefer visualizing things and communicating their ideas through drawings instead of merely talking about them. Your architect is looking for the optimum arrangement, the one that makes the most of all the program criteria while starting to define spaces and develop an architectural concept. This kind of analytical problem solving and three-dimensional thinking allows the architect to ask "what if" questions, examining many

FRONT ELEVATION
1/4" = 1'-0"

scenarios, evaluating each while envisioning the spatial consequences as he goes. He may use sketch paper or a computer sketching program to run through many possibilities quickly. He'll flip things around and alter shapes in his mind. Considering the three dimensional mental dexterity this requires, it's no wonder the inventor of Rubik's Cube was a professor of architecture. Working out a building design is very much like working out a puzzle.

You can count on the fact that this process will change the initial list of design criteria and objectives listed in the program that you have developed. That is natural and should be considered a good thing. This is only the early stage of design and is the point in the process where I feel I am just beginning to understand the opportunities and the problems that the site, the house program, and my client's desires present. This is a diagramming exercise to organize concepts and strategies. While doing this, it is best to avoid making anything too rigid. Keep in mind that the lines on the paper are not walls or spatial boundaries, yet. They are only potential edges of spaces.

Assess each arrangement and then try another one. Every version should teach you something more about what *Your* Perfect House "wants" to be. You should start to realize a great deal about the various rooms and spaces and how they will best interrelate.

You'll see what issues control and influence the design. Here's an example of what a design might look like at the bubble diagram level:

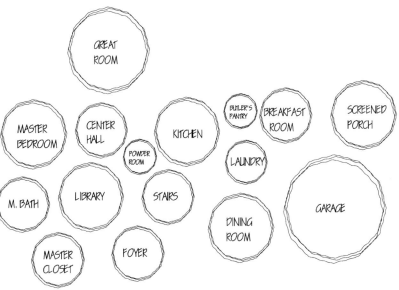

Bubbles represent the rooms and spaces that the house must include. The size of each bubble roughly indicates the relative size of the room it represents.

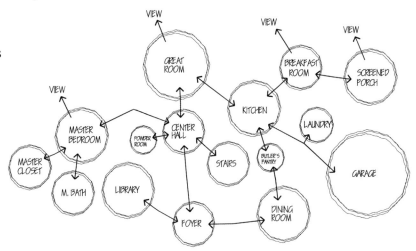

Links are drawn indicating how one room relates to another. If there is no connection, no link is drawn. Additional arrows indicate views and which rooms should have them.

Remember, right now you are only creating a diagram, not a floor plan. Don't get too caught up in details. Don't worry about where the powder room will go or whether or not there is a coat closet. We're just trying to figure out which rooms are going to connect with other rooms. This is not the exercise for deciding whether there will be an island in the kitchen or how big the fireplace will be. Do, however, consider where the staircase might go. It is a key element in determining how the circulation works. That's the architectural term for the path of travel we take when walking through the house.

The architect will probably develop his or her bubble diagram for the house while laying the tracing paper over the site plan or site analysis. By this process, drawing the diagram at the same scale as the site plan, either electronically or with good old fashioned paper and pencil, you and the architect will discover immediately and precisely how the house you are imagining matches up with the building site you've chosen. Remember all those issues we learned about while doing the site analysis? This is where they come into play. If you diagram the plan separately from the site plan, you may find out

WHY YOUR ARCHITECT USES SKETCH PAPER

A good architect is willing to make changes to a design. Change is actually how designs are born. An architect tries out idea after idea, sketching and assessing numerous concepts until one emerges as the most appropriate. An architect uses a pencil and sketch paper or a "sketching" program on his computer during this process because these are loose and agile media. This kind of non-rigid method lets his mind work freely rather than casting his initial designs in the proverbial stone. "Getting it right" requires trying things in different ways. At this point we are only discussing the positioning of rooms, but an architect will use this same sketching process as he gets down to the level of designing the fine details, such as the cabinetry or fireplace mantels. No matter how good a concept may seem at the time it is created, your architect knows not to cling relentlessly to that design. It may simply be a stepping stone on the path to the real solution.

To that end, your architect will keep a roll of transparent sketch paper on hand and frequently roll out piece after piece, overlaying the previous drawings and roughly sketch out other options or ideas. He should do this in front of you, so you can partici-pate in the process. If something is making you uncomfortable in a design, it is your right and re-sponsibility as the client to say so. Otherwise, your architect is likely to charge blithely ahead, without a clear sense of your true desires, all the while thinking that everything is meeting with your approval. He will welcome your input, particu-larly during the design phase. Keep in mind that changes on sketch paper don't cost anything. Changes to the actual construc-tion, after the walls are up, cost plenty. Make your thoughts known while your architect is still designing.

too late that your garage has all the best views or that the land outside the first-floor master bedroom is exactly wrong for the private garden you want to have. All of these site issues and opportunities are just as important as all of the interior relationships and considerations we wrote into the program.

WHAT IS A CHARRETTE?

Instead of "pulling all-nighters," architects say they are "on *charrette*." The term "*charrette*" evolved from the pre-1900 Ecole des Beaux-Arts (School of Fine Arts) in France. The most famous of all was the Ecole Nationale Superieure des Beaux-Arts in Paris. There was an extremely strong emphasis on classical design and elaborate, hand-painted presentation drawings. Architecture students were given a design problem to solve within an allotted time. Much of the work was done at students' residences, in lofts and garrets throughout the city. When the deadline came, a cart called a *charrette* would be pulled through the town, picking up the students' drawings. Just as architects still do today, the students would work right up to the deadline, often jumping in the cart to finish drawings on the way. The term *charrette* evolved to refer to the intense design exercise itself. Today it refers to an intense, creative design process and the long hours spent by architects to develop solutions to a design problem when trying to meet a deadline.

A bubble diagram can teach you a lot about the design. Suppose you have a site with a lovely view in one particular direction. In an effort to maximize the site's potential, you decide to line up all the rooms across the site so that you will be able to enjoy the view from each and every room. You look at your diagram and see that it resembles a freight train. You will quickly see that the interconnections and flow between rooms you noted in your design program cannot work. Using this bubble diagram, you can sort things out, moving rooms around until you get the ones that should have the view positioned on one side of the house and the rooms that can work without the view on the other side of the house. You'll have to prioritize and compromise. Rooms such as dining rooms, powder rooms, master baths, or master closets can often be relegated to the non-view side. This may sound like an obvious example that would never happen, but it always astounds me how often these "non-view" rooms end up in the best locations. It happens because no one has bothered to think things through. It also happens when a stock plan from some book is imposed upon a site without consideration for the opportunities a site presents.

If you haven't yet selected a site, you can still begin this diagramming process in a more abstract way by assuming some characteristics of the site you are searching for. The programming and diagramming process will help you understand your house and what it should be. That

DESIGNING YOUR PERFECT HOUSE

information can help with the site selection. But your architect will not want to start the actual design in a vacuum, i.e., without a specific site.

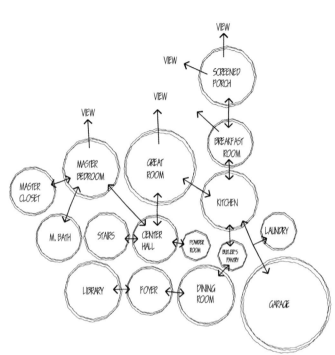

Through trial and error, plus some deductive thought, the bubbles and spaces are moved to tighten up the relationships between rooms and to consolidate the spaces.

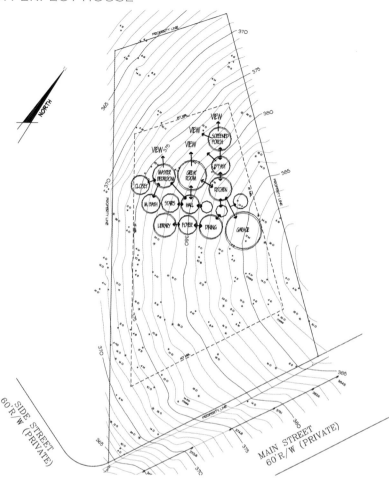

The bubble diagram is sketched on the site plan. In each step of this process, adjustments are made and various ideas are tried out. Rarely will the first idea work best. Each trial is a learning experience that helps the architect "discover" where each room or space might best be located.

Where to Park?

If I were to ask what you thought the largest space in the house would be, chances are you'd mention the living room or perhaps a kitchen/dining room/play area combination. In reality, unless you have an exceptionally large house, the biggest space in your entire house will be the garage, especially when you combine the garage with the portion of the driveway needed to back the car out and turn it around. Very often, people want a three-car garage, which consumes a great deal of space. A three-car garage and the turning space in the driveway adjacent to it often take up as much as 2,200 square feet. Rarely is there any other room or group of rooms in a house that demands this large an area. To make matters worse, all of this area, approximately 40 by 55 feet, needs to be essentially level. A typical family room might be 20 by 25 feet, only one quarter of the size of this automobile area, and a family room can be easily built over a slope.

Where does an 800-pound gorilla sit? Anywhere it wants, as the old joke goes. It is certainly not the sexiest part of the house, but because the garage is the biggest single design element and therefore the proverbial 800-pound gorilla, my planning generally starts with the location of the driveway and the garage. You have already figured out the likely direction of approach to your house when you developed the site analysis. This is where the cars will come from, and the garage is where they are ultimately going. Although dealing with the automobiles first may not seem very artistic, they demand the largest portion of your site and cannot be ignored. If you can't get in and out of your garage, it won't matter whether you're living in the most beautiful house in the world; it won't be *Your* Perfect House.

I urge you not to fool yourself with regard to turning radii and backing-out areas. Do not plan this area based on minimal dimensions or you will regret it later. Also, don't overlook the need for possible guest parking. If your community does not allow on-street parking, you will need to provide an area for this on your property. Keep in mind that there may be more than one possible place to put the garage. I usually consider several garage locations and assess the merits of each, weighing how each one will

influence the rest of the design before choosing one location. Make your garage and driveway as big as they need to be and not an inch smaller. For the rest of your life, you'll thank yourself for having done so.

It's a Sequential Thing

Once you have your garage situated, the kitchen location is next. After all, people are going to be bringing groceries from the garage into the kitchen on a regular basis, and the shorter the distance between the garage and the kitchen, the happier they will be. As such, the location of the garage usually dictates your options for the location of the kitchen. At the same time, the kitchen will have its own requirements. Maybe you are intent on capturing that great view from the food preparation area. That kind of program criterion may exert some reverse pressure on the process and influence the garage location, causing its position on the site to be altered. The entire process of establishing the basic room layout is a cyclical thing. As we said at the outset, nearly everything in *Your* Perfect House can affect something else. We are looking for the ideal balance of all of those issues.

After the kitchen you may plan the dining room since the house works best, for obvious reasons, when the kitchen and dining room are adjacent to one another. You can see already this is not rocket science. It's just common sense…which is often harder to think through than rocket science. You might want a butler's pantry between the kitchen and dining room. I usually don't worry too much about these smaller spaces at this point. There is time to work those things in later. Right now I am interested in arranging the big elements, the major rooms.

The next step in the flow of a well-designed house is to locate the family room, breakfast nook, playroom, and any other communal areas of the house. Are these adjacent to the kitchen? Are these near the dining room? Is the dining room not a separate, formal room at all but perhaps a portion of the family area? This is often the case in an open living concept.

It's a natural progression to have the dining room near the living room, as they are both areas in which you may entertain guests, so the placement of the living room generally comes next. You also may have other shared spaces, such as a foyer, a library, or a game room to consider. You can see this process is a little like stringing beads on a necklace or arranging cars on a train. One part must follow the next part in a sensible progression.

Your architect may bring you several bubble diagrams he has developed. Together, you will assess the merits of each. Keep in mind when you are reviewing the diagrams that there really are very few cases of something being absolutely right or absolutely wrong. For example, it may not be the end of the world if your garage doesn't connect to the house immediately adjacent to the kitchen. This is not necessarily a fatal flaw; it is just a design choice. Just be cognizant of the fact that every design choice has ramifications that affect other possible choices.

I never tell my clients, "This won't work." Instead, I show them the implications of the decision and say something like, "It's okay to move the staircase here, but that means there won't be a good view from the dining room. Is that a consequence we want to have?" In other words, choice "A" always creates impact "B." Don't be afraid to think through exactly what you'd like to see and what you'd like to have in your house. You can always change things in the design later. We haven't poured a single yard of concrete or hammered a single nail yet.

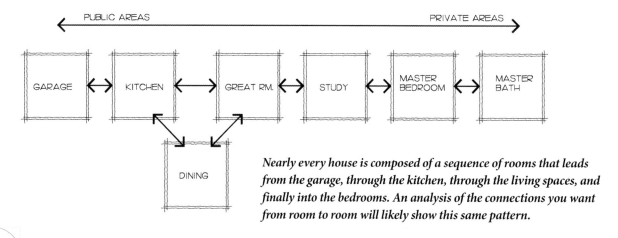

Nearly every house is composed of a sequence of rooms that leads from the garage, through the kitchen, through the living spaces, and finally into the bedrooms. An analysis of the connections you want from room to room will likely show this same pattern.

This is also not the time to become overly concerned with what the house itself is going to look like. The "look" of the house will emerge from the sort of planning you and your architect are currently doing. Yes, you want to keep the look of the house in mind, but instead of focusing on the outside of the house, this is the time to think seriously about the issues that will drive everything else in its design.

Be sure to consider the staircase and its location in the diagram. You might not think of this as a "room," but it occupies nearly as much space as a room, and it has important implications for the design. Do you want to see it, or do you want it hidden? Should it start in the foyer, the living room, or somewhere else? It is a good idea to have the top of the staircase end up somewhere near the center of the second floor so that access to all of the bedrooms will not be too difficult. Is the staircase going to be a grand statement, or will it be secondary to other elements in the house? Should there be a double staircase that creates an impressive entrance? Is there a back staircase in your program? Where should it go?

The rooms of this house revolve around this central, two-plus story central hall. The curving, custom-designed and custom-built staircase is both elegant and artful. Architectural features like these can only be created when working with exceptional craftsmen.

You will probably have several meetings with your architect during which the bubble diagram will be evolving into a real floor plan. Doors and hallways will gradually appear. Closets will emerge. The details of bathrooms, such as the soaking tub you wanted in the master bath, will find a place in the developing plan. You will almost certainly find yourself re-evaluating some of the things you included in your program. Maybe the exercise room is awkward on the main floor and will work better on the lower level. Maybe you will remember that you wanted an outdoor sitting area off of the master bedroom, so you amend the program and add this to the diagrammatic plan. These are all good things to think of, and it is a good time to think of them. These are the sorts of design elements that are appropriate to consider right now.

Your bubble diagram has grown up and become a sketch plan. Architects call this a schematic design.

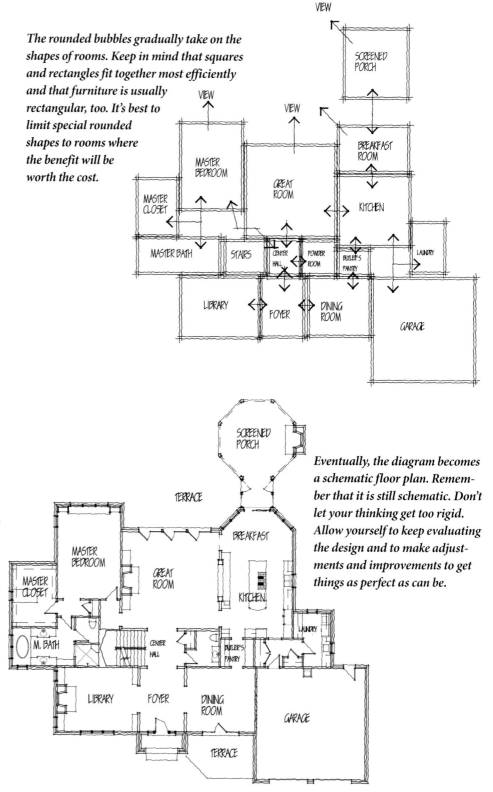

The rounded bubbles gradually take on the shapes of rooms. Keep in mind that squares and rectangles fit together most efficiently and that furniture is usually rectangular, too. It's best to limit special rounded shapes to rooms where the benefit will be worth the cost.

Eventually, the diagram becomes a schematic floor plan. Remember that it is still schematic. Don't let your thinking get too rigid. Allow yourself to keep evaluating the design and to make adjustments and improvements to get things as perfect as can be.

Here's a look at what this diagram (at left) eventually became.

You now have a game plan for the entire first floor of your house. Remember, you are not locked into that plan, but at least now you and the architect have a very clear, precise vision of how the main floor of your house will appear and how it will be situated on the building site. Now it's time to imagine what it would be like to actually live in that house, what it might look like—and it's also time to start thinking about what you'd like to change. Change is a natural part of the design process. Pencils truly do have erasers. The "delete" key is even easier. What happens if you want to make small or large changes to the design that you just created? That's the subject of our next lesson.

Drawing upon thoughts of old stone houses of the northeastern United States, this house captures an unpretentious charm. The sunroom to the left is a bit of nostalgia, designed to seem as if built at a later time than the original structure.

Lesson Ten

DESIGNING THE HOUSE

"Architecture starts when you carefully put two bricks together. There it begins."
—LUDWIG MIES VAN DER ROHE

In the previous lesson, I told you that the architect will probably begin by drawing a bubble diagram of the programmed spaces on tracing paper while overlaying his sketch on the site plan or site analysis plan. Let me drop back a bit and discuss the impact of the site on the building design in more detail.

The program indicates the ideal relationships the rooms should have, and the initial diagram graphically shows the interrelationship of all the spaces. The hypothetical diagram of your new home now has to work on the actual site. The characteristics and opportunities of the site offer another layer of design criteria that must be addressed. Integrating the house diagram with the site plan will probably require making at least a few modifications to the diagrammatic plan.

169

Designing the Site Concept— Working with the Land

In the last lesson, we talked about positioning rooms on the site to capture the best views. We discussed how some compromises might be required to maintain the flow from room to room while maintaining the view from the most important rooms. We also talked about how any important outdoor spaces you wish to create should be included in the building program. You should have determined whether these spaces need to be oriented toward the view or concealed from neighbors and whether they should relate to any of the interior rooms. These kinds of issues are examples of how the site and its limitations and opportunities start to influence the design—and that is a good thing. It may feel like the puzzle of designing this house has gotten a bit harder, but this is a key step toward creating a house that fits the site properly.

It's important to use the slope of the building site to your advantage. If you wish to have the ability to walk out of the kitchen directly to the backyard, you may have to move the kitchen to the end of the house where the ground is going to be higher, thus allowing the access you desire. If the slope falls away in one direction, you might want to take advantage of that by creating a lower level playroom for small children or an exercise room with windows and doors leading out to the yard. The nature of the slope of the land helps determine where certain rooms should be placed.

If you will excuse me for returning to the mundane topic of the garage, I need to point out that it is generally best to place it on the uphill side of the house. I tell you this because usually none of us likes to have many steps to climb from the garage to the house. Also, you don't want to have to build up the soil under the garage or the driveway in order to get the floor of the garage up to the level of the main floor. Filling in a site is an expensive, time-consuming, and often unnecessary process. The garage and driveway will be less prone to cracking and settling if they are built on what your builder and architect will call "undisturbed soil," i.e., original, unexcavated soil that has not been filled in. My recommended rule of thumb is to follow the shape of the land.

Like most design rules, this is not a completely hard-and-fast rule. Structurally speaking, a garage floor can be built as an above-ground deck, creating a basement or storm cellar below. This might be a desirable thing, especially if you live in a tornado-prone area. Building an above-grade garage is considerably more expensive, however, so there needs to be another benefit if you decide to accept the expense. I always look for ways to eliminate unnecessary costs since building a house is expensive enough as it is. Like everything else we are discussing, just consider each decision thoroughly and make sure you are getting an appropriate benefit from each investment you make in your new house.

Watch the Weather

Consider climate and weather factors when positioning a house on the site. The garage, the utility room, or other non-living spaces can serve as buffers against the weather. Rooms for living and sleeping usually have many windows and doors, which causes them to be more vulnerable to severe weather. In harsh climates, you may want to protect those rooms by positioning the garage on the "weather side" of the house. Consider the classic farmhouse built in the middle of the American prairies. The barns and outbuildings would often be located to the northwest, to serve as a windbreak. The farmer would plant some shade trees to the south, giving the house shade in summer and then, when the leaves fall in autumn, needed sunlight and warmth could come through branches and into the house in winter. This kind of design, simple as it may be, is quietly responsive to the environment in which it is situated. The barns and outbuildings placed to the northwest mean that the farmer and his family will stay warmer in the winter with less concern for the winter winds howling through their house.

An even simpler way to think about how to situate parts of a house with regard to climate and weather is to imagine yourself standing outside on your site on a sunny, windy winter day. To stay warm, you would naturally turn away from the north wind and face the southern sun. You might even turn your collar up. By making this simple adjustment, you would be sheltering yourself from the wind and maximizing the solar heat gain from the sun. Well, that's exactly what architects do for houses when they place the garage in the way of the prevailing wind and position the windows toward the sun. The house is responding to the climate in the same way you would. These ideas are the first steps in passive solar design. Best of all, there's no added cost for any of this. By merely acknowledging and responding to the climate of the site, the house will live in harmony with the natural world around it.

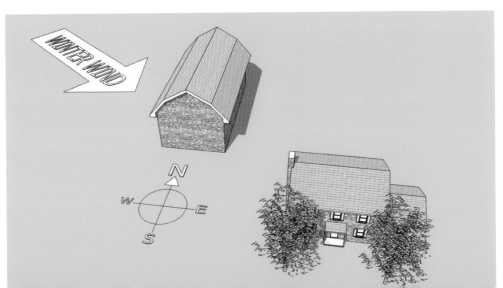

Farm buildings were often places to buffer the house from winter winds. Deciduous trees were planted on the south side of the house to provide cooling shade in the summer months.

Approaching the House by Automobile

Many of us aren't thrilled about the fact that in our modern society, unless we both live and work downtown, we are inexorably tied to our cars. It is critical that we recognize this reality as we design our homes. Many unsuccessful house designs fail because the architect or the client did not want to bend to this reality of how we live every day. In many unsuccessful home designs, the garage is tucked around the side of the house, presenting the delightful illusion that we are living in another century, in a more charming, bygone era, and at a position in society where the coachman drops you, the landed gentry, at the front door and then takes the horses and carriage around to the carriage house. I know I told you earlier that nostalgia is a good thing, but sometimes it needs to be tempered with reality. The facts of life in the twenty-first century are that you and your guests will be coming and going from your house by automobile and you park your car yourself.

When the garage and the parking area of the driveway are tucked around to the side of the house, you are forcing your guests, not to mention yourself, to drive around the house before actually feeling like they have arrived anywhere. Then they have to circle back on foot to find the front door. It's a common problem that looks dreadful and feels awkward. You may currently live in a house like this. If so, ask yourself how many times anyone has actually come in through your front door. This situation feels so clumsy because there is really no "there" there.

Somewhere between the time when you are driving into the driveway and when you walk through the front door, there is a point in space that is the "there" space. This location is called "the point of arrival." It is a critical place where you and your guests feel that the journey has ended and a critical first impression has been made. It is the place where you step out of your car or turn in from the sidewalk to head toward the front door. It may sound overly simplistic, but the number one key to a successful point of arrival is that your guests can actually find the front door! If the entrance to the house is not understood at this point, the house will not have an especially welcoming feel. Too often we see houses where the front door is hidden behind hedges, located somewhere around a corner, or may actually be located some distance from the guest parking area and around on the other side of the building. Sometimes there may be an additional door that opens out from the kitchen or from the side of the house. The way that secondary door is situated may cause confusion over which door really is the main entrance to the house. Strive for clarity. This may all seem painfully simple, but if you start looking around, you will notice plenty of examples of houses that make this common mistake and "disguise" the front door.

There is a basic principle that can help you avoid this design pitfall.

As in many European country homes, vehicles are brought close to the front door. Two projecting wings embrace a wide front terrace, providing an appropriate transition in the arrival sequence.

Creating a Sense of Arrival—SAAPE

The acronym SAAPE stands for these words: See, Approach, Arrive, Park, and Enter. Each is a portion of the proper sequence of events that should take place as we travel to and arrive at *Your* Perfect House. Let's take a look at each in turn.

See. This is the moment you first become aware that you've reached your destination. This is the long-distance view we discussed earlier. You've been driving on the freeway or on some other large street, and then you find the right neighborhood and the right street, and then there comes that wonderful "Ahh!" feeling—there's Joe's house! We've found it! At that moment, the nature of our journey changes. We are no longer en route. Instead, we have made our first psychological and perceptual connection with our destination.

173

Approach. This is the part of the journey between the time when you first see your destination and when you actually arrive. The approach has a psychological significance all its own. It is the foreground of the presentation. Who among us has not been impressed and enchanted by a tree-lined drive leading to an estate, farm, or other building? This kind of allée of trees is a classic, grand example of an "approach," but it is possible to create this sensation of approach even in a modest context. Landscape plantings that frame the driveway, a gentle curve to the drive itself, or twin post lights can create a brief but important approach to your house.

Arrive. The point of arrival is the point at which you actually feel like you are "there." It needs to have some delineation in architectural terms. It could be marked by a widening of the drive or a change in the pavement. It could be marked by a quartet of surrounding trees that enclose an outdoor space through which the driveway passes. Any of those design features will trigger in the visitor's mind the thought, "This is where I should stop. I am at my destination." One classic arrangement is to create a center circle in front of the house. The circle is the obvious point of arrival.

Park. This is the physical act of parking your car, as opposed to the psychological feeling of having arrived. If the house is created in such a manner that you park before you've arrived, it will feel awkward. The house doesn't quite seem welcoming although the visitor is not likely to be able to articulate reasons for having that feeling.

Enter. This is not merely the act of walking through the front door, but it is the entire process of walking up the path, stepping onto the porch, passing through the door, and hanging up your coat. The way the spaces are arranged outside and inside the house in an ideal design will enhance that sense of arriving and moving from a public space into increasingly more private spaces. We'll get further into that discussion later in this book.

When you give yourself and your guests this series of psychological and physical demarcations—See, Approach, Arrive, Park, and Enter—you're providing a sense of orderliness and comfort. When this sequence is out of order, the whole thing feels wrong. If you park before arriving, such as is the case

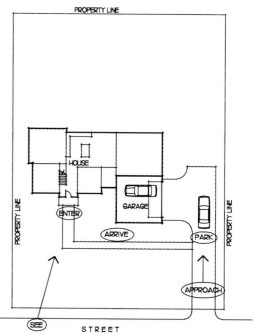

In this all-too-typical driveway and house arrangement, the "See-Approach-Arrive-Park-Enter" sequence is out of order. Guests must park before there is a sense of arrival at the house. The guest is confused, and the actual front door of the house becomes an unused relic.

when the front door is not visible from the parking area, and you have to walk around the garage to find the door, and only when you finally get there do you have any sense that you have arrived, the entire thing feels clumsy. This is such a basic principle, but now that I've pointed it out to you, look around at houses in your neighborhood and see which ones get it right. My bet is that those are the houses that feel the best.

Here's another car issue. Do you have an appreciation for how much room cars need to turn around? I have many clients who would like a circular driveway in front of their house. That is a good sign that they already appreciate the SAAPE principle, even if they cannot articulate it. But they often experience a sense of shock when they realize just how much room cars need in order to park and turn around. Let's say you want to have a circle in front of your house. You'll need space for a circle that is sixty feet in diameter. Imagine three full-sized SUVs, end to end to end, or the size of the infield at a Little League baseball field, and you'll have a pretty good picture of the amount of space it takes in order to create a circle that a car can drive around without backing up.

Something less elaborate, such as a pull-off from the drive large enough to park, will still need at least ten feet by twenty feet per space for guest parking, but the average suburban building lot may have enough space to allow this. Many people want their garage doors to face sideways instead of to the street. If this is part of your plan, the point of arrival that we discussed above must come prior to the garage doors. I often recommend creating a slight bend in the driveway, to keep you driving toward the front of

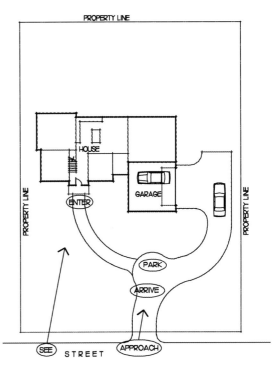

This driveway and house arrangement creates an important place for you to feel you have arrived at your destination. The entrance to the house is visible, and the parking location is nearby. With the addition of a bit more driveway length and a thoughtful placement of a guest parking area, a much more gracious presentation of the house is achieved.

the house and not directly around to the garage doors. Adding some shrubbery on each side at that bend will help define a space. Within that space, the guest parking area can occur, and the point of arrival will be defined. Something as simple as this can make a great deal of difference. I see too many houses built on sites that actually had enough room for a welcoming type of driveway, complete with an approach and arrival area, but apparently no one thought this through. Sadly, the driveway leads straight to the garage on the side of the house, and the real front door is a forgotten memory.

175

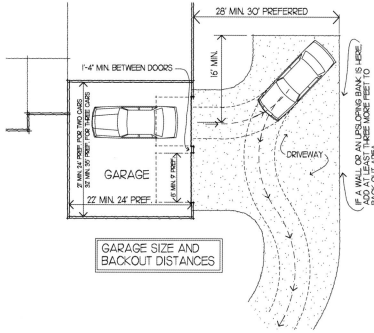

Plan enough room for maneuvering your car comfortably. If you allow less room than what is shown, you will need to make multiple turns to get in and out of your garage.

Sequence of Interior Spaces

In times gone by, gracious halls, often with sweeping staircases, greeted the homeowner as he entered the house through the front door. Today, though, most of us enter and leave our houses through our garage. Regrettably, most people who go through the garage also have to climb through their kids' bikes, around the laundry facilities, step gingerly among boots in various states of muddiness, and then finally make their way into the kitchen. There's really no place in the average garage for you to feel as though you've "entered," in an architectural sense, your home. You've been too busy dodging the

emblems of domesticity the typical garage contains. The front foyer, the traditional entryway or greeting point, all too often goes unused for days or weeks at a time.

If your budget and site can stand a few extra square feet next to the garage, do something nice for yourself. Add a hallway, perhaps even with a window, a built-in bench, some nice furniture, and even a closet between the garage and the kitchen. This is a place where you can drop your car keys and hang up your coat. That small hallway will dramatically change the feeling you have when you enter your home because, even if it is small, it will denote a place of entry.

Most of us come and go through our garage and not our front door. But that passage need not be uninteresting or uninviting. A window lets in sunlight and provides a view of the cutting garden. There is room enough for a bench for pulling on boots or flipping off shoes. The actual door to the garage can be seen beyond the back staircase.

In larger houses, say four thousand square feet or more, you can create some wonderful side entrances, charming spaces, and cozy areas that will make you, your family, and your most familiar friends and relatives feel more at home as they arrive. You might have a back staircase and a door leading to a side garden or a side porch in this back hall.

If you have a house with small or school-aged children, you'll definitely want to have places where your kids can dump their book bags. Frequently, I design cubbyholes or lockers for the children of my clients to get all that clutter out of the way. Think about creating a mud room or other transition space adjacent to the back hall so that your children can get their boots off instead of tracking mud over the clean kitchen floor.

Stairways Need to Communicate Correctly

It's traditional to have an impressive stairway as the center of attention in the foyer of a home. These kinds of stairs are often the focal point of the entire house and can be quite elegant. But here's another point of view. Let me suggest that a central stairway may subliminally send a message you do not wish to send. In a sense, a large, central staircase actually "invites" you to come up to the bedrooms, which is probably not the invitation you really want to extend. You may only mean to show off the beautiful woodwork. Instead, think about placing the stairway in an adjacent, yet convenient and appropriate place in the front hall that is not quite front and center. Or design the stair so that the bottom of the staircase does not face the front door.

If grand, central stairs send the wrong—albeit subconscious—message, why is it that we so often find staircases front and center in the foyer? It's a tradition held over from European houses. In old English houses, a well-to-do family lived on the second floor, away from the smells and sounds of the street, and the servants occupied the first floor. The main living level of an Italian palace is called the *piano nobile* and is also raised above ground level. A grand center staircase was positioned right at the main entrance to these houses for the very purpose of inviting guests into the family quarters, where a "receiving room" played the role that a formal living room plays today. The purpose actually was to invite guests upstairs. We no longer live in an "upstairs, downstairs" world in which the servants occupy the first floor of our houses, yet this type of staircase, something of a throwback to earlier times, remains in most house designs, still in its central location in the main foyer.

Of course, it doesn't have to be that way. Some of my clients prefer to have the staircase located closer to the family's entrance in and out of the house, nearer the garage and kitchen. Such a "back" staircase can still be well-built and handsome, serving as the main staircase, while also serving guest rooms, but it's not the main event. In one of my client's houses the staircase is actually in a very atypical location, beyond the front foyer and beyond the living room. It is in a central hall dominated by a skylight of old-fashioned design and an impressive balcony served by a massive, curving staircase. Halfway up the grand stair, sitting on a landing and in an alcove, a large grandfather clock looks back down on the grand hall's floor below. A visitor never sees this staircase until he or she has gotten deep into the house, inasmuch as this center hall is sandwiched between the living room, library, dining room, and kitchen. It serves the occupants of the house and goes unseen by all guests except those who are the most familiar to the family. This unusual positioning of the staircase works very well in that house, and non-traditional stair locations can work very well in yours.

A Stairway to Heaven

The staircase is often a focal point of a house, no matter where it is located in the plan. Well-designed and well-built railings can be a signature element. A thoughtful banister can be a statement about the quality of the craftsmen that built the house and a testament to the taste of the owners. The staircase design is a place to have some fun. Scour books and magazines to find inspiring images that reflect your preferences, and then work with your architect to create something special. Keep in mind that curved staircases, while very dramatic, are significantly more costly than straight staircases. Apply your budget wisely. A nice compromise between the high cost of a curved stair and the simplicity of a straight stair is one with landings. Shorter, straight sections can turn at these landings, creating a nice effect and giving the staircase some added style.

This staircase serves only the guest suite above and a single basement room below. Because of its secondary importance, it was located at the end of the crossing hallway. The windows provide a great amount of daylight, keeping the cottage ambiance that is the theme of the house.

This staircase and its custom-designed and custom-built railing are statements of style. The tall window on the landing gives the space a unique character and provides a focal point.

One word of caution: Too often I find stairs that are either too steep or just plain awkward. How sad it is to see an otherwise well-planned and comfortable house with a tight, steep staircase or clumsy level changes from one portion of the house to another. Here are a few simple rules that will guarantee your stairs are comfortable to walk up and down;

in addition, they will be safe to use. These are just guidelines. You should consult your local building code for any additional regulations.

For a typical interior staircase:

1. Avoid risers that are more than 7¾" high. Back stairs or attic stairs can have taller risers, but for the main staircase, try to stay between 7" and 7¾" high.

2. Avoid treads that are less than 9½" deep except possibly on back staircases. I prefer to make treads 10" deep. You might think that making treads even deeper, say 12" deep, would be even better, but combined with a 7¾" riser, these would feel excessively large for most people to walk up and down.

3. A primary staircase should be between 3'-4" and 4'-0" wide. Wider stairs could be used where a more dramatic effect is desired. The width of the stair does not usually affect the comfort of use as long as it is not too narrow. Building codes usually require a minimum width of 3'-0".

For interior steps along a hallway or between rooms, such as into a sunken living room:

1. Avoid risers that are more than 7" high. I prefer 6" risers here.

2. Avoid treads that are less than 11" deep. I prefer to make treads 12" to 14" deep. We tend to walk up and down these types of steps differently than we do on a full staircase. Instead of getting ready to go up or down, most of us simply stroll along. If the treads are too narrow, people will trip and fall.

This classic circular staircase dominates the large foyer of this elegant, traditional home.

Never have a single riser. This is a tremendously dangerous situation. Single risers are too often overlooked and cause people to stumble or fall. I prefer steps in groups of three risers (two treads) for steps placed between rooms. You can get away with only two risers if the materials of the floors are different, thus helping you see that a level change is happening.

For typical exterior steps and staircases:

1. Avoid risers that are more than 7″ high. I try to make exterior stair risers only 6″ high whenever I can. Risers that are less than 5″ high can feel awkward and will not match the normal stride of a person.

2. Avoid treads that are less than 10″ deep. I prefer to make exterior treads 12″ deep. Remember, exterior stairs are often used when they are wet or even covered with ice or snow. On the other hand, avoid treads that are excessively deep. We all have walked up stairs that have treads so deep that you can not step from one step to the next without taking a "baby" step between. Just remember how uncomfortable those were.

3. Avoid a single riser wherever you can. I prefer steps in groups of three risers (two treads). Single risers are too often overlooked and cause people to stumble or fall. Also keep in mind that in most areas the building code requires a handrail to be installed for steps with four or more risers.

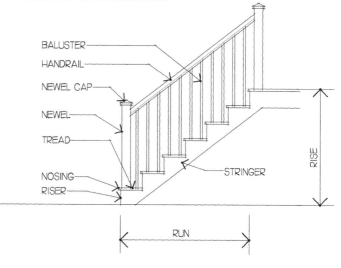

STAIRCASE TERMINOLOGY

Developing the Plan

How a conceptual floor plan evolves into a design of an actual three-dimensional house is something I will have trouble explaining. I do not have a formula or a step-by-step method for growing a real house up from a two-dimensional plan. The process I go through is often inexact and loosely planned. It goes a little like this. I sketch out an early idea, evaluate it, give myself a critique, revise the concept, and then repeat the process as many times as necessary. Once I have something I like or when I need feedback from my clients, I review it all with them. Following that meeting, armed with comments, both good and bad, I go "back to the drawing board" and begin the process again.

You might think this is a frustrating thing to go through, but it really isn't. Each iteration of the design, each critique, invariably improves and strengthens the design. Every round of this cyclical process gradually involves more of the fine detail as the larger scale aspects settle into place in an overall design concept. Every decision takes me a step closer to the final design. I continue making changes and refinements even while creating the construction drawings. The considerations of structure and the realities of construction need to be thought through just like any other aspect of the design.

At some point the floor plan becomes fairly well established, and the process shifts to being one of refinement. The volumetric, aesthetic, and qualitative considerations evolve in the same manner as the floor plan developed. First, there is a skeletal massing of the building form, and then the windows and

Located in the center of this home, this staircase connects four floors. Notice the curve of the railing between the upward flight and the downward flight. Features like this give a staircase individuality.

doors are added, materials are determined, rooflines are refined, and the finer details are addressed.

Do not be afraid of changing what you and the architect have already created. If you find yourself clinging to your initial ideas and early designs even after you feel they are not exactly right, step back and take a cold, hard look at where the design has gone. Don't hold on to ideas that are no longer valid simply because it was a lot of work creating them in the first place. More importantly, don't worry about hurting the architect's feelings. He is striving for the best possible design, just as you are.

From Plan to House

As the architect begins to give the schematic plan a shape in the three-dimensional world, he will first test out concepts of massing. This is the study of the bulk and shape of the building. Here is where I begin designing the upper floors of the house. The location of the second-floor and possibly third-floor rooms will determine where the house is tallest and shortest. I sometimes draw little elevations (views of exterior walls and roofs) or perspective (three-dimensional) sketches to experiment with the composition of the major forms of the house. These drawings are quick and lack much detail, but they are informative, teaching me what works and what does not.

The roof line is one of the most prominent features of a building. It sets a tone and character. We "read" the building partly by its roof. We might see a craftsman style bungalow as being sheltering because of its low-pitched roof and extended eaves.

A classic revival house stands stately and dignified with its simple, large-gabled roof punctuated in front by an entry pediment. Some houses, like a Gothic revival with its steep, pointed gables adorned with ornate, cross-bracing details at the peaks, might even be described as poetic. Although all of the building details contribute to the overall personality of the architecture, it all starts with the massing and the roof lines.

If your program and the images that have inspired you express a particular style you are striving for, do some homework and learn what the key elements of that style are. A terrific book that can help you identify and understand the proper elements for each style is *A Field Guide to American Houses* by Virginia and Lee McAlester. It is full of sketches and photos that explain things nicely. It is also a great travel companion when you are touring American cities and historic villages.

The creation and development of the design are parts of this home-building process in which an architect can be indispensable. As I have said, there is no simple formula for these tasks. Here is where experience and expertise can be extremely valuable.

Some Rules of Composition

Although this is not canon law, here are a few simple rules for composing a cohesive and pleasing building.

The primary portion of the house should be the tallest. In the classic Pennsylvania "telescope" farm house, the main block of the building is usually two stories tall. The adjacent building segments are capped with lower and lower roofs. This is where the term "telescope" house comes from because the entire building looks like you could push the end in toward the center and the segments would collapse like a telescope. No matter what style of house, this concept of a central, prominent roof, flanked by diminishing, ancillary roof segments provides a solid basis for good composition.

Houses built with additions of diminishing size, such as this, were known as Pennsylvania telescope houses because they resembled a collapsible telescope.

CALCULATING ROOF PITCH...AND WHAT IT MEANS

Roof pitch is the angle of the slope of the roof. A layperson might describe this in terms of degrees from horizontal such as a "thirty-degree slope." But carpenters, builders, and architects, at least in the United States, do not. We use a system that evolved from the way carpenters lay out and cut the rafters. Roof pitch is expressed as the number of inches the roof rises for every twelve inches you measure horizontally.

If your architect or builder says the roof is "6 in 12" or "6 and 12," this means that the roof rises six inches for every twelve inches you go horizontally. This is written "6:12" or "6/12." The framing

carpenter lays out his rafter cuts using a carpenter's square, which is an "L-shaped" tool with inches marked along each edge. It is easy for him to mark the appropriate number of inches in each direction and cut accordingly. He doesn't commonly use a tool that measures degrees of an angle, so degrees are not used in the United States for determining roof pitch.

Incidentally, a 6:12 roof is actually an angle of about 26½ degrees, a 9:12 roof is about a 36-degree angle, and a 12:12 roof is exactly a 45-degree angle, but I'm sure you were ahead of me on that last one.

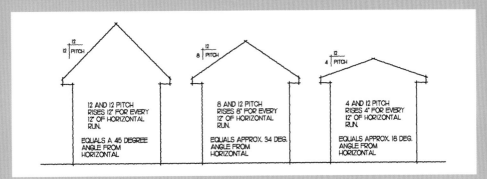

Strive for balance but not necessarily symmetry. We discussed this earlier. Symmetry can be stiff and static. Balance can be achieved by the placement of opposing elements. For instance, if you have a large, single-story element on the left side of the house, such as a garage, you might want to place a smaller, two-story element on the right side of the house.

Good buildings need a good foundation, both physically and visually. The house must look "grounded." Rules of classic architecture require a base, a middle, and a top. Greek and Roman architecture always started up from the ground with a substantial base, often built of oversized blocks of stone, for the building to stand on. The columns and more delicate walls of the actual building were then built upon that base. Visually, the building could not tilt or sway, thus appearing solid and permanent. Your house should share in these principles. Place heavy, large-scale materials low and near the ground. As the building rises, the materials used can become lighter and smaller in scale to create the middle. The cornice and the roof above become the top.

When changing materials on the face of the building, make those transitions in logical places. If only a portion of the house is to be stone, for instance, do not stop the stone at an outside corner. If you do, the thin edge of the stone will be visible, and the stone will look "glued on" to the wall. Material transitions should always occur at inside corners so that the entire "box" of that part of the house appears to be built of the same material. A corollary to this rule is that when you change materials, change planes. That means you should not arbitrarily change from brick to wood siding midway along a straight wall. If you must change materials, make the wall jog a foot or so to create a logical place for one material to stop and the next one to begin.

Windows and doors should align with the openings above and below. The centerlines are the best guides to use for this alignment, thus allowing narrower windows to be properly placed above wider ones. Windows and openings should diminish in height as they move up the wall. Keep in mind the concept of "windows of appearance" that we discussed earlier.

Windows Are the Eyes and a Door Is the Mouth of the Building

A window is first and foremost an expression of the use that lies beyond. From outside, windows entice us to wonder about what lies within. From inside, windows can frame a view by blocking out unwanted parts and focusing attention where attention is deserved. Windows can be broad and expansive if the view is panoramic or they can be small and restrained, tightening the view to a single object. The overall shape of the assembly of windows should relate to the shape of the view. Horizontal openings work well with a view to the horizon, and vertical arrangements might be best for a view to the woods.

The placement of windows must be considered in terms of what can be seen through the window, how they will work as a source of light and air, and how they punctuate and enhance the appearance of the building.

From the exterior perspective, placing windows in a wall is a bit like hanging pictures on a wall. You are not necessarily trying to fill up the wall, but you are striving for a cohesive and orderly pattern. Muntin patterns can be used to regulate scale. Shutters, even if not actually functional, are a useful "peopling" tool, expressing the presence of other people within.

Doors are the portals that welcome and connect. There is a subtle anticipation of what lies beyond that clings to each door. The detail and articulation of doors express the importance of each. Front doors command embellishment. Others are simpler and thus suited to their rank and purpose. French doors, i.e., doors with panes of glass, are the chameleons of the openings. Sometimes they behave as doors, and sometimes they behave as windows. They allow us both to look and pass through them. Unlike windows, French doors have the added power to allow our psyche to feel as though it can move through to the other space that can be seen through the glass. Even if you have never actually walked through a French door to the patio or terrace beyond, the mere fact that you could enhances the sense of connectedness we feel to the space beyond.

Front doors are signature features in any home. They offer the opportunity to express the style of the architecture and the personality of the owners.

Using the Right Stuff

A mistake I see all too often in house design is the inappropriate use of materials. Please don't put heavy materials such as brick and stone above lighter materials such as wood siding on dormers above the roof or in visually unsupported bay windows. It is structurally possible to do this, of course, but these heavy materials look funny there because there is nothing beneath them that looks substantial enough to support the weight. Heavy materials should be the foundation and primary walls of the structure. Chimneys should have the massive, permanent look of masonry. Bay windows, porches, and items like that should be built of the lighter weight materials like wood and should read as appendages or supplemental elements to the central structure of the house.

Materials must always be used in appropriate locations. Here is an example of an attractive home that makes the mistake of attempting to support a heavy material with a light material. There is no logic to supporting heavy bricks with wooden columns. Although it can be accomplished structurally, the visual logic is appalling. The heavy balustrade only makes matters worse. Think how much nicer this house would be if the porte-cochere was pulled down and hauled away.

HOW MUCH DOES YOUR HOUSE WEIGH?

A two-story, wood-framed house, excluding the foundation and basement, weighs somewhere around forty or fifty pounds per square foot. That means that a 3,000-square-foot house weighs 120,000 pounds! If it has a stone or brick exterior and if you add in the basement or foundation, it could weigh over 300,000 pounds! That's about 110 pounds per square foot.

Maybe instead of thinking your house costs $150 to $200 per square foot or more, you should think of it as costing two bucks a pound. That sounds like a bargain—especially when you compare it with, say, a pound of top sirloin.

Another disconcerting look is having chimneys built out of combustible materials such as wood siding. Granted, a wooden chimney can actually enclose a metal flue pipe that meets the building code and be perfectly safe. But it's hard to shake the nagging sense that hot embers and smoke should not be anywhere close to highly combustible wood siding or framing. If brick or stone is too heavy to support or is cost prohibitive, consider sheathing the chimney with thin brick, thin stone, or stucco. You can now install real stone and real brick in places where the weight of brick or stone would be problematic. Thin bricks and stone are glued to the wood frame and sheathing with high-strength construction adhesives. Mortar is installed between the bricks and stone. The result is a masonry wall that not only looks real, it is real, except it is missing the weight of the full thickness material.

Chimneys Are Spatial Markers

We spoke earlier about how vertical elements can command and denote a certain space around them. In a residence, chimneys do just that. Their verticality and height act as exclamation marks for the language of the building. They hold portions of the building within their influence. Chimneys can also mark the spaces within the house that we cannot see from outside. They indicate that beneath them sits a hearth where the family gathers.

The almost forceful anchoring effect of a chimney can be used to define various portions of the building. Pairs of chimneys, located on opposing ends of the structure, can serve as bookends, embracing all that lies within.

I'm not opposed to building a false chimney to make the design you want. There is a long and distinguished history of false architectural elements. This is not "cheating." Not only do false chimneys complete a design, they can be used to conceal the necessary roof protrusions, such as plumbing vent pipes and water heater vents.

The classic lines and simple elegance of a New England-style house are forever appealing.

Lesson Eleven

THINKING THROUGH THE PLACES WHERE YOU LIVE

"The space within becomes the reality of the building."
—FRANK LLOYD WRIGHT

We have looked at what rooms and spaces the house should include, where the house should sit on the land, and how the rooms and places should interact. From the bubble diagrams and conceptual plans, you should have a good sense of the interrelationship of each room and the relative position of each to the other. You have notes and inspiration images that are important to the character and features of each space. But we still need to look at each space or room and design it in more detail. When I am at this stage, I often have no particular plan for the kitchen layout or the master bath and closet arrangement. I will have space allocated for these functions, but the actual cabinet arrangements, doors, windows, and even the exact shape of the room will not yet be determined.

Each room and space is a little design project of its own. Many factors will influence the configuration and shape of the room, not the least of which is the room's position within the overall building. Because each room is a piece of the overall puzzle that is the house, each one must "interlock" with the adjoining rooms—and not just in two dimensions. Eventually, these rooms will have to become a part of the three-dimensional building. If rooms are going to be taller than a single floor or have shaped ceilings of some kind, they will have an impact on the rooms above on the next floor, actually becoming a part of the plan of that floor. If a first floor room needs to have a ceiling height that is a foot or two higher than the basic ceiling height throughout that floor, the upstairs room that will sit above it will have to be up a few steps. If a first-floor room is planned to be two stories tall, there can be no room above it at all.

The more influential consideration when designing any room is the function that the room will contain. There are many things to think through for each room. I'll try to outline some of the more important issues. Feel free to add to these lists. Remember, this needs to be a house that is specifically tailored to *you*.

WHEN COUPLES DISAGREE

Recently, a client asked me how to go about breaking a deadlock between herself and her husband. They had reached an impasse over a critical decision, and both felt strongly about it. Unfortunately, they each held totally opposing opinions. What I suggested was trying to determine who had the most at stake in the decision. By that I mean that if the decision involved an element of the house he would be using or interacting with more than she, then he should have the tie-breaking vote. If it was a decision that involved one of her special spaces or things, she should break the tie.

Often couples can step back and evaluate the relative value and importance to themselves and to their partner of each decision. When that happens, the decision becomes clear. Sometimes a compromise is reached. It might even end up being an "Okay, I'll go along with you on this fancy spa in the bathroom, but I get that built-in outdoor grill I've always wanted" type of arrangement.

An outside, unbiased opinion can sometimes help. This is often the role of the architect. But it might be a friend or relative who can take a more objective view, add an opinion, and help clarify things.

Try not to keep score on who prevailed the most times. That is not productive.

If all else fails and you find you just can't break the tie, you could always try a round of "rock, paper, scissors."

This kitchen, keeping room, and breakfast room flow together to create the "heart" of this house. It's the place where the family congregates.

Kitchen—The Heart of the Home

Frank Lloyd Wright redefined the American house. He changed how we see our lives and how our houses should respond to our modern lives. But, throughout this transformation, he preserved the essence of the "home." He knew that every house has a "heart," and that heart is the perceived center of the house. The heart of the house is the room that provides the greatest sense of security, even if that sense is only on a subconscious level. This is the place where we feel most comfortable. In virtually every design, that heart needs to be the starting point of our day. It is where the family congregates. Wright felt the heart of the house was the fireplace. This is the concept of "hearth and home." I would contend that in the last few decades this has changed. Today, the heart of the home is the kitchen. Often, it's not simply a place to prepare food.

The kitchen is the congregating place for the family as well as the family dining spot. It's sometimes the place where we want to put a small sofa or a comfortable chair so someone can sit and chat with the food preparer. Today, the idea of the "country kitchen" or open kitchen is extremely popular. Such a kitchen provides for food preparation, eating, family interaction, and relaxing. It's more than just a kitchen. A fireplace is often a part of this space. I usually refer to this kind of room as the keeping room. I believe this term derives from the word "keep," which was the stronghold of a medieval castle. That would be appropriate since this is the place where the family is kept safe and sound. It is intended as an extension of the traditional kitchen, and it becomes the focal point of family life. It is a space that is designed for more than efficiency. We're talking about designing for livability.

No room in the house has gotten as much print over the decades as the kitchen. It is easily the most complicated room in the house, containing cabinetry, appliances, utilities, and special finishes. It is also the room that must accommodate a myriad of functions. This is the place for food preparation, utensil and food storage, cleaning, entertaining, and dining. Although many have tried to create the *ideal* kitchen, it really cannot exist. Here is where you must closely examine how you live and how you wish to live on a day-by-day basis.

There are a number of good kitchen planning resources in bookstores and on the Internet, but here's a list to get you started.

KITCHEN PLANNING—TWENTY QUESTIONS:

1. Is the kitchen a central part of family life?

2. Is your kitchen an extension of the family living area?

3. How do you use your kitchen? Is it used by one person, two people, or by the entire family?

4. When you have guests, do you want them in your kitchen, in the kitchen but not in the work areas, or not near the kitchen at all?

5. Do you like morning light in the kitchen?

6. Does the kitchen "connect" to any other spaces, such as a screened porch or great room?

7. Is there a view or connection to the outside?

8. What style do you see in your mind's eye?

9. Do you need multiple workplaces within the kitchen?

10. How many days a week do you cook dinner? Is it a complex or simple meal?

11. Do you often cook for large groups? If so, how many people?

12. Should there be a place for sitting at a counter? Or for sitting at a table? Or should there be some comfortable seating, maybe for television viewing or family games?

13. Is there a television? Is there a computer? Is there an Internet connection?

14. Is your present kitchen adequate for working and storage? If not, what would you change?

15. Is there an island in your dream kitchen? If so, are there any appliances or a sink in or on the island? Is it one level?

16. What appliances do you need? Is the oven a wall oven or is it a part of a range?

17. How many sinks do you want?

18. What material(s) is (are) the countertop(s)?

19. Is the primary dining area adjacent to a part of the kitchen? Is there a separate, formal dining area?

20. Are there any special features in your kitchen, such as a fireplace, bake center, pastry slab, appliance garage, etc.?

You may have already addressed a number of these issues when you did your programming. Consider creating an additional program just for the kitchen. Include every detail you can imagine. Remember, even if a detail will not need to be addressed until months later, write it down when you think of it or it will slip out of mind until it's too late.

As we said earlier, kitchens are a competition for wall space. I like to decide first the connections a kitchen should have with the neighboring spaces, plan on window locations, and then create the actual kitchen layout within the parameters left over after these other requirements are met. This may mean revising the doors, openings, and windows later, but every design should have the flexibility of revisions. Don't feel at all concerned if you find yourself dropping back and rethinking things several times.

When laying out the actual countertop and cabinet arrangements, there are a few basic rules to follow. First, there is the infamous "work triangle." Personally, I think this gets over-emphasized. At its core, however, the concept is valid. The work triangle is the imaginary triangle formed between the kitchen sink, the cook top, and the refrigerator. Conventional wisdom says the three legs of this triangle

Sometimes called a "country kitchen," a keeping room that is open to the kitchen and breakfast room creates the traditional feel of "home."

should add up to no more than twenty-six feet. The obvious concept here is that this minimizes the number of steps you must take between functions. The work triangle should be arranged so that the sink is generally in the center of the two distant ends of the triangle. The leg of the triangle between the cook top and the sink should not be interrupted by an island or peninsula. The leg between the sink and the refrigerator can be interrupted by an island if the island can be used as a work area or a place to lay down items taken out of the refrigerator.

Arched openings allow communication between the kitchen and family room while maintaining a pleasant sense of separation.

In many larger kitchens a prep sink is included. In this case, think of the prep sink as part of the work triangle since it is the water source for the cooking function. The main kitchen sink becomes a clean-up area, instead of part of the cooking function, and can drop out of the original work triangle. A kitchen like this should be thought of as having "work stations." One work station would be for cooking and food preparation while the other would be for cleanup. Each work station needs its own work triangle with the components of the kitchen necessary for the particular function of that work station conveniently located and arranged.

The classic "galley" kitchen is unquestionably the most efficient arrangement possible. Everything is nearby and readily accessible. Although a galley kitchen is only feasible in a smaller area, the concept of the galley can also be employed in an island-type kitchen. The island and the row of cabinets and countertop along the opposite wall form the basic galley, plus additional counter space and cabinets are gained on the other side of the island. Add another row of wall cabinets and countertop along the other wall, and you now have a double galley with two work areas, one on each side of the island. Another variation on this design is an island within an "L-shaped" cabinet and counter arrangement. No matter what the final shape and no matter how large and complex the kitchen becomes, the original work triangle must be maintained to some degree. If not, the entire kitchen will become disjointed and awkward to use. The emphasis should be on maximizing counter space and not maximizing floor space. You don't want to add unnecessary footsteps just to get from one work area to another.

You will need to find places to position what I call the "big boxes." These are the refrigerator, wall ovens, and a freezer, if you have one. Because the refrigerator and a wall oven cabinet are so large, they break the visual and functional flow of the kitchen. Any counter space that is on the other side of the refrigerator, away from the majority of the counter space, will feel isolated and cut off from the rest of the kitchen. Because of that, I like to place the "big boxes" at the ends of the lengths of countertops. I also take care not to place the big boxes in positions where their bulk is obvious or where they interrupt any sight lines.

Here is a checklist of things to consider and things you may want to include in your kitchen and your butler's pantry:

1. How many work stations?
2. Dish storage cabinets in uppers or lowers?
3. Extra deep upper cabinet for chargers or serving plates?
4. Glassware storage cabinets?
5. Utensil drawers?
6. Pots and pans drawers?
7. Storage container and miscellaneous object storage cabinets?
8. Spice storage?
9. Appliance garage?
10. Other small appliance storage?
11. Food storage cabinets?
12. Food storage pantry closet?
13. Under cabinet lighting?
14. Countertop material(s)? In which areas?
15. Broom and cleaning equipment storage?
16. Primary kitchen sink?
17. Prep sink?
18. Pasta pot filler?
19. Dishwasher? One or two? Right or left of sink? Drawer type or standard?
20. Disposal for each sink?
21. Window above main sink?
22. Refrigerator? Conventional or cabinet depth? Width?
23. Refrigerator type, side-by-side, over/under, compartmented?
24. Refrigerated drawers?
25. Oven? How many?
26. Oven location? Under cook top as part of a range? Wall? Under counter away from the cook top?
27. Oven type and fuel? Gas, electric, convection, dual fuel?
28. Steamer oven?
29. Warming drawers?
30. Built-in coffee maker?
31. Ice maker?
32. Wine cooler?
33. Freezer? Width?
34. Cook top? Type? Fuel?
35. Venting? Visible Hood? Hood liner within cabinetry? Downdraft?
36. Cabinet panels on appliances?
37. Cabinet style and finish? One or more style or finish?
38. Appliances on island, or none?
39. Is the island a table look?
40. Bookshelves?
41. Wine rack?
42. Pot rack?
43. Linen storage cabinetry?
44. Liquor storage?
45. Cooking fireplace?
46. Eating countertop? How many seats? What height?
47. Table in kitchen?

While planning your kitchen, ask yourself questions about how you will use each item. Be sure there is counter space next to or nearby each appliance for setting things down, like a pitcher of milk or a hot casserole. Think through which side of the sink your dishwasher should be on and then plan where the clean dishes that come out of the dishwasher will be put away. You don't want to be walking clear across the room to put the glasses away every day. It is always a good idea to measure your present kitchen to determine how many lineal feet of lower cabinets, upper cabinets, and countertops you have. Then use those measurements as "yard-sticks" to evaluate the plan of your new kitchen. It helps always to have a real-life reference point for all of your house planning.

Obviously, there is much, much more to consider when designing a kitchen, and I do not have enough room in this book for all of that. There are many good kitchen design books and magazines available that can provide you with more detailed information.

Dining—Breaking Bread Together

Next, ask yourself how your family eats. Is it a bucket of chicken on the run or do you prepare a "sit-down" meal and all eat together? Is mealtime a time of family interaction? Should the room be conducive to conversation? Maybe you have two dining places, one for daily meals that is light, airy, and casual and another for holidays and dinner

French doors lead to a terrace adjacent to this dining room. Even without actually opening the doors, a sense of connection with the outdoors is achieved that could never be matched with windows alone.

parties that is formal and more dignified. Maybe the informal room has a big, heavy trestle table and benches or perhaps it's a booth-type eating nook with windows all around. Maybe it's part of a big country-style kitchen. The formal dining area might be the place for grandma's antique dining table and Chippendale chairs.

From a spatial standpoint there are not too many considerations for a dining room. Primarily, the furniture has to fit into it. There needs to be adequate room for getting in and out of chairs, and there should be wall space for side furniture, such as buffets or servers. A formal dining room might need a butler's pantry between it and the kitchen to aid in serving, storage of the good dinnerware, and simply to form that transition space that feels right between the acts of preparing the food and enjoying it. A butler's pantry can have a good double use as a bar.

A dining room is one of the rooms that can actually be too big. There is a definite limit to the space around a table and chairs. If it's too large, the furniture feels out of place. Personally, I feel that two-story high dining rooms are never comfortable. I think that a space designed for sitting across from others around a table has real, psychological limits in three dimensions.

Dining rooms usually contain one clear example of a focal point that defines space. The chandelier is often a dramatic element, both when illuminated and when turned off, and it clearly defines the center of the space. Because of the impact of the chandelier, the table must be centered beneath it. It follows that the window at the end of the room and the painting

Delicate onlays surround the chandelier, transforming a plain ceiling into something special.

or side table at the other end must be centered. In dining rooms that are somewhat narrow, sideboards or buffets that need to be positioned along the longer side wall can end up crowding the chairs on that side of the table, but moving the table over will mean the chandelier ends up off-centered over the table. One solution for this dilemma is to build a wider dining room. Another less expensive and clever solution is to create a wide alcove that the buffet can sit back into. This will let you still center the table in the room while only adding a foot and a half or two to the width of the room on one side and not four feet (two feet to each side).

A dining room can have windows on only one wall and still feel right. You need some wall space for artwork, anyway, so a blank wall can be an asset.

Think about tray ceilings, chair rails, and cove lighting in the dining room. These features can enhance the formality while also keeping the space intimate and pleasing.

Living—What We Do between Work and Sleep

In your program you have already identified spaces for living. You also know where these rooms should be placed in relationship to the other rooms in the house. These might be called living rooms, family rooms, libraries, or great rooms. You should have an idea of the specific features you want. Will there be a fireplace? How many people will the room be able to handle? Will the room be oriented toward the view or toward the rear terrace? Will it be a quiet room for an evening of reading or television viewing? Will it be the room where the ballgame is on the giant screen television? Whatever it is, we now come to the time where we must "concretize" the program and start to turn it into an actual room.

Living spaces present us with another set of competing factors. What will be the focus of the room? Which way will the furniture be arranged? Often, the three competing focal points in living spaces are the view, the fireplace, and the television. It is nearly impossible to set up the furniture to relate optimally to all three. It is also impractical to be rearranging the furniture continually since sofas don't swivel very well. You, and only you, can determine which focal point is the most important. Try to think about the way you actually live. Don't try to

Living spaces should be sized to be appropriate for the intended number of occupants.

deny the fact that you actually watch television when you know you do. One arrangement that is currently popular but that I find to be particularly unworkable is placing the television above the gas fireplace. This lets you hide the television behind doors when not in use, preserving the "magazine photo" aesthetic of the room. But, when you do actually watch the thing, you have to sit in a very uncomfortable, neck-craning position to do so.

Living spaces should be sized to reflect the number of people who might usually be in a given room. Great rooms might be just that, great. This is the place where the whole family and your friends will congregate. If the room is large enough, a higher ceiling can be a plus. If you are considering a two-story space with a balcony overlooking from above, keep in mind the potential sound transfer problem that can happen when the sounds from downstairs reflect off of the walls and reverberate into the bedrooms above. You can help ameliorate this by making sure the bedroom doors are somewhat remote from the second-floor balcony.

Cozier rooms, like studies or libraries, are often best sized with nine- or ten-foot ceilings. Here we often want a room for just two to four people. There might be bookcases, paneling, or a fireplace. Incidentally, paneling is an expensive item. That might be another reason to keep this type of room from getting too large. Libraries can be the second living room for the family member who wants a quieter place away from the noise. That desire for silence might influence the position of this room in the overall plan. A library can also serve a double

function as an office. Doors might be needed. These can be pocket doors, either solid or French doors, especially if they will be closed only infrequently.

Libraries and studies are often intended for only a few people and not large groups. Warm wood paneling and hand-crafted woodwork make this room cozy even for one person sitting alone.

Wood cross-beams create coffers in a library ceiling. Although expensive, beamed ceilings are elegant and wonderful.

Sleeping—Retreat from the Day

The bedrooms and bathrooms are the most private rooms in the house and should be located in positions that help control sound transmission. You might also want to think about what orientation—north, south, east, or west—the room should have. This has an impact on the amount of daylight that will come into the room. Bedrooms are not just places for sleeping. A child's room is his or her personal space or "zone of retreat," a concept we discussed earlier. It might be the place where homework is done. Bedrooms might be shared by more than one child. The master bedroom might be the place the parents retire to in the evening when they want a quiet place away from the kids and the television. Your concept of "bedroom" may be unique and different from another person's, so take some time and ask yourself how the bedrooms in your house will be used.

Bedrooms range from those that are quite small to ones so large they should properly be called suites. No matter how large each bedroom is, it should have at least one wall long enough for the headboard of the bed, including one or two night tables. Of course, a king-sized bed needs more length than a queen or double bed, so the master bedroom will need a longer headboard wall. If at all possible, try to place the bed either on the wall with the bedroom door, on the wall across from the bedroom door, or on the side wall of the bedroom away from the bedroom door. Avoid placing the bed in a position such that when you walk into the room you are looking directly at the side of the bed. The room will present itself better this way. It's a good idea to have another wall for some furniture on the opposite wall from the headboard for a dresser or armoire. Many bedrooms have a television, so plan its location along with the other furniture.

Whenever possible, I try to position closets between bedrooms, and I also try to avoid having bedroom doors situated directly across the hall or right next to each other. This gives each bedroom additional sound and visual privacy. Another good idea is to keep the guest and children's rooms away from the master bedroom, unless you have small children to whom you want to be close. If you have a master bedroom suite on the first floor, it is best not to place the guest rooms directly above the master bedroom. Creating some separation enhances privacy.

Master bedrooms, and sometimes other bedrooms, especially those that will be used as guest rooms, may also include sitting areas. These can be as simple as an extension of the main room or can be a space separated by a large opening or doorway. Once you add this sitting area, the room instantly becomes a bedroom suite. Often, the sitting area has the majority of windows within the bedroom suite. Building codes usually have a requirement for light, air, and a secondary means of egress for bedrooms. A means of egress is a way out of the room in an emergency. The bedroom door is the primary means of egress, but if that is blocked by a fire, the window must be large enough to be an escape route. These building code requirements will dictate a minimum size and height above the floor that at least one bedroom window must be.

Bedrooms are certainly rooms where having windows on two walls is a plus. Consider window seats. These fun places to sit can be the "away" places for the bedroom's occupant without the need for adding a lot of square footage.

Bedrooms are best shaped as rectangles, unless they are quite large. The reason for this is simple. Beds, dressers, and other large pieces of furniture are rectangular or square, so these items fit into a rectangular room more efficiently.

Bathrooms—Just Functional or Luxurious?

In these, the most private spaces in the house, the trend today is toward more elaborate bathrooms for the master suite and individual, private baths for each bedroom. Just like the kitchen, the master bathroom will be its own little design opportunity. Bathrooms are one of the most expensive rooms in your house. Even the open floor area is costly because it is usually covered with tile or stone. First and foremost, a bathroom must be functional. The overall layout of the house will impact the location and shape of the master bath. How the bath interacts with the bedroom and the closets is another influence. Before making too many assumptions about the bathroom, re-read and possibly edit your program. Ask yourself how you will use the bathroom and what appointments you want and need.

BATHROOM PLANNING—20 QUESTIONS:

1. Do you and your partner use the bathroom at the same time, e.g., one person shaving while another is bathing?

2. Do you want separate vanities, and should they be near each other or far apart?

3. Should there be a "sit-down" makeup vanity?

4. Should the sinks be in a separate room from the shower and tub?

5. Is the toilet going to be isolated in an area separated from the rest of the bathroom by a door?

6. Do you want a bidet?

7. Will you have a whirlpool tub?

8. Does the bathroom need to be "officially" handicapped accessible or should it provide "practical" accessibility for you now or in your later years?

9. Do you want a shower that needs no door?

10. Will the shower be used by one or two people?

11. Does the shower need a bench or seat?

12. Do you want the closet to be directly accessible from the bathroom?

13. Do you want a linen closet?

14. Do you want medicine cabinets?

15. What kind of lighting do you want? Should it be overhead recessed lights, sconces, wall lights above the mirror, or Hollywood lights around the mirror?

16. Does the bathroom have a view, and if so, what portion of the room should enjoy the view?

17. What should the floor materials be?

18. Should the floor be heated?

19. Does the bathroom "connect" to the outdoors, e.g., to a private garden or an outdoor shower?

20. Are there any special components, such as a sauna or a steam room?

When you design a bathroom, you are putting a lot of things into a fairly tight space. Consider how you will actually move around in the space. I sometimes see serious errors in bathroom designs. Often, as the space of the bathroom grows, the toilet gets located farther and farther from the bedroom. This certainly must be inconvenient in the middle of the night, especially if the path from the bed to the toilet is winding. Another inexplicable feature I sometimes see is having the bathroom either a few steps up or down from the level of the bedroom. I just can't imagine this being very safe in the dark at two o'clock in the morning.

This brings up another point—accessibility. The current term for handicapped accessibility is "universal design." Many people who are designing and building their dream homes are so-called empty nesters. These are people whose children have grown and who are building the house that is the culmination of their careers. They have made their last job relocation move, or they no longer need the house they raised their children in. But they worry that if they ever become wheelchair bound, they will be forced to move out of this dream home simply because they cannot get from one room to another. If this is your concern, it is essential that you plan for this eventuality, particularly in the bathroom.

If you look up government guidelines, you will see requirements for doorway widths that are very large. Clear widths through opened doors must be at least 32″. This necessitates using a 36″ wide door, which can be overwhelmingly wide inside a normal house. You can size the doors to be that wide and be "officially" accessible, but for "real life" living,

Here is a checklist of things you may want to include in your master bathroom:

1. One or two sinks?
2. Sink at makeup vanity?
3. Sit-down make-up vanity?
4. Medicine cabinets?
5. Mirror above sinks?
6. Full length mirror? Lighted make-up mirror?
7. Linen closet or cabinet?
8. Toilet? Separate his and hers?
9. Bidet?
10. Bathtub alcove, free-standing or in raised platform?
11. Whirlpool tub—for one or two people?
12. Shower combined with tub?
13. Hand-held shower for tubs?
14. Walk-in shower? With or without a door?
15. Two mixing valves? Two shower heads?
16. Rain-head shower?
17. Hand-held shower?
18. Body sprays?
19. Shower seat? Fold-down seat?
20. Shampoo niche?
21. Steam room? Steam generator in shower?
22. Heated towel bar?
23. Sauna?
24. Heated floor?

32″ wide doors work just fine, and they don't overwhelm the rooms they serve. Other universal design items you do need to plan into your bathroom are grab bars. Make sure you have adequate wall space for these and that the builder provides good reinforcement within the walls so the grab bars can be properly supported.

The most critical, and often overlooked, universal design component is maneuvering space. A wheelchair needs an unobstructed 60″ diameter circle to allow for turning within the room. Bathroom doors should swing outward from the space so that should a person fall out of his or her wheelchair and block the door, someone else can still open the door and enter the room to help him or her. For other requirements regarding universal design, consult your architect or refer to government guidelines. It is not necessary for you to incorporate each and every government requirement into your private house. Select the ones that can be most effective for you and the ones that can be implemented without compromising the aesthetics and non-handicapped functionality of the house.

Design of the bathroom is highly personal. Bathrooms range from basic, purely functional spaces to luxurious personal spas. Your desires and your budget will determine what is perfect for you. Searching through photos in magazines and online is a great way to prod your thinking. Discover what makes you feel good.

Many people wonder whether they really need a bathtub or whirlpool in their master bathrooms. The bathtub is often merely an interesting object in the space. By including one, you are increasing the size of the space. This can be seen as a good thing since it makes the room feel more spacious without merely adding empty floor area, even though the whirlpool might only get used once or twice a year. It can add to the spa quality of the bathroom because of its stone or tile surround and possibility of a nice window above the tub. A whirlpool tub conveys the message of relaxation, even if your busy schedule does not allow you actually to use it very often. If you really don't want or need a tub, consider expanding the shower and adding some space for a bench outside the shower.

A general planning rule these days is to compartmentalize the master bath, at least to some degree. Almost always, the toilet gets placed in a small room by itself. Whenever possible, include a window in this room for natural light and a possible view, if privacy will allow. You might also wish to separate the sink vanities from the wetter components, like the shower and bathtub, which can help keep steam off the mirrors and also allow one person to be showering while another is fixing her hair.

For your other bathrooms, consider keeping them fairly basic. Unless you want to create another "master suite" for yourself or for your guests, the bathrooms serving your other bedrooms do not need to be elaborate. I often tell my clients to think of a nice hotel bathroom as a good model for just how big or elaborate a guest bath should be. I mentioned Jack-and-Jill baths earlier. I prefer—and the resale market prefers—to have private baths for each bedroom. Keep in mind that you may need a bathroom that can be entered from the hallway. If you have a bonus room above the garage or an office on the second floor, you will not want to have to go through one of the bedrooms to get from the office to a bathroom. If this is the case, consider adding a second door to the bathroom that serves your least used guest room. One clever arrangement is shown on this sketch. This configuration allows the bedroom door to be closed for privacy while leaving the bathroom door accessible from the hall. In nighttime situations, when this bedroom is occupied, the door to the main hallway can be closed, thus giving the occupant of the bedroom private access to the bathroom.

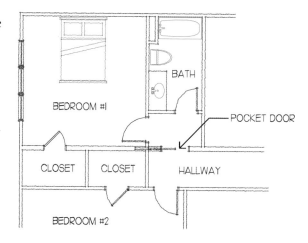

This arrangement offers two options. The pocket door can be left open, allowing access to the bathroom from both bedrooms, or, when bedroom #1 is occupied by an overnight guest, the pocket door can be closed, creating an en-suite bath.

Entry—The Guest Starts Here

The entry hall or foyer of your house is the first impression of the interior your visitors will have. Everyone from the pastor to the pizza delivery guy will be greeted here. This is the place to make that critical first impression.

From a purely functional standpoint, this space must be large enough to accommodate at least six people. This is where you will say goodbye to your guests. You don't want to have someone standing halfway up the staircase while trying to put on a coat. Aesthetically, the foyer can make a grand statement. It can even serve as an additional room when you entertain many guests. In one large house I recently designed, the sizeable foyer has an intricate, mosaic marble floor and makes a wonderful dance floor during large parties.

The foyer is one of those transition spaces we discussed earlier. It is clearly inside the house, but it often retains some of the exterior characteristics,

This striking, articulated archway separates the foyer from the hallway that leads to the master bedroom, strengthening the sense of separation and privacy.

When stepping through the front door, a guest is presented with this view through the "floating" staircase to the trees beyond. When the leaves are gone in the winter-time, the view changes to a twenty-mile vista to the distant horizon.

This staircase "floats" free of the bank of windows, adding lightness and interest. The entire staircase, including the railing, is built out of a wood called cumaru.

such as a hard-surface floor. It is the most public space in your house. As such, it should be placed near the less private spaces, like the living room or dining room. A very uncomfortable situation is created when a bedroom door opens directly into the foyer. Give some consideration to where the powder room is located and try to avoid a direct view of the toilet from the foyer. I also like to avoid a direct view of the family living space from the foyer, and you never want to look directly into the kitchen from the front door.

Ask yourself whether you would like to see through the house from the foyer. Do you want to present the distant view? This can be a dramatic effect, and it conveys the importance of the view in the overall design of the house. The main organizational axis in many houses originates at the front door and runs through this distant view. It can serve as the backbone of the house.

Remember, the foyer is experienced in two directions, once as you enter the house and once as you leave it. The design of the entry door and the view you see when you step outside are both important.

Other Places—Work, Hobbies, Etc.

Use the same sort of critical thinking to develop designs for the other rooms and spaces. Where do you work on your hobbies? Do you work from home? Do you love movies and need a home theater? Each of these rooms will have its own list of requirements and considerations beyond the simple length and width. Each one should be designed in a responsive way, recognizing and evolving from the fulfillment of those parameters.

Your outdoors "rooms" should not be ignored. How many people should your screened porch accommodate? Will this be a place for sitting or eating or both? Use the same spatial criteria we discussed earlier.

Don't Forget the Closets

You should not forget to allocate square footage for closets when you prepare your program. These take up floor space quickly. We all know the value of adequate closet space, but these days a lack of closet space in a master bedroom suite can affect the resale value of a house dramatically. In a larger house it is more appropriate to think of the master bedroom closets as dressing rooms since they often include dresser drawers and shelving. These kinds of closets are no longer meant simply to be places to hang up a few clothes anymore.

Here are some rules of thumb for closets. Walk-in closets are highly sought after, but they use up more floor area. That's because they need both the area for hanging the clothes and what amounts to a hallway between the hanging rods. If you are trying to limit the size of your floor plan, consider using standard closets that only provide enough room for the clothes hanging. The space where you stand while perusing the closet, however, is actually shared with the space of the bedroom or the hallway into which the closet doors open.

THE DOORS

Here are a few rules and suggestions for door swings and placement:

1. Front doors to houses should be 36" wide at a minimum. You can certainly make them larger if the size and scale of the house can handle it.

2. Doors for bedrooms should be 30" wide at a minimum, but I prefer to make them 32" to allow convenience for moving furniture and to keep the house from feeling tight.

3. Bathroom doors should be 28" minimum, but 30" or 32" is preferred, especially on the master bath where future accessibility may be a concern.

4. Closet doors can be smaller. But I don't like them any narrower than 30" on a walk-in closet. Twenty-eight inches wide is tolerable in a pinch, especially if this is in a seldom-used bedroom.

5. Pocket doors are great where they will be opened and closed infrequently. If you have a doorway leading from the kitchen to the dining room that you will only close when entertaining guests, then use a pocket door. But for bedrooms and bathrooms, pocket doors are awkward and cannot be locked easily for privacy.

6. If you use pocket doors, remember that any type of door can be hung as a pocket door, such as a French door (one with panes of glass in it). This is something to consider for doorways to libraries or even dining rooms.

7. Doors are best arranged with the hinge side toward the nearest corner of the room. That way you won't feel you will be walking around the door to get into the room.

8. Plan a good place for the door to "park" when opened. It should lie against a wall and not be sticking out into the space of the room.

9. Never position a door to swing forward over a descending step or stair. This creates a dangerous situation.

10. Doors should swing into rooms and not out into a hallway. An exception to this rule might be on a bathroom where handicapped access is desired. Out-swing doors on handicapped bathrooms will allow access for assistance if the handicapped person were to fall to the floor and block the doorway. An in-swing door would be impossible to open.

11. Even though 36"-wide doors are required in public buildings for handicapped access, I feel they are much too wide for interior doors in a residence. A 32"-wide door, when opened at 90 degrees, will give a clear space of about 30" to pass through. A typical wheelchair is 24" wide. If you are a very large person and need an extra large wheelchair that may be 31" wide, you should plan on the extra wide door, too. For full accessibility (universal design) guidelines, consult your architect or refer to government guidelines.

GOOD DOOR ARRANGEMENT

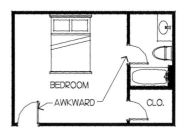

BAD DOOR ARRANGEMENT

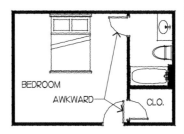

ANOTHER BAD DOOR ARRANGEMENT

The first drawing shows doors that are properly placed. Each one has a wall to lie against when open. The swing of the bedroom door allows you to walk into the room at an angle that leads you to the center of the room. When open, the bathroom door reveals the vanity and mirror. The closet door can open either into or out from the closet. Both options are acceptable.

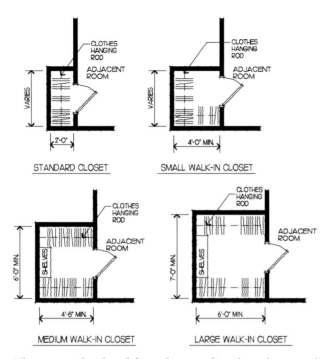

STANDARD CLOSET

SMALL WALK-IN CLOSET

MEDIUM WALK-IN CLOSET

LARGE WALK-IN CLOSET

There are no hard-and-fast rules regarding closet shapes and dimensions, but these sketches will provide you with some basics to build upon.

If your budget and program will allow walk-in closets, think through how you will use them. Provide enough space to actually move around. Maybe you need a bench to sit down upon while tying your shoes or to lay out your suitcase when packing or unpacking. Stacks of shelves help maximize the storage capacity and can provide areas for folded garments. Use double (upper and lower) hanging rods for shirts and skirts. These can double the usefulness of a closet. Generally, people only need a limited amount of single-rod, "long-hanging" for full-length dresses, robes, or trousers hung from the cuff.

To get a feel for what you need, try measuring the lineal footage of hanging and shelving you presently have. Use that as your "yard stick" to determine whether your new house will provide you with adequate closet space.

Trade-Offs

Every design is a series of compromises. There are no elements of the house that do not impact other elements in some way. By "impact" I mean that doing or including one element causes a physical, structural, or aesthetic adjustment to another element. The trick is to get 90% of everything, not 100% of some things and only 50% of others. Strive for an optimized design while maximizing your highest priorities.

Here is a list of some typical trade-offs:

1. Many trade-offs involve money. Cost directly affects the size of rooms; the quality of materials, finishes, and fixtures; the quality and features of mechanical systems; special features, such as built-ins or paneling; and special systems, such as home electronics. Reduce the cost, and the quality usually goes down and vice versa.

2. Wall space is always a point of compromise. In kitchens there is never enough wall space for wall cabinets, tall appliances, windows, doors, and openings to other rooms. If you include more of one item, you reduce the wall space available for another.

3. Layouts of rooms often compete for the primary points of interest or focal points. For example, is

the large group of windows, the fireplace, or the television the focal point in a room? How will the furniture be arranged? How can we focus on the outside view without turning our backs on the fireplace?

4. Bathrooms need daylight and privacy. Often, adding windows for light makes privacy more difficult to achieve. The big window above the whirlpool in the master bath lets in terrific light, but what if the window faces the neighbor's backyard?

5. Initial costs often compete with long-term costs. A material that costs less during original construction can often cost more in maintenance as years go by. Analyzing the long-term costs of a material is known as life-cycle costing, which takes into account the costs of maintenance and/ or replacement over a number of years. Some materials with a very high initial cost can actually look like a bargain when viewed on a life-cycle basis. Stone or brick exterior walls are examples of more expensive materials that require little or no maintenance over the long term.

6. Classic, traditional materials, for lack of a better description, often compete with a desire for low maintenance. Real wood moldings and exterior details look better than plastic parts, but they require periodic painting. Stone countertops look nicer than plastic laminate, but they require periodic sealing. There are some exceptions to this rule that look better and last long. Porcelain tile is one of those exceptions.

7. Openness competes with privacy. The less the floor plan is divided into distinct rooms, the more open and airy the spaces feel, but privacy from space to space is compromised.

8. High, soaring spaces work against cozy comfort. A room that has a two-story-high ceiling and balconies overlooking it from above can turn out to be cold, full of echoes, and uncomfortable to be in. Creating distinct, cozy rooms can sometimes make a house feel chopped up and restricted.

9. Efficiency of structure and economy of construction costs are often at odds with architectural interest. The simple box is the most cost-effective shape to build, but it's the most visually boring. Overly complicated designs with roofs going all over the place and lots of curved and angled walls might be very dynamic and spatially exciting, but the construction costs will be dramatically higher.

10. Rooms with lots of glass openings to the outdoors compete against the energy efficiency of the house.

11. Sometimes the preferred orientation competes with other issues. The classic example is a house situated on a site with a dramatic western view. The design of the house will have to find a compromise between enjoyment of the great view and control of the hot, glaring, low western sun in the afternoon.

LIGHTS, CAMERA, ACTION

Before the builder begins to hang the drywall, you need to address the *lights* and the *camera*.

When designing the house, while the plans are still just lines on paper, and again while the framing is still visible, you should review all the proposed light fixture locations with the builder and architect. This is best done when the framing is nearly complete and before any electrical, plumbing, ductwork, or insulation has been installed. Check that fixtures are where you will need them. Spend a morning walking through each room and confirming which switch operates which fixture. Be sure you have adequate lighting on art walls and countertops.

Speaking of countertops, I like to align the recessed fixtures in the kitchen ceiling directly above the front edge of the countertop. This allows light to reach the inside of the wall cabinets as well as the countertop surface. If you place them too close to the upper cabinets, the shelves will be in shadow. If you place them too far back from the edge of the countertop, over the kitchen floor, they will be essentially behind you, causing your head to cast a shadow on your work when you are standing at the counter. Recessed lights can be more centered over the countertops, where no wall cabinets are located, and above kitchen islands.

Too often, light fixture locations are decided after the framing is totally complete. This is where Murphy's Law applies. Undoubtedly, a floor joist will be running directly above and in line with the front edge of the counter, forcing you to compromise the lighting positions. This also seems to happen often in the center of hallways, forcing the hall lights to be placed awkwardly off center. If you want to win the "Plan Aheader of the Year Award," you will determine the places where this framing-versus-lighting conflict might happen and see to it your builder frames the house so as to leave a space between the joists where you need it so your lights will end up perfectly placed.

As for the *Camera* part of all of this, it is a great idea to videotape or at least photograph every wall and ceiling after all the mechanical and electrical stuff has been installed. This will give you a fantastic reference for the future when you need to find or avoid anything that is buried in the walls or ceilings.

Now that you have done the *lights* and *camera* parts, it's time for the *action*—installing the drywall. This is where you can put on your beret and yell out, "Roll 'em!"

The "Other Guy Syndrome"

Sometimes clients say to me, "If I add something that's quirky or a little different, isn't that going to affect the resale value of the house?" I understand their concern, but if you worry about this too much, you are falling victim to what I call the "Other Guy Syndrome." In other words, you are designing the house not for yourself, but for some other person who will buy your home years or even decades hence. My general sense is that if something's quirky, that is rationale enough for including it in the plan. After all, we are designing a true custom house. It should not end up being plain vanilla and look like every other house on the market. That unique feature you love could turn out to be the very thing that attracts the next buyer.

Keep in mind that we are designing *Your* Perfect House, so don't compromise on your desires or goals simply for the sake of resale value. People build swimming pools in their back yards knowing full well that there is a large segment of the market that will not even consider buying a house with a pool. There are, however, certainly still a good number of people who view a swimming pool as an important plus.

There are limits to this point of view, of course. I would never recommend building a house with only two bedrooms, for instance. One of my professors in college designed a house for himself with no doors at all—not on the closets, not on the bedrooms, not even on the bathrooms! Personally, I thought that was taking individual preference a little too far. He definitely designed the house the way he wanted, but if he ever has to sell it, he'll have to find people who have the same "open" attitude he does.

Aging with Your Perfect House

Time goes by and, like it or not, we all age. Instead of ignoring this fact, it is wise to plan for it. Here is a checklist of some universal design considerations that can allow you to age comfortably in *Your* Perfect House and not "outgrow" it. These are not requirements; they are simply food for thought. Most of these considerations can be designed without any compromise to the aesthetics or budget.

Exterior:

- Low-maintenance exterior (cement siding, brick, stucco, stone)
- Clad, non-painted windows and doors
- Low-maintenance landscape design
- Steps down through exterior doors should be as small as possible without compromising weather-tightness

General Floor Plan:

- Main living spaces on a single story, including full bath
- No steps between rooms and spaces on the same level
- 5′ x 5′ clear turning space in living area, kitchen, a bedroom, and a bathroom
- Hallways minimum width of 42″; wider is preferred
- Well-lit plus possible built-in night lights
- Lever door handles

Entrance:

- Accessible path of travel to the home with few or no steps
- If exterior steps are needed, they should be at least 12″ deep and no more than 6″ high
- Provide at least one "no-step" entry with a cover
- Wide enough aisle in garage (48″) for wheelchair access to cars
- Door to house must be at least 32″ wide
- Non-slip flooring in foyer
- Provide a surface to place packages after the door has been opened

Garage or Carport:

- Wider than average garage or carport to accommodate lifts on vans
- Door heights may need to be 9′ to accommodate some raised roof vans
- If code requires the floor to be several inches below the entrance to the house to block garage fumes, possibly slope the entire floor from front to back to eliminate the need for a ramp or step; provide a ramp to the doorway if needed
- Install a handrail if steps are required

Faucets:

- Lever handles or pedal-controlled
- Thermostatic or anti-scald controls for hot water piping
- Pressure balanced faucets

Kitchen and Laundry:

- Upper wall cabinetry 3″ lower than conventional height
- Base cabinet with roll-out trays or lazy Susan
- Pull-down shelving
- Glass-front cabinet doors
- Open shelving for easy access to frequently used items

Appliances:

- Easy-to-read controls
- Washing machine and dryer raised 12–15" above floor
- Front-loading laundry machines
- Microwave oven at counter height or in wall
- Side-by-side refrigerator/freezer
- Side-swing or wall oven
- Raised dishwasher with push-button controls
- Electric cook top with level burners for safety; when transferring pans from burner to burner, front controls and downdraft feature to pull heat away from user; light to indicate when surface is hot

Miscellaneous:

- 30″ x 48″ clear space at appliances or 60″ diameter clear space for turns
- Multi-level work areas to accommodate seated cooks or cooks of different heights
- Open, under-counter seated work areas
- Loop handles for easy grip and pull
- Pull-out spray faucet; levered handles

Bathroom:

- At least one wheelchair maneuverable bath on main level with 60″ turning radius or acceptable T-turn space and 36″ x 36″ or 30″ x 48″ clear space
- Bracing in walls around tub, shower, shower seat, and toilet for installation of grab bars to support 250–300 pounds
- If stand-up shower is used in main bath, it can be curbless and minimum of 36″ wide
- Make bathtub lower for easier access
- Fold-down seat in the shower
- Adjustable/handheld showerheads, 6′ hose Tub/shower controls offset from center
- Toilet 2½″ higher than standard toilet (17–19″) or height-adjustable
- Slip-resistant flooring in bathroom and shower

Stairways, Lifts and Elevators:

- Adequate handrails on both sides of stairway
- Increased visibility of stairs through contrast strip on top and bottom stairs, color contrast between treads and risers on stairs, and use of lighting
- Multi-story homes may provide either pre-framed shaft (i.e., stacked closets) for future elevator or stairway width must be minimum of 40″ to comfortably allow space for lift
- Residential elevator

Storage:

- Adjustable closet rods and shelves
- Good lighting in closets
- Easy-to-open doors that do not obstruct access

Electrical, Lighting, Safety, and Security:

- Light switches by each entrance to halls and rooms
- Light receptacles with at least two bulbs in vital places (exits, bathroom)
- Light switches, thermostats, and other environmental controls placed in accessible locations no higher than 48″ from floor
- Rocker or touch light switches
- Battery-powered emergency lighting system
- Audible and visual strobe light system to indicate when the doorbell, telephone, smoke, or carbon monoxide detectors have been activated
- High-tech security/intercom system that can monitor the heating, air conditioning, and lighting from any TV or control pad in the house
- Easy-to-see and read thermostats
- Flashing porch light or 911 switch

Flooring:

- Smooth, non-glare, slip-resistant surfaces, interior and exterior
- If carpeted, use low pile, high density, with firm pad
- Color/texture contrast to indicate change in surface levels

Heating, Ventilation and Air Conditioning and Energy Efficiency:

- HVAC should be designed so filters are easily accessible
- Energy-efficient units
- Windows that can be opened for cross ventilation, fresh air
- Sealed crawl space for air quality control
- Properly sealed duct work

Reduced Maintenance/Convenience Features:

- Easy-to-clean surfaces
- Central vacuum
- Intercom system

There may also be the eventual need for a live-in caregiver. One of the guest rooms could be designed for this additional use, requiring some added provision for a living area and possibly a small kitchen facility. A suite such as this can perform an additional function as living quarters for an aging parent or any other family member who may require additional care. In my own home, we have a suite just like this, with a separate exterior door but still with an interior connection to the house, where my mother lives. I have another past client who wanted a guest suite to use as a lock-out guest apartment for out-of-town business guests who often visited even while he was away. We provided a way for him to lock the remainder of the house while allowing his business guests the use of the suite and swimming pool.

Design Tidbits

Here are a few random thoughts you might want to consider while designing *Your* Perfect House.

1. A word of caution about over-lighting a space. This is easy to do, and you can end up with lights you paid for but never turn on. Also, try to consolidate the switches for lights so that one switch controls a group of lights. Think through your realistic use of the lights so you don't end up with large banks of switches and redundant lighting.

2. Measure your large furniture, and be sure you have enough room for it in your new house. Cut out "paper doll" furniture to scale and try out layouts in each room to be sure there is enough wall space and floor area. Pay attention to the traffic flow, and avoid clumsiness.

3. If you have a great view from your site, maybe you will want to look out at your view from your whirlpool bath. You will need a window with a low enough sill. This compromises privacy, but that can be solved by having a window shade you can operate from the bath so that you can get into the bath with the shade down, and then, once you are in the tub and discretely below the window sill height, you can lift the shade to enjoy the view while you soak. Reverse the process when you are ready to get out, and you will avoid giving the neighbors a show.

4. Think about where the televisions will go. One near that whirlpool might be a decadent luxury you could give yourself. How about one in the kitchen? Or the garage, if you like to work on the car while the ballgame is on? It's a small expense to run a coaxial cable to several locations during construction, but it's a headache to do it in a completed house.

5. Do you want a small sink to provide water at your make-up vanity?

6. Groups of three or five windows side-by-side look better than groups of two or four. Why? If you are standing in the center of the group, such as at the kitchen sink, you will be looking out of glass in a group of three or five and not at the vertical bar between units as you would with a group of two or four.

7. It is also a good idea to have your builder order a little extra brick, tile, or stone to give you spares for the future in case replacements are ever needed. Tiles made later will not match the ones you bought even just a few months earlier. The color "lots" will not be the same. Marble tiles that are quarried later than the original order will be cut from a different part of the mountain and may well vary in color. Or, they may simply be discontinued by the time you need that one tile to replace the one Uncle Louie cracked when he dropped his bowling ball.

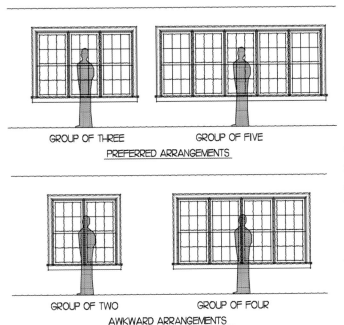

GROUP OF THREE   GROUP OF FIVE

PREFERRED ARRANGEMENTS

GROUP OF TWO   GROUP OF FOUR

AWKWARD ARRANGEMENTS

Groups of windows meant to be looked through, such as in a living room or above a sink, are best when grouped in threes or fives rather than twos and fours. An odd number of windows allows a pane of glass to occur in the center instead of a wooden window frame. This principle applies to groups of columns, as well. Think of the spaces between columns as the "windows" you look or walk through.

A large cupola rises above the foyer, admitting copious amounts of natural daylight.

Lesson Twelve

OH, YES...
THE BUDGET

"The home should be the treasure chest of living."
–LE CORBUSIER

Now we need to talk about dollars and sense. The checkbook is the place where the dreams and aspirations for our perfect new home can crash headlong into reality.

Of all the aspects of creating a perfect house, perhaps the most unpleasant has to do with money. It often happens that people who are having their dream houses built don't really want to focus their attention on the financial ramifications of building a home. Sometimes there is a denial of reality. Some individuals will invest a serious amount of money and make an equally serious emotional investment in the home of their dreams, spend a great deal on architects and designers, and spend even more for the right piece of property, only to overlook in the early critical stages whether they will be able to afford this dream!

Face Reality

I suppose this oversight is a function of the all-too-human tendency to hear only what we want to hear. Selective perception works this way: The builder tells the client, "We can build this house for somewhere between $150 to $200 a square foot." The builder might even tell the client that the high end is more likely, especially if the client wants a lot of special extras in the building of the house. But the client might simply seize on that "$150 per square foot" figure, ignoring the fact that this number represents the low end of a range. Quite frankly, when it comes to building one's own house, no one ever wants to stay at the low end. After all, you want it to be as good as you can get it. I always hear things like, "If I'm going to go to all of this trouble, I may as well do it right." This is admirable, but the usual result is that the house ends up costing 20 to 40 percent more than the client had originally imagined. And that may be 20 to 40 percent more money than there is in the client's true budget for the house.

It's essential to avoid that sense of selective perception, and it's essential to deal in the real world when it comes to dollars and cents in building houses. The alternative is just too painful to contemplate.

The first step in determining the true cost of a home is to consider two separate figures. The first is how much you can put into the house. How much do you want to spend? What's your maximum? How high are you willing to let costs go before you feel uncomfortable about the cost of the house?

The other side of the coin is to determine, with the guidance of the architect and builder, how much the house of your dreams *really* will cost. We ascertain this number by listing all the program requirements for the house—the land, the design, each of the rooms, and the basic sense of the complexity and special features of the home. Once you've worked out the basic program of the house, the architect and the builder can come up with a fairly accurate, though not precise, range for the cost of your house. Obviously, if you decide to put in Sub-Zero and Viking appliances and curved kitchen cabinets, the cost per square foot of the house will rise. But for the time being, you can get a rough sense of how much *Your* Perfect House is going to cost.

Now you've got two numbers, what you want to spend and what the house you have in mind will actually cost. This is the moment of truth. This is when you have to determine whether these numbers are basically in balance. If not, this is the time to change the budget. Not everyone can do that, so if you are in the majority who can't simply change the budget, it's time to start prioritizing your needs and desires for the house. Start asking yourself what is essential and what would you not miss if it weren't included? Once you've got these two numbers—how much you want to spend and how much the house will cost—in rough balance, you can proceed confidently to the next stage of designing and building.

I understand that thinking about the cost of the house is probably the least appealing thing you can do. It's a lot less fun than thinking about all the features of your master bedroom and bathroom suite or the beautiful new dining room in which you'll be entertaining your guests or the sweeping foyer and beautiful staircase where you will greet your guests. But it's truly necessary to take a cold, hard, objective assessment of the cost early on, when it's still easy to make adjustments to the program and to your own expectations. I simply cannot emphasize this point enough. Avoiding that unpleasant wake-up call later on, when it turns out that the house is growing much more expensive than you might wish, must be a real priority.

There's another way many people run into trouble when thinking about the price of their house. They compare the plan they want for their house—the square footage and basic design elements—with the cost of resale houses currently on the market in their communities. These individuals will say, "Why, they're selling a house like the one we want to build for $850,000. So our house shouldn't cost more than $850,000, right?"

Unfortunately, the answer is that constructing a new house is invariably more expensive than buying a resale house. There are a number of important reasons for this. First, the typical resale house was most likely constructed by a developer who was building a large number of similar houses in that community or perhaps in other communities around the state or even around the nation. Anything that's mass-produced is going to be cheaper to create than something that is custom-designed. Even if all the materials and features were identical on the resale house and on your house, someone who is building a large number of houses can build each house for less money than an individual could.

A large homebuilder benefits from the economies of scale that come from mass production. But it is highly unlikely that the house you design will use the same building materials and design features as a mass-produced house. Quite simply, your house is going to be much nicer. Individuals who design houses generally are looking to create something unique, special, impressive, and delightful to the eye. A mass-production homebuilder is not looking to create architectural masterpieces. He is looking to build houses as economically as possible and sell them as quickly as possible. He will include the ubiquitous "eye candy," but he doesn't want to spend the money that it's going to take to create unique properties. Also, the very aspects of a house that make it unique and desirable to one group of buyers would make it undesirable to others. The builder is aiming at a broad market, so he has absolutely no stake in creating a home that would be as personal, personable, and perfect for you as the house you design.

There's another important factor to consider as well. A builder putting up a spec house might make choices in terms of building materials that will save him money in the short term and cost the homeowner more money in the long term. He just wants a house that looks good for the time it takes to sell it. He's not worried about your long-term cost of upkeep.

Consider windows as one example. A home builder working on a spec house would be more likely to put in windows that need to be painted on the outside every five or six years. Such windows will cost him less, but the ultimate cost of maintaining and painting those windows for the homeowner will be much higher over the long haul. You might choose to spend more money initially on windows for *Your* Perfect House. You might want to get the kind that come with an aluminum cladding or another maintenance-free finish, thus saving you the cost and hassle of painting them in future years. When you build a house for yourself, you will make different value judgments than a builder who is building a house with the objective of selling it to someone else.

A key term to consider here is "life-cycle costing." Life-cycle costing means you evaluate the cost of a product or a material over the duration of the life of the house. Again, clad windows may be more expensive initially, but they actually cost less to maintain over their life cycle because they don't have to be painted. If you are thinking about living in *Your* Perfect House for the next twenty years, life-cycle costing will be important to you. A builder is focused only on keeping his initial costs as low as possible, to maximize his profit. Life-cycle costing will not be a factor in his decisions unless the marketplace is demanding it. This concept will apply to many items in the house. Eventually, these extra costs will add up to significant amounts of money. *Your* Perfect House will be significantly better, built of higher quality materials, but more costly to construct than the builder's spec house.

It is for these reasons and others that the custom house you build is far more likely to be attractive and distinctive than the mass-produced homes in the area. So using the resale value of currently existing homes similar in size and scope to the house you're thinking about is rarely an accurate guide to the true cost of building your new home. Working with such a figure can only lead to heartache, in the form of sticker shock, down the road.

The good news about creating a house with more attractive materials and a more personal design is that your custom house will eventually resell for more money than a production house of equal size. Your custom-designed house will also hold up better. The uniqueness of its design, the appropriateness of the way the house fits onto the lot, and the overall correctness and thoughtfulness of the design will all shine through. As we all know, crystal balls can be somewhat cloudy when it comes to predicting short-term or long-term trends in real estate, but, historically, custom-designed houses command a premium over their mass-produced and less thoughtfully designed brethren.

The Murkiness of Cost per Square Foot

Earlier, when we were discussing programming and figuring out how big your house should be, we discussed the fact that cost per square foot can mean different things to different people. For example, some builders will seek to deflate the cost per square foot by including in their estimates the garage, the patio, or other areas that don't require as much labor and materials as interior, heated and air-conditioned spaces. It's essential to make sure that you, the architect, and the builder all refer to exactly the same kind of space when you talk about how many square feet are in the house and how much the house will cost per square foot. In my practice I consider cost per square foot to be the amount of heated and/or air-conditioned space in a house. I do not include unconditioned spaces. You must make sure that the builder is going by the same standards as you and the architect are. At various points along the way, as I develop the design, I check how many square feet the floor plan now includes. I compare it with the program and see whether everything is on track.

We also said earlier that builders use the "cost per square foot" only as a rough estimate. They never sign a contract binding them to build a house at a particular cost per square foot. They'd go broke if they did that because there's no way for them to know precisely what a house will cost until they know precisely what has to be ordered for the house and precisely how much labor it will take to build the house. There are just too many variables. You may want a stone exterior for your house. That will drive up the cost per square foot of your home considerably. Or you may want a certain kind of roof shingle that requires more labor and materials than a simpler one. That's why some builders quote the estimated cost per square foot as a range. They won't know precisely how much the house

HOW TO CALCULATE SQUARE FOOTAGE

The most commonly used formula for calculating square footage, and the one used by real estate appraisers, is to include only the heated and air-conditioned areas of the house in the equation. That excludes the garage, attic storage, unfinished basement, porches, and other such spaces.

The total square footage includes not just the areas of the rooms, but also the area occupied by the walls between the rooms. The area the walls occupy seems small, only a few square inches, but it adds up fast. It can be as much as ten percent of the overall square footage.

You need to measure square footage from the outside faces of the outside walls and include the areas of the stairs. Count only spaces that have a ceiling height of more that seven feet. Stair areas count as a part of the floor from which they rise. Areas that are open to the rooms below do not need to be counted. Don't worry about fireplaces, small mechanical closets, and such since these areas amount to a tiny fraction of the overall space.

Remember, the heated square footage is generally used in conjunction with a very rough estimate of the cost per square foot for preliminary cost estimating. It is not what determines the actual cost of your house.

Caution: Be sure the builder you are talking to defines "square footage" in the same way you do. Once in a while I run into a builder who wants to include the garage and porch areas. Or sometimes builders will count in the garage at half its square footage. This serves to "dilute" the overall cost per foot average. It can make the cost of construction seem lower, but it can make matters confusing. I prefer the appraiser's method of counting the "heated square footage."

is going to cost until they know exactly how many and what kind of toilets, sinks, bricks, roofing material, appliances, flooring, and all the other things that go into the house will be.

I know I just said that the builder puts a price together by adding up every single item that is actually going into the house, plus the cost of the labor to install the items and assemble the pieces, instead of working off a cost per square foot basis. Let me clarify that a few of the building tradesmen, like painters, do charge for their portion of the work by the square foot. Most, however, use their own formula to calculate what they need to charge. Plumbers might charge based on how many fixtures are in the house, for example. The brick mason charges based on the surface square footage of the brick facing or the number of bricks he must lay. And even at that, he might charge more for brick on the second floor than brick on the first floor since the cost of scaffolding and the labor of lifting his materials need to be taken into account. He will add in more for any special details, too. The actual, ultimate cost of your house is a function of how much each item costs and how many of each item you'll need for your house.

Bang for the Buck

The typical starting point for adding extras to a house is to think in terms of resale value. Frequently, clients ask me whether a particular design concept or idea they have will make a difference in the resale value of the house. My response to them is that we want to avoid what I've called elsewhere in this book the "Other Guy Syndrome." Remember, we're not designing a house for the other guy—we're designing *Your* Perfect House. So the real return on investment from a particular design idea isn't how much money that element will net you twenty years from now when you sell the house. The real return on investment comes right now and in the years to come as you enjoy that particular feature of your house. Instead of focusing on the question of what will make *Your* Perfect House more attractive to somebody else decades from now, I'd rather share with you some ideas about how you can enjoy a very big benefit right now, for a relatively small amount of money. These options will not cost much, but they will add enormously to your enjoyment of the house. And, yes, they will make a difference at resale time.

1. Interior sound insulation. How much would you pay never to hear your teenager's stereo echoing through the walls of your home? Or foot traffic from rooms above you? Or, for that matter, what would it be worth to you to be sure that sounds didn't emanate from *your* bedroom? You can have the builder install interior sound insulation between the studs in the walls of your house and in the ceilings and floors of rooms. Interior sound insulation works very well to deaden sound transfer between rooms. Special sound deadening gypsum wallboard, a relatively new product on the market, stops sound as effectively as eight layers of normal wallboard. This product is good for encasing the home theater. The cost of these features, from which you will benefit every single day that you and at least one other person occupy the house, is remarkably low. The cost of adding interior sound insulation is only $1,000 to $4,000, depending on how large your house is. The value of not hearing the plumbing echoing through the house every single day is certainly more than that.

2. Cast iron plumbing drops. We have all heard the Niagara Falls sound effect that occurs when a toilet is flushed upstairs and the waste water surges through plastic PVC plumbing pipes. This can also be avoided. For a few extra dollars, ask the plumber to use old-fashioned, cast iron piping for the "drops." Drops are the vertical pipes that run from floor to floor. They are the culprit for the rushing water sound when they are made of lightweight plastic. The heavy cast iron deadens the sound effectively. All of the piping should also be wrapped with insulation to reduce water sounds further.

3. Flush wood thresholds. I happen to like these quite a bit. In a typical hardwood floor, the boards are two-and-a-quarter inches in width. You can put in a few boards that are four to six inches in width across the openings from one room to another, especially those rooms that have a doorway but no door, like between the foyer and the dining room. You can choose a different species of wood to get a color difference, and these wider boards that you place at the thresholds to rooms should be flush with the rest of the floor, not raised. They serve as a line of demarcation and are extremely attractive. To put in a whole floor of six-inch-wide boards would be expensive. You might wish to do that, too. But you can obtain the attractiveness and elegant qualities of flush wood thresholds for very little money, gener-

Flush thresholds of sapele, inset into the oak flooring, help separate one room from another. This is a relatively inexpensive detail that can provide an elegant look. The intricate inlays in the foyer are more difficult and more costly.

ally only a few hundred dollars. This might be a very wise allocation of a relatively small amount of cash.

4. Steel beams that eliminate columns. It often happens that builders go a little bit berserk at the idea of introducing steel into a wood-framed structure. I've never really understood their reluctance to use steel beams. But because steel is stronger and the span of a steel beam can be significantly longer than a wood beam, using steel beams means that you can eliminate columns in your garage or in your basement. In the garage you won't ever have to open your car door into a steel column and dent the door of your shiny, new vehicle. You also won't have as many unsightly columns breaking up your basement into smaller and less useful spaces. It turns out that adding steel beams to your garage or basement can be accomplished at practically no net cost increase. Since you won't need as many columns or the concrete footings the columns would sit upon, you won't need to pay to have those items installed. This saving should offset much of the cost of the larger steel beams. The net cost of installing steel beams to eliminate columns? Maybe a few hundred dollars, at most. Again, this is an extremely savvy use of a small amount of money with benefits that will last forever.

5. *An especially nice brick.* The rule of thumb for bricks is that the more attractive they are, the more visual character they offer—and the more they will cost. Hand-formed bricks are simply more expensive than tumbled bricks, which in turn are more expensive than wire cut bricks. Fancier bricks, however, aren't all that much more expensive in real terms. The labor cost is the same to lay most bricks, whether they are attractive or ugly. You might be surprised to know that the bricks themselves aren't the bulk of the cost of a brick wall. Certainly, good-looking bricks will make a huge difference in the appearance of your home. Let's do the math and see why this choice can work out well for you.

At the time of this writing, bricks cost from $220 to $250 per thousand in North Carolina. Uniquely attractive bricks cost between $290 and $350 per thousand. Brick prices are typically quoted "per thousand." Your builder may shudder at the idea of an extra $100 per thousand for the bricks, because he is interested in keeping his costs and yours as low as possible. Yet a typical house might need 25,000

bricks. Doing the math, you can see that even if you jump up to a very expensive, good-looking brick for an extra $100 per thousand bricks, the added cost is only $2,500. There are few places where you can spend an extra $2,500 on a house and have it make as big a difference as choosing attractive bricks. A couple of thousand bucks can make your house look like a million dollars.

6. *The occasional angle.* Angled walls definitely make a difference in rooms. They can open up a space, take away a hard corner, and add visual interest to a room. I don't advise going crazy and tossing in angles every few feet in every single room. You don't want your house to look like a geometrical maze. But the occasional angle can enhance the character of a room and therefore a house. It may also cost nothing at all to add that extra angle.

7. *Tray Ceilings.* Tray ceilings that are built by dropping the ceiling around the perimeter of a room can add drama and interest. These are relatively inexpensive in that the framing required is filling in the corner where the ceiling and wall join and is not structural. Dining rooms, family rooms, and even the master bedroom are good places to use this feature. Consider adding another strip of crown molding and possibly a concealed rope light above a molding to provide a glow of light into the tray.

8. *Dimmers.* Dimmers, also called rheostats, are controls at light switches that allow you to reduce the amount of light a fixture emits. Although dimmers add a small expense, they provide a tremendous degree of control and are an elegant enhancement.

It only costs a few dollars more to have the electrical outlets placed in the baseboard instead of partway up the wall. Consider this option for rooms where furniture will not hide the outlets, such as in the foyer, living room, or dining room. Bedrooms are usually less of an issue because beds and dressers hide the lower portions of most walls. The fixture to the right is the central vacuum connection, and the fixture in the center is a nightlight.

Wooden air registers, inset flush with the floor, are not expensive and add a look of refinement and thoughtfulness. Registers made from metal can be faux painted in tile floors to help disguise them, as well.

What most people do not know is that dimmers actually save you money two ways. By reducing the wattage of the light, they reduce the electrical consumption and extend the life of the bulb. Ten percent dimming of the light level reduces the electrical consumption by half. Additionally, most bulbs burn out when the switch is flipped because of the surge of power that occurs. Dimmers act as a filter for this and thus further extend the life of the bulb. I've been told that simply having a dimmer on a switch, even if it is turned all the way up, will double the life of the bulb.

Elements with Significant Cost Consequences

It's possible, as we just saw, to spend a little and create a significant difference for your home. Alas, the reverse is true as well. Some items can end up costing considerably more money than you ever imagined. They might be wonderful to have and greatly enhance your home, but don't let yourself be stunned by the cost. You may still want to have these things, just be sure you are aware of the costs before making your decisions.

1. Curved walls. Somehow, the idea of a curved wall seems like it shouldn't be that big a deal. And yet it is. Curves are incredibly expensive when it comes to home design. When clients bring up the idea of curved walls, I remind them that the curve is the same shape as a dollar sign! Curved dry wall is expensive. Curved baseboard, curved crown moldings, and any other materials that are usually flat are expensive to make curved. Every time you add another curve you are adding a large number of dollars and an equivalently large amount of work. Curves are just

A staircase is a signature item in many homes. This example goes beyond mere functionality and is a piece of original sculpture.

Built of "standard" stair parts, this railing separates itself from the ordinary—but at a reasonable cost.

plain tough. Also, rooms with curved walls are difficult to furnish. A bowed breakfast room or a turret stair are truly exceptional architectural elements, but be sure they are really important to you before you include them in your design.

2. Curved cabinets. These are unbelievably elegant and unbelievably expensive. They are extremely difficult to manufacture, and it can take a couple of days just to make one single curved face cabinet. Yes, they are gorgeous, but are they really always worth

the expense? For most people, the answer may be "no." If you can find them, pre-manufactured curved cabinets, while still expensive, can be a lot more economical than ordering a one-of-a-kind cabinet. Since the setup to build a curved cabinet is the bulk of the cost, producing numerous units causes the cost-per-unit to drop. It's the economy of scale.

3. High spaces. Quite simply, high spaces are more costly than rooms of traditional ceiling height. Are they attractive? They can be if, as we discussed earlier, the grandeur of the room doesn't dwarf its inhabitants. High spaces are costly because it's more expensive for the builder to frame a high room and put up dry wall on the ceiling and tall walls. Expensive scaffolding is needed. It is harder to paint the walls and ceiling. Installing crown moldings is harder and more complicated. There is added cost for the heating and air conditioning. Even lighting is harder to supply to a room with high spaces. The cost of a room with a two-story ceiling is almost as high as if you'd put in a floor up there and created another room. I always advise my clients to be cautious about the casual use of high spaces in home design.

4. Exterior stone walls. Stone is the most expensive facing you can put on a house. Stone on the inside, such as on a fireplace and mantel, would be a good, cost-effective investment. A hundred square feet of stone would be enough to take care of a truly grand fireplace, and the expense wouldn't be all that great. But a hundred square feet of stone on the outside of a house is a relatively insignificant area. Yes, stone is very attractive, but at three or four times the cost of brick, the expense can be stunning. Don't get me wrong—I am not against using stone. Just make sure the benefit is worth the expense to *you*.

5. Porches. Sometimes a client will say, "Bill, I'd like a porch in front and in back and a veranda on the side. That can't cost all that much, right? After all, they don't add to the square footage of the house." Somehow, people cling to the impression that porches and verandas don't cost anything, simply because they are traditionally more simply finished than interior rooms and don't have windows, heating, and air conditioning. The fact is that porches require roofing, framing, trim, and floor surfaces, just like interior rooms. They are not free. And yet the costs of porches and verandas typically are not acknowledged when calculating the cost per square foot of a house, especially when comparing the cost of one house to another. If a small porch costs $20,000 to add and the house is 5,000 square feet, that porch adds $4 per square foot to the cost of your home. Is it worth it?

This screened porch, complete with a gas "campfire" on a stone hearth, is large enough for dining and living.

Frequently, the answer is yes. Porches and verandas are very attractive design features in a home and are often the favorite rooms of the owners. My point is simply that they are not free. You've got to pay for a porch. It's not an "easy throw-in" to the construction without a cost consequence.

A stone fireplace helps extend the useful seasons of this screened porch while also adding character to the space. The screened porch of this house serves as the owner's cigar room, making his wife happy that the aroma remains out of the house.

6. Brand names. Not long ago, a builder and I were walking through the kitchen with the owner of his newly-constructed home. It just so happened that the Sub-Zero refrigerator had arrived with a spare nameplate. The builder and I jokingly asked at the same time, "Can I have that nameplate?"

The Sub-Zero nameplate itself could easily be worth more than a lot of standard refrigerators! I tell this story to illustrate the point that brand-name appliances can add a great deal of cost to a house, as well as a high perceived value at resale time, but they may not always be sensible additions unless they have a perceived value to you. This goes back to the "Other Guy Syndrome." Do not do things simply because everyone else is doing them. If you don't want or need a brand-name refrigerator, you shouldn't feel compelled to buy one. If you hate granite countertops, don't put them in. Go with copper or even Formica if that's what you prefer. Go with what you like; don't worry about that "other guy" who may or may not buy your house twenty years from now. And don't worry about what other people will think when they come into your kitchen. Chances are they'll be thinking, "What an incredibly beautiful kitchen!" So why not have the kitchen on your terms? After all, it's the most expensive room in the house, and it's one in which you're likely to spend many hours.

There are benefits to Sub-Zero refrigerators. They are, after all, the "top of the line" of refrigerators. They are designed to be the same depth as your kitchen cabinets so that they don't project out past your cabinets, the way most conventional refrigerators do. They have two separate compressors, one for the refrigerator and one for the freezer, so they don't mix air from the refrigerator to the freezer. On the other hand, they cost $6,000, instead of about $1,200 for a good "regular" refrigerator. And because they are more mechanically complex, they can require more frequent and more costly repairs.

Sub-Zero appliances definitely improve the resale value of high-end spec houses. If someone walks into a multi-million-dollar house and sees a Sub-Zero refrigerator, that person comes away with the feeling that everything in the house is of high quality. But you're not in the business of building yourself a spec house. You're building a house that will be perfect for *you*. Rather than spend $6,000 on a high-end refrigerator, maybe you can design the wall behind the refrigerator with a recessed pocket so that your conventional refrigerator's backside can fit in nicely. That way, the refrigerator doors can be flush with the cabinets, which is the most compelling design feature that Sub-Zero refrigerators offer. You'll be spending a whole lot less money.

Every decision you make will require you to balance cost against both quality and quantity.

Meet the Builder

Since we're discussing the budget, you might be wondering when we should select the builder. I'm hoping you took my earlier advice and retained an architect for the design of your house. Or at least you have chosen a design/build firm and are working with a professional architect or experienced designer. Either way, sooner or later you will need to decide upon a builder. Although this book is primarily concerned with designing *Your* Perfect House, I thought it prudent to discuss some selection criteria for the builder.

First and foremost, find out how happy his past customers are. Ask the builder for a list, and call them. Ask them specific questions. Was the builder organized? Did he and his subcontractors show up on time? Was the project properly staffed? Did they do good work? Was the builder a good guy to work with? That last question is important. You'll have a long-term relationship with your builder, so you want someone you actually enjoy being around, someone who respects you, and someone who also understands your financial objectives. You may not want a high-end house builder to build a house on a tight budget. He won't know how to throttle back, and even though his subcontractors will likely be the best, they may also be the most expensive ones in town. Similarly, you don't want someone who has been building tract homes or additions to take a shot at building your custom-designed dream house. It's fine to help a nice young man develop his business, and his lower price may be attractive, but you don't necessarily want *Your* Perfect House to be his first project above his normal level. It will cost you more in the long run.

Check into the business ethics of your builder. Does he have a reputation for honesty in the business community where you live? Does he take on too many projects at once, not giving enough focus to each individual project? This is the kind of information you can easily get from past clients, who will be more than happy to share their success stories—or horror stories—with you.

If his business ethics and organization meet your standards, you will then want to see some of his work. I recommend going to houses he has completed, preferably in the same price range as your prospective house and similar in the level of detail you are expecting. It is also enlightening to visit a project that the builder is still working on. This will give you an idea of how neat or messy his job site is. I find the condition of the building site gives me insight into the builder's overall thoroughness and attention to detail, as well.

Things to Check Out in a Builder's House

Here is a list of some things you should take note of when you are touring a potential builder's past work. This would usually be a house that the builder is showing you to illustrate his level of workmanship.

1. If the house is still under construction, how neat is the job site? Has it been swept recently? Has the framing been open to the rain for a long time? Is there trash blowing around? Is there a trash bin or a dumpster on site?

2. If still under construction, how good is the site preparation? Are tree protection fences in the proper places? Are silt fences in place, and are they being maintained? Has the rough grading been done so that rainwater drains away from the house and not toward the foundation?

3. If still under construction with some finished work in place, such as cabinets and floors, are these items properly protected from damage by other workers? Is there protection for the tubs and showers to prevent scratching? Are countertops covered? Are finished floors covered? Are "no smoking" signs posted? Have windows been kept closed to prevent damage from rain? Is the glass on the windows covered to protect them from damage if brick, stone, or stucco work is being done nearby? Are the sills of the doors relatively clean and undamaged? Are the driveway and garage floor undamaged and free of stains?

4. How good are the surfaces? Are the moldings and trim boards tightly fitted, or do the joints rely heavily on caulking to close gaps? Do the edges of countertops meet the walls properly? Do the floors feel level when you walk across them, particularly at doorways between rooms? There should be no humps or tilting. Are the tile floors set with even joints and the corners of the tiles not sticking up relative to the adjacent tiles? Are wood floors properly installed, without gaps between boards and with tight, even end cuts? Do the floorboards lay flat without cupping or humping?

5. How well are the stairs built? Are the risers all the same height, especially the top and bottom risers? Are the railings fitted smoothly, with no humps or dips where straight sections join curved sections? Are the balusters (pickets) aligned, straight, and evenly spaced? Are the treads, risers, and other parts fitted together neatly?

6. How is the general fit and finish? Are the light fixtures installed level and without gaps at the drywall? Are electrical outlets level and not protruding from the walls or recessed into the walls? Are there nicks or dings in the woodwork, especially the window sills? If there is brickwork, is the mortar neatly done and not splattered on the other bricks? Do the roof shingles lie flat, without humps of broken shingles? Is the paint done without drips and sags and without excessive brush and roller marks? Is the drywall finished smoothly? Do the doors operate smoothly, especially sliders?

TWENTY QUESTIONS TO ASK A PROSPECTIVE BUILDER

1. How many projects do you have going at once?

2. Will you supervise my project yourself? If not, do you have a full-time superintendent who will be devoted to my project, or will my project be one of two or three or more that one superintendent will handle? Can I meet the superintendent?

3. What other staff do you have?

4. What type of contract do you use? Is it "cost plus fee," "cost plus percentage," "fixed sum," or some other format?

5. Do you require a deposit? If so, how much?

6. Do you work with a retainage until final completion?

7. How can you assure me that the subcontractors and suppliers will be paid and that I will not be at risk for mechanic's liens?

8. What type of schedule do you provide? How do you show me where the progress of the work stands relative to the schedule?

9. How are changes handled?

10. How are allowance items handled? Do you charge a mark-up on overages in allowances?

11. How long will the construction take?

12. What would you estimate the approximate cost of construction to be, based on your usual projects? Or based on the description I have given you of the types of appointments and finishes I will want in the house?

13. Do you have an unlimited contractor's license? (Licensing in some regions will vary, but many places have a limited form of contractor license that restricts the types of construction a contractor can do. More experience and financial stability is required for the higher level of licensing.)

14. What are your limits of insurance?

15. How long have you been in business?

16. Can you provide me with a list of references and a list of all the projects you have done within the past five years?

17. Can you provide me with credit references and bank information?

18. How would you want payments to be handled?

19. How will you document progress, schedule, selections, costs, and other factors through the course of construction?

20. When can you realistically start my project?

Retainage

Retainage is an amount of money, usually a percentage, deducted and withheld from each month's payment request you will receive from the builder. A retainage is your "insurance policy" against the builder leaving you with an unfinished project when he's been overpaid for the work done to date or for other deficiencies that may become apparent later on in the construction process. This is often set at five percent and may "cap out" at some fixed amount of money. When the work is complete, not counting warranty work, the retainage is paid in full to the contractor.

Retainages are common in commercial construction but not in residential work. Often, the builder will actually request an initial deposit from you before beginning his work. This deposit goes to pay the subcontractors and suppliers on a weekly basis during the current month until the builder receives the next month's payment from you. If you find a builder who will work with a retainage, great. If not, you will have to depend on his reputation and your architect's advice and his review of each monthly payment request to help protect you from getting into a payment problem if the builder fails to do the work properly.

When reviewing the builder's requests for payment, the rule of thumb I use is to look at how much work has been accomplished and then compare this with how much money is being requested. Toward the end of the project I look at how much work is left to be done and compare it with how much money is left to be paid to the builder. You want to be sure there is more money left to be paid than work left to be done. This protects you in case the builder fails to finish and you have to go hire another builder to finish the work. If your initial homework has been done properly and you have hired a responsible builder, this should not happen. Still, you are better off safe than sorry.

Types of Construction Contracts

There are three basic types of construction contracts: fixed sum, cost plus a fee, and cost plus a percentage.

A **fixed sum contract** is one where the builder gives you a total, bottom line cost for the project and nothing other than the designated allowances can vary in cost. This type of contract gives you the best assurance of what your final costs will be, but the builder will certainly have some contingency amount built in to protect himself from unforeseen expenses. For this reason, a fixed sum contract is not necessarily going to be your lowest cost contract, but that may be preferable to you in order to have the assurance that costs cannot go up.

A **cost plus a fixed fee contract** is one in which the builder gives good faith estimates on all the categories of the work, such as concrete work, carpentry, plumbing, etc., and then he adds on a fixed amount of money for his services, overhead, and profits. In this case your costs can go up or down depending on the accuracy of his estimates and the vagaries of the construction market for materials and labor. But you will have the assurance that your builder will not profit from any unforeseen cost increases since his fee is fixed and will not go up if the raw costs go up. Also, you may benefit if things go better and costs are lower than estimated.

A **cost plus a percentage contract** is the most common cost/plus type of contract. In this case all the costs can fluctuate from the builder's estimates, and the builder will charge you a fixed percentage on all of the costs. His percentage might be anywhere from 8 to 25 percent, depending on the size of the project, his experience, overhead, region of the country, and whether any supervision or other costs are included elsewhere as "line items" in his cost estimate.

Both types of cost plus contracts give you the potential of enjoying any savings that might come up along the way, but you also assume the risk for cost overages. I would advise you only to enter into contracts like these with builders who have extensive experience and a good reputation for adhering to their estimates. Your architect can be quite valuable in determining the best contract form for your project.

Where Do We Go from Here?

We have reached the end of this book, but this is certainly not the conclusion of the home design and construction process. As you have seen, there are many, many issues to deal with and decisions to make. And we haven't actually built the house yet! Still, look how far we've come. We have selected a building site and figured out how to use it to its best advantage, we have determined how big is "just right" for *Your* Perfect House, and we have discovered what will make this house your home. We have even come to grips with the difficult issue of budget. You are armed with the knowledge you need to keep control of the process and handle each step along the way. You have a vision of what is ahead. Best of all, you have discovered what *Your* Perfect House should be.

What's next?

The journey forward from here should be enjoyable and rewarding, and it will be if you approach it in the same manner we have approached the process up until now. Do your homework, try to understand your options, get good advice where you need it, and look at things as opportunities, not problems.

Here comes the fun part. Dream your dreams. Fantasize. Indulge your imagination. Work confidently with your architect to turn your dreams into reality. Enjoy the magic that happens when your visions become *Your* Perfect House. Go ahead and make your new house better than you had ever hoped it might be. Don't settle for "okay." Your new house can and should soar above the ordinary. You have the knowledge and understanding to make it so. Have fun along the way, knowing that you are in control of the process. Exceed your expectations. Make your family and yourself happy.

Thanks for reading. But this show is not over. For this Second Edition, I've added an encore. A bonus lesson entitled "Building Green, Naturally." Enjoy.

Bonus Lesson

BUILDING GREEN, NATURALLY

"Always design a thing by considering it in its next larger context—a chair in a room, a room in a house, a house in an environment, an environment in a city plan."
—ELIEL SAARINEN

The word "green" is rapidly becoming the most overused word in architecture and homebuilding. It is being applied to everything from building materials, to paint, to furnishings, and more. Because the marketplace is demanding it, every manufacturer is compelled to claim their products are "green" in some way or another. Add to that the fact that claims can be exaggerated or just plain false, and we consumers can no longer differentiate one product from another in terms of their environmental impact. This kind of overblown hype is now termed to be "greenwashing." Watch out for it. It pays to be a bit skeptical of every claim and do some homework on your own before making your choices.

Fortunately, there are things you can do to design and build—or remodel— in an environmentally responsible way that will also pay you back more quickly than others. Some of these may not be the first things you think of when you start your design process.

For example, when we think of building "green," most of us instantly jump to solar panels, also known as photovoltaics, on the roof or a geothermal heating system. While these are good ways to reduce your dependence on outside energy sources, they are probably the most expensive "green" options and have the longest "pay back" period. In other words, it will take a very long time for you to save enough money on your energy bill to cover the initial cost of buying and installing these systems.

Other green building strategies will not pay you back personally at all. But they will pay back the overall community in significant ways. Building green is about much more than just the energy your home consumes each day. It is about the "embodied" energy in the materials you use, the consumption of resources in the manufacturing of materials, the waste produced during the production of materials and the building process, and the final disposition of the materials when the house has ended its useful life and is torn down.

Building green can be accomplished in four ways:

1. Design a House that is Naturally Energy Efficient

2. Use Energy Efficient Building Materials

3. Use Materials that are Sustainable

4. Power the House with Renewable Energy Resources

Some aspects of green building will fall into more than one of these categories. But for our discussion here, we will consider them one at a time.

Design a Naturally Energy Efficient House

Because this is a book about *Designing Your Perfect House*, I will focus on the design aspects of building green and only briefly mention the technical and material aspects. I truly believe that the most effective green houses are designed to coexist "naturally" with their environment and use energy "gently," thus reducing long-term energy consumption. This method is under-appreciated, perhaps because good, naturally green design is subtle and not flashy. Maybe it's because you can't show it off to your friends as easily as you can show off your array of solar panels. Maybe because it is so inherently simple, it just doesn't seem overt enough to "count." But it does work. Best of all, many of the strategies for designing and building a naturally energy efficient home do not require much added cost. They merely require some added thought and planning.

There is a long list of steps you can take to make your house consume less energy. The "payback" period will be short, and the savings will be real. I can vouch for this effect from personal experience. In my house, I implemented a number of the design strategies and other "green" tactics we will discuss. The result was that my house uses much less electricity than comparably-sized houses built without these considerations. But, I still thought it might be a good idea to add solar panels, so I had a solar-electric contractor evaluate my house. He looked at my past electric bills, only to conclude that the payback period for the solar-electric system would be over twenty years! And that was after including both state and federal tax credits. I had already reduced my electric bill so much while designing and building the house there just was not that much more money to be saved.

The Five Secrets to Designing a Naturally Energy Efficient House

1. Design the house so it tends to stay at comfortable temperatures without mechanical assistance (such as heat and air conditioning)

2. Build a tight and well-insulated house

3. Use low-energy fixtures and appliances

4. Design the house to take advantage of natural light

5. Design the house to naturally ventilate

Secret #1 — *Design the House so it Naturally Tends to Stay at Comfortable Temperatures without Mechanical Assistance (heating and air conditioning)*

This is the most important secret of all. Your house should "want" to stay cool in summer and warm in winter. And it all starts with the land and the sun.

It is critical to place your house on the land with the correct orientation relative to the sun. The sun provides free heat. In what is called a "passive solar"

design, we don't worry about converting the solar radiation from the sun into electricity and then powering electrical heat pumps or lights. We use the sun directly for heat and light. Of course, you want to consider your climate when determining how to best utilize all that free energy from the sun. This means that if you are in a northern, cold climate, you want to let more sun into your house. Your house will have the majority of the windows on the south side to maximize the heat gain when the sun is shining. You will want fewer doors and windows on the north and northwest sides of the house because that is the direction the harsh weather usually comes from. If you live in a hot, southern climate, you will

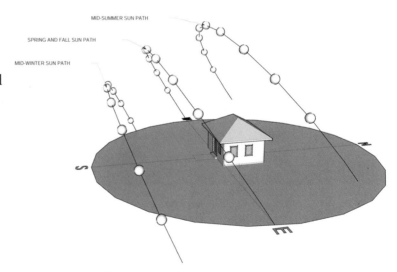

MID-SUMMER SUN PATH

SPRING AND FALL SUN PATH

MID-WINTER SUN PATH

S

N

E

Due to the earth's tilted axis, the sun's position relative to your house's location changes dramatically with the seasons. This needs to be considered when designing a house so as to take advantage of the sun when you want it and provide shade from the sun when you don't. It costs no more money to build a house that works well with the sun than it takes to build one that fights with Mother Nature.

want to make sure to effectively shade your south-facing windows with roof overhangs. Limit the windows on the west side where the sun will be so low that roof overhangs are ineffective and the hot afternoon sun would overheat your house. The majority of windows should be on the north side where they will remain shaded. Of course, I am referring to houses in the northern hemisphere. In the southern hemisphere the orientations would be reversed.

Orienting the house on the land properly, relative to the sun angles, will cost virtually nothing extra. It is only a matter of thinking things through at the outset and not simply plopping the house down on the site with no thought about the sun angles. If you have not selected your property yet, make sure to consider the orientation of the house before buying the land. Some sites are better than others. I see far too many houses that end up baking on late summer afternoons when the low western sun pours in through the windows. This problem is a result of a stock house design being placed on a building lot with no concern for orientation. Windows that were intended to view backyards and glass doors that lead to porches and terraces unexpectedly turn the house into a solar furnace with the air conditioner churning away trying to keep the house at a comfortable temperature. I look at these and shake my head. If only a little thought had been given to the sun angles, the energy consumption would have been much lower and the house would have been considerably more comfortable, all with no additional cost.

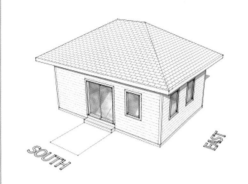

10:00 am, December 21

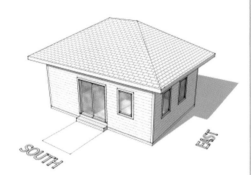

Noon, December 21

These illustrations of a house located at the latitude of Atlanta, Georgia shows how the shadow pattern of a 24" roof overhang effectively shades the south wall in the hot summer while letting the sun warm the south wall during cold winters. Using three-dimensional shadow studies like these can help you determine the optimal house orientation and how much roof overhang is appropriate.

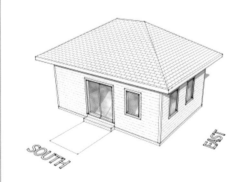

2:00 pm, December 21

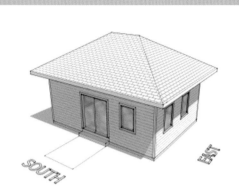

10:00 am, June 21

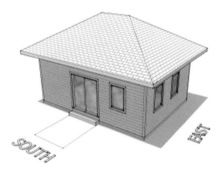

Noon, June 21

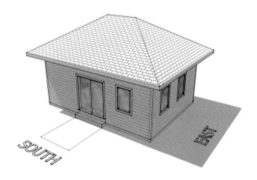

2:00 pm, June 21

BUILD GREEN WITH ROOF OVERHANGS AND PROPER ORIENTATION

For houses in the northern hemisphere, the south-facing side of the house is the easiest side for controlling the sun angles (the north side in the southern hemisphere). The reason for this is that the south sun is at its highest point in the sky at midday and the angle varies predictably with the season. In other words, the sun is never close to the horizon in the southern sky. Since the sun is never too low, any wall or window that faces within thirty degrees of due south can have its "sun exposure" controlled with properly-sized roof overhangs. The sun rises higher in the sky in summer and lower in winter as the earth tilts on its axis. Because of this, a roof overhang can be sized so that in summer the shadow it casts will shade the windows on the south wall, keeping the house cool. Then, in winter, it can allow the sun to shine through the windows to naturally warm the house.

This same seasonal shading effect can help the walls themselves warm up in the winter sun and stay cooler in the summer, thus transmitting more or less heat into the house in the appropriate season.

This shading from roof overhangs is not possible on the eastern- or western-facing sides because the sun is simply at too low an angle for roof overhangs to be effective. You would need an extremely long overhang to provide any useful shading. Usually, the low, eastern morning sun is not a big problem because it occurs in the cooler part of summer days. However, the low, hot western sun occurs at the hottest part of the day. If you need to have west-facing windows because of a great view or other site restrictions, consider placing a porch on the western side of the house. This would effectively give you a very long roof overhang to shade the west-facing windows and wall. But keep in mind that you may still need to install shades on the west side of the porch to make it useful on those hot summer days.

Another often overlooked factor that can help a house stay at comfortable temperatures is thermal mass. You probably have noticed that old, uninsulated buildings built with solid stone, brick, or concrete walls tend to stay cooler on hot summer days. This happens because the concrete and masonry materials have a lot of mass. These materials are dense. It takes a long time to heat them up, and it takes them a long time to give up their heat once they have been heated. If a house has a lot of thermal mass, the rate of temperature change—especially from day to night and to day again—will be much slower than the rate of change in a wood framed house, even a well-insulated one.

One of the principles of passive solar house design is to utilize these materials as a "heat sink" to hold heat gained in the daytime and allow it to slowly release through the night. The reverse process is utilized in summer where the thermal mass is kept out of direct sun to remain cool. It thereby gradually absorbs the heat from warm air in the house and slowly cools again overnight.

You can put some of this same principle to work in your energy efficient house by using concrete floors instead of wood and having some stone or brick walls in key areas. To optimize this natural cooling method in the summer, don't open your windows early in the day. This will let the thermal mass stay cool and absorb heat from the air in the house. Then at night, open the windows to allow the thermal mass to cool back down in order to absorb more heat the next day. This all requires some planning and effort, but it does actually work.

Secret #2 — *Build a Tight and Well-Insulated House*

A basic principle of green building is to build a house that doesn't leak too much air. We all can easily appreciate the problem when cold air is leaking in during winter. Cold drafts are easy to feel and make you uncomfortable, but stopping leaks is just as important in the summer as it is in the winter. After all, you would not dream of leaving your refrigerator door open just a little bit. Everything inside would spoil, and the fridge would run constantly. Imagine the electric bill if that happened!

A typical, reasonably well-built house has enough cracks, gaps, open vents, and other leaks to lose the same amount of air as if you left a window open all the time. The U.S. Department of Energy estimates that cracks in floors, walls, and ceilings account for 31 percent of air leaks, air ducts cause 15 percent, fireplace flues account for 14 percent, plumbing entry points are 13 percent, and doors and windows contribute 21 percent. Caulking, good quality windows, weather-stripped doors, direct vent fireplaces, and other sealing methods can greatly reduce this air loss. While you do not want a house that is hermetically sealed, you can seal up a lot of leaks before you are in any danger of creating an unhealthy air situation.

You also need to properly insulate the house. If you go outside on a winter day and want to stay warm, you put on a warm hat and coat. Your house needs a good hat and coat, too! Of all the building materials that go into a house, one of the least expensive is insulation. The more insulation you have, the more your house will tend to stay at a steady temperature. Don't skimp here. You might be surprised to know that the cost of insulating a house reasonably well amounts to only about two to three percent of the overall cost of construction. The cost to upgrade that insulation, and even to "super-insulate" the house, is still relatively small compared to the overall budget. In fact, it is only a fraction of the cost of a solar power system or a geothermal system, yet the resulting savings in energy consumption can be dramatically more. Additional insulation beyond the building code minimum will pay for itself through lower energy bills and greater comfort in a short time.

Insulation in the wall is not as critical as you might think, relative to some other measures you could take. Consider that adding to the wall insulation probably will require thicker walls that will cost more because of the additional material, labor, and extensions on the window and door jambs necessary to fit into a thicker wall. Back in the 1970's, during the Arab oil embargo and energy crisis, the federal government put out a number of documents to help consumers understand how to save energy. We were not "saving the planet" then, but we did have the oil embargo and the energy crisis. In one of those documents, the government listed things you should do to save energy when building. Listed in order of priority, the first item that would provide the most benefit relative to cost was to insulate your attic; second was to use good windows that were tight and had double-paned glass; third was to use a more efficient heating system; fourth was to put insulation in your walls. As counter-intuitive as it may sound, having any insulation at all in your walls was less critical than having a more efficient heating system.

The message here is that when enhancing insulation, your house needs a better hat before it needs a better coat. When improving your home's energy efficiency beyond the industry standard, you need to follow the same order of priorities just as the government recommended so long ago. First, upgrade your attic insulation, a lot. Most of the heat you lose in winter will be through the attic and roof. In summer, much of the heat your house will gain will be through the roof and attic. Just think of how hot your attic gets during that time of year. Next, upgrade the windows. Then, choose an even better heating and air conditioning system. Only after all of that, think about enhancing the wall insulation.

Be aware that not all insulation is the same. There are several methods and materials to choose from. Do your homework and select the best one for your energy efficient home design. Just make sure you increase the R-value as much as is practical. Fiberglass insulation has been the tried and true insulation for decades, but dense-pack cellulose, rock wool insulation, and spray foam insulations offer their own advantages. Consider your options, learn all of the facts, and balance that information against the cost so you can make an informed decision.

STUDY YOUR R-VALUES

The ability for insulation to resist the transfer of heat is described as its R-value. The "R" stands for "resistance" to heat movement. You will see R-values listed on insulation either for the thickness of the product or per inch of thickness. Interestingly, the resistance to heat transfer is not due to the material itself, but rather to the material's ability to hold dead air. Air that cannot move is a great insulator. In an open cavity of wall, the air can move, rising as it gets warm and falling as it cools. It actually makes a vertical loop within the wall known as a convective loop. The more the air moves, the more heat is transferred. Placing insulation within the wall cavity restricts air movement, preventing a convective loop from forming. Fiberglass, if properly installed and fit tightly into the space, prevents these convective loops from happening. Foam insulations do the job even better, as the dead air is within all of the tiny bubbles in the foam. A shortcoming of fiberglass insulation is that if wind can penetrate the exterior surface of the wall, the air in the wall cavity can start moving. As a result, the effective R-value of the fiberglass insulation is substantially reduced. Here's a chart of some typical R-values per inch. Multiply these figures by the total thickness you will need to get the total R-value.

Insulation R Values

Fiberglass (batt)	3.1 – 3.4 per inch
Fiberglass (attic)	2.2 – 4.3 per inch
Fiberglass Blown (wall)	3.7 – 4.3 per inch
Polystyrene Board	3.8 – 5.0 per inch
Polyurethane Board	5.5 – 6.5 per inch
Polyisocyanurate (foil-faced)	5.6 – 8.0 per inch
Open Cell Spray Foam	3.5 – 3.6 per inch
Closed Cell Spray Foam	6.0 – 6.5 per inch

These are approximations. Consult the insulation manufacturer's data for exact R-values.

Beyond considering proper orientation, insulation, and air-tightness, you should position the house on the site and arrange the floor plan so the living spaces are protected from the winter wind and the late afternoon summer sun. A hill or a group of trees can do this nicely. A thoughtful arrangement of rooms will do this, too. Place the garage and other service rooms on the windward side of the house so they can naturally buffer your living spaces from the cold wind and winter storms. In a warm climate, place the garage on the west side to buffer the house from the heat of the late afternoon sun. In a cold climate, try to avoid placing the rooms that have large windows on the north or west of the house. In a warm climate, try to avoid placing large windows on the west side where the low, hot late-day sun will be most intense. Use those locations for rooms that need small windows or none at all. This will improve the house's defenses against heat gain and loss by ensuring a greater percentage of those walls will be solid and well-insulated and not have too much glass. Notice that in all climates, the west side of a house presents the most challenges for climate control. Remember that the R-value of glass, even double- or triple-paned, is far less than the R-value of an insulated solid wall.

The energy needs of a house are also influenced by human behavior. You need to do a few things to get the best result. Just as roof overhangs shade your windows to limit heat gain, so do window coverings. These can be in the form of blinds or curtains. Blinds have the advantage of being adjustable so as to cut out the direct sun while still admitting indirect daylight, while curtains insulate the cold window glass in the winter. A nice compromise between the two are insulating pleated shades with an enclosed edge. These shades hold air in the pleats and provide some insulation.

Secret #3 — *Use Low-Energy Fixtures and Appliances*

Using appliances and fixtures that consume less energy is the same as driving a car that gets better gas mileage. There are no mileage ratings for appliances and fixtures, but there are Energy Star ratings that can help you compare one product to another. Energy Star is a rating system that serves as a guide to let you know the real cost of operation of fixtures or appliances so you can compare them on an equal basis and choose the most efficient ones.

Remember, light fixtures consume a lot of energy because there are so many in a typical house. With the continuing drop in the cost of LED lights,

PICKING THE RIGHT LED LIGHTS

Things have changed rapidly in the world of LED lighting. Not only have the prices dropped considerably, the quality of the light has improved dramatically. It used to be that LEDs cast a garish blue light—not something you would want in your home. Now they are available with light production that matches our beloved incandescent lighting. To get the ones that look best, you should check the "color temperature" of the light. Color temperature is expressed in degrees Kelvin. This is not actual heating temperature. LEDs produce much less heat than incandescents. But the Kelvin scale tells us the range of the color spectrum the lights emit. Look for LEDs with color temperatures of 2700K to 3000K. Avoid the blue versions with color temperatures of 5000K.

Also check the Color Rendering Index (CRI), a scale of 0 to 100 that indicates the "completeness" of the spectrum the light emits. You will want a CRI above 80 to ensure enough of the light spectrum is produced so your fabrics, paintings, and people look natural and vibrant.

LEDs are now clearly worth the investment. Generally speaking, they will use about one-eighth the electricity of a comparably bright incandescent fixture and will last up to ten times longer. An added benefit is they give off much less heat. So your air conditioning costs will go down, too.

The largest appliances in your house are your hot water heater and your heating and air conditioning system. Select a water heater that is highly insulated. A water heater's efficiency is dependent on its ability to store hot water and not on its ability to heat the water. Simple physics tells us it takes the same amount of energy to heat water, regardless of the fuel, but only a well-insulated water heater will hold the temperature of the hot water efficiently. Check the water heater's label for comparative projected energy costs.

TANKLESS WATER HEATERS MAY NOT BE WHAT YOU THINK

I give the same speech about tankless water heaters to my clients on every project. There seems to be a couple of misunderstandings about what tankless water heaters are and what they do. First, they are not "instant" hot water as some people believe. They do heat the water "instantly" as it flows through the units. But the hot water still has to get to the fixture. The time that takes is dependent on the length of pipe between the water heater and the fixture, regardless of whether the water comes from a tankless heater or a hot water tank.

The primary benefit of a tankless water heater is that it will supply an "endless" amount of hot water. There is no tank to run dry. If you have a big hot tub to fill up or lots of people living in the house taking showers in rapid succession, this can be an advantage. Tankless water heaters also cost a bit less to operate than a traditional hot water heater because there is no storage of hot water required. Naturally, when storing hot water, it will tend to cool down and have to be reheated to maintain its temperature. However, if you get a high-efficiency tank-type water heater, it will be well insulated and not lose heat as fast as older models. The tankless water heater will still have an advantage in lower operating costs, but not as much as you might expect. In fact, according to the U.S. Department of Energy, tankless water heaters will save you less than 9% in operating costs over a storage tank-type water heater.

Tankless water heaters have two significant disadvantages, in my opinion. First, they cost a lot more than a tank-type heater. Maybe more than $1000, depending on the unit size. You could buy three conventional water heaters for the price of one tankless heater. The second disadvantage is that in order to maintain the efficiency of the tankless unit, you need to have it serviced annually to remove scale that can build up on the heating elements. That also comes at a cost.

Lastly, tankless water heaters operate on natural or propane gas. This can present a big problem if you do not have gas available. So unless you need endless hot water or have no place to put a water tank, you may not really want a tankless water heater after all.

Heating and air conditioning systems are given energy efficiency ratings. Furnaces are rated with an AFUE rating, air conditioners get a SEER rating, and heat pumps get an HSPF rating. Standard furnaces might have an AFUE rating of 80, which means 80 percent of the fuel goes to heat the air while the remaining 20 percent goes up the flue. You will want a high efficiency furnace with an AFUE rating of over 95.

The SEER rating (Seasonal Energy Efficiency Ratio) for air conditioners typically ranges from 13 to 18. Choose a system with a SEER rating of 15 or higher. You can go higher, but the initial cost goes up fast. I would suggest that the extra money you might have spent on the highest SEER air conditioner would be better spent on more insulation. The payback will be quicker.

Heat pumps are actually air conditioners that are reversible. In summer, they act as traditional air conditioners, taking heat from inside and moving it outside. In winter, they reverse the process, taking heat from outside and moving it inside, effectively "air conditioning" the outdoors and depositing the waste heat indoors. Yes, there is actually heat outside in winter, even on cold days. But in northern climates, there is a lot less, so a heat pump cannot efficiently move that heat indoors, and you'll end up running the backup heat (usually power-hungry electric resistance heating strips) frequently. This is why you usually see heat pumps being used only in regions with more moderate winters. As with the other types of equipment, the higher the HSPF (Heating and Seasonal Performance Factor), the more efficient the unit.

Secret #4 — *Design the House to Take Advantage of Natural Light*

LED lights might be the most efficient electric lights on the market, but natural sunlight is completely free and abundant. It makes sense to use as much natural daylight as possible in your energy efficient home design. With natural daylight, the challenge is to get the light where you want it, keep it out of where you don't want it, and keep it from overheating your house.

Natural light comes in two forms, direct sunlight and indirect sunlight. Direct sunlight is wonderful to sit in on a cold winter day, but most of the time it is hot, glaring, fades fabrics, and makes seeing electronic screens tough. It is generally a good idea to limit direct sunlight unless you are developing a passive solar design and have appropriate sun-spaces to accept the direct sun.

Indirect sunlight is what we all like. Light through north windows has been cherished by artists for centuries for its even and accurate color. If your energy efficient home design uses roof overhangs properly, you will gain natural sunlight through most of your windows with only occasional direct sunlight entering your house. Keep in mind that sunlight reflects off of light colored surfaces. A light-colored patio or wall can reflect the indirect light into a room even if the windows are on the north side of the house, thus multiplying the daylight in the house.

Skylights and solar tubes can introduce natural light deep into a house where windows cannot be placed. But place these carefully. They can bring in a lot of excess and unwanted heat while also being a "hole" in your insulation. Skylights are usually best if the direct sunlight that comes through them is then reflected off of a light-colored surface before it can reach the furniture and people below. Placing

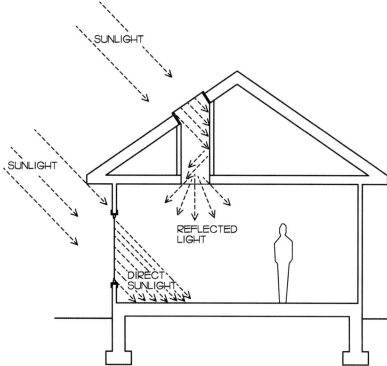

SUNLIGHT

SUNLIGHT

REFLECTED LIGHT

DIRECT SUNLIGHT

A light shaft beneath a skylight can relieve the potential problem of admitting too much direct sunlight. The shaft reflects light several times before the light can enter the room. This provides gentler, diffused natural daylight deep into the house without admitting excess heat and harsh light that can fade fabrics and make parts of the house uncomfortable during a portion of the day. I've found that painting a skylight shaft a pale yellow will create a pleasant ambiance in the room. As an added bonus, consider placing LED lights in the shaft so that light still comes from this source even at night.

skylights on the high part of the roof with a light-colored shaft down to the room below will provide such a buffer for the direct sunlight.

And of course, the orientation of the house and windows is critical to optimizing natural light. Consider your climate and place windows and skylights accordingly.

Secret #5 — *Design the House to Naturally Ventilate*

Long before houses were air conditioned, great attention was paid to ventilating houses. Windows were placed at opposite ends of halls, proper over-hangs were built so windows could remain open during rains, and whole-house fans were common. And, just as we've already seen, the placement of the house on the land was important. When developing your "green" house, pay attention to the direction of the prevailing breezes.

Old southern houses often had a whole-house fan in the attic. The fan would blow air out through a large vent, and each room in the house would have a hatch or opening to the attic that could be opened or closed. The windows around the house were opened only slightly, and the hatches were opened fully. When the fan was running and blowing air out of the attic, it would simultaneously pull air into the attic through all of the hatches and windows in order to replace the exhausted attic air. The result was that the house was evenly ventilated, and a gentle move-ment of air through the house would keep everyone cooler.

This whole-house ventilation would be best done during the night when the air was cooler. Then as the day warmed, the windows were usually closed on the sunny side of the house so that the hot, midday heat would not come in. When you think of southern houses, you think of porches. Those porches served a purpose beyond being a nice place to sit and sip sweet tea. They shaded the exterior walls and provided cooler air around the house.

Unfortunately, we have become so dependent on mechanical air conditioning, we no longer design houses with ventilation in mind. That is a shame, since proper ventilation will keep your house cooler with very little energy consumption and will greatly improve the quality of the air in your house.

If you want to dig deeper into ways of cooling your house by natural ventilation, read up on solar chimneys. These induce a flow of air through the house by means of a solar activated convective air current. Combined with an earth-cooled intake pipe system, solar chimneys are wonderfully effective in hot locales with low humidity.

One other item we can borrow from southern houses are ceiling fans. These are very helpful in energy efficient home design. By keeping the air moving, we can feel comfortable in air that is somewhat warmer than what we might usually want. By using ceiling fans, you can keep the air conditioner set at a higher temperature, saving a substantial amount of energy and money.

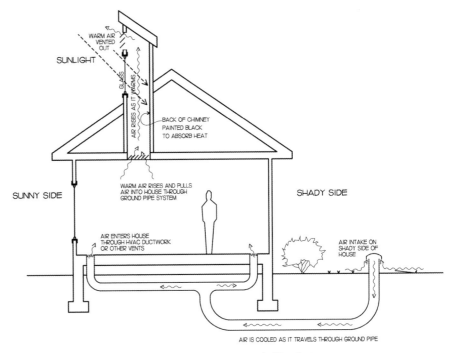

In hot, dry climates, a solar chimney can provide "free" air conditioning. When sunlight enters the glass on the sunny side of the shaft and hits dark surfaces on the interior, the air in the shaft is warmed significantly. Warm air rises, naturally. A vent at the top allows the warm air to escape. Vents at the bottom of the shaft allow the air in the house to rise and replace the escaping air. This, in turn, pulls replacement air into the house through a vent on the shady side of the house. This replacement air is naturally cooled as it travels through underground piping. No fans are needed to move the air. Convection does the job for free. And yes, even in a desert climate, the earth is cool only a few feet down. Unfortunately, this system does not work well in humid climates because condensation can form in the underground piping and promote the growth of mold. But in arid climates, that is not a problem.

In my opinion, these five secrets are the most cost effective and practical steps toward green building and energy efficient home design. Start out making use of these and add in things like programmable thermostats, radiant barrier roof sheathing, energy recovery ventilation systems,

247

heat-reflective roof shingles, and many of the long list of energy reducing building products, and you will greatly reduce your energy consumption while making your house a more pleasant place to live.

Energy Efficient Building Materials

A key component in truly building green is the use of energy efficient building materials. A building material could be considered energy efficient if it has one or more of these seven attributes:

1. It helps the final building use less energy during its useful life

2. It has a very long useful life

3. It is made from raw materials that regenerate and grow quickly

4. It is made from raw materials that are recycled from discarded products or waste materials

5. It is made from raw materials that are so plentiful, it is impossible for the raw materials to be exhausted

6. It requires low amounts of energy to produce

7. It is easily recycled or can be disposed of without harming the environment

Here are some of the best energy efficient building materials to consider using in your green homebuilding project.

Light Gauge Steel Framing

You have probably seen steel studs used in office buildings and other commercial construction. Steel studs are a recycled building material and are made from recycled steel that comes primarily from cars. According the Steel Recycling Institute, it takes between 40 and 50 trees to supply the lumber required to frame up an average 2,000 sq. ft. house (186 sq. meters). A similar house framed with steel studs and joists can be made from only six scrapped automobiles. The institute estimates that 75,000,000 tons of steel are recycled every year. That's more than two tons per second!

Recycled steel and aluminum can also be found in other building products such as metal panels on appliances, gutters, and metal flashing. Consider also that steel has a very long useful life, and you can see what an important energy efficient building material it is.

Insulating Concrete Forms

This technology has been around for decades and uses simple, relatively low-cost materials. Insulating concrete forms are much like traditional concrete forms, except these have additional layers of rigid foam insulation lining them. The concrete is poured into the form, and when it cures, the entire wall, forms, insulation, and concrete are left in place. The result is a very strong wall with integral insulation enclosing the concrete. It looks kind of like an Oreo cookie with the icing on the outside.

A wall constructed with insulating concrete forms is a good insulator and is clearly an energy

WHAT IS LEED CERTIFICATION?

We've mentioned Energy Star as an energy efficiency evaluation system. One other program that is gaining in public awareness is the U.S. Green Building Council's LEED® (Leadership in Energy & Environmental Design) green building program certification. Based on "points earned" for its green building aspects, a building can be certified as silver, gold, or platinum LEED certified.

This program was originally aimed at commercial buildings, but now there is also a certification for residential buildings. The certification serves no purpose other than validating the quality of the house in terms of environmental responsibility. There are no discounts on electricity costs nor tax credits, but the satisfaction of knowing that your new home has achieved a level of energy efficiency and environmental responsibility can be gratifying. And the certification can be beneficial when it comes time to sell your house.

Green building involves many considerations, and some may seem to contradict others. And, of course, there is the cost versus benefit analysis you must perform. Choose wisely and prioritize things so you not only design and build an energy efficient home, you also spend your budget wisely and see a real return on your investment. Although there is a fee for actual LEED certification, the LEED list for points can be used as a good guide for improving your house's "green-ness."

efficient building material. But you might lower its score as a green building product just a bit due to the fact that the foam insulation is usually an expanded polystyrene.

Plant-Based Polyurethane Rigid Foam

Because of the concern about the toxic off-gassing of certain plastic and foam products, you might find yourself shying away from foam insulation. Those worries may not be a problem for much longer. Malama Composites has developed a foam made from bamboo, hemp, and kelp. This organic-based polyurethane rigid foam could potentially replace petroleum-based foams and plastics. It also boasts a higher R-value than polystyrene.

Cool Roofing

Have you noticed that most school buses now have white roofs? This helps reflect the radiant energy of the sun and keeps the buses from becoming metal ovens on sunny days. It is the same principle you might employ by wearing light colored clothes on hot days and dark colored clothes on cold days. White reflects the sun's energy, and black absorbs the radiant energy and turns it into heat. Cool roofing is traditional shingle roofing made to reflect and repel the radiant energy of the sun. These types of shingles cost more than traditional shingles, but you could make the argument that they will save you enough money on your air conditioning bill to offset the added cost, especially in warm climates.

Metal Roofing

At first glance, installing metal roofing might not seem like a way to keep your house cool. You might think of the movie title, *Cat on a Hot Tin Roof*. But actually, metal reflects a good deal of heat, and it also is "low mass" so it does not retain heat like asphalt shingles do. Metal roofs lose their heat quickly at night, whereas asphalt remains warm for much longer. Metal roofs can be installed so as to leave a small space beneath it, holding it above the roof sheathing and allowing air to flow under it, keeping its heat from transferring into the sheathing. Plus, light colors, especially silver, will reflect much of the sun's radiation.

Radiant Barrier Roof Sheathing

Radiant barrier roof sheathing is an oriented strand board (OSB) with a reflective foil layer on the inside surface. This product was invented forty years ago during the oil embargo energy crisis. It replaces the traditional plywood sheathing installed on roof rafters and under shingles. The reflective foil layer blocks a good deal of the radiant heat that otherwise would penetrate the shingles and roof structure. For a small added cost over regular sheathing, this

This house is being framed with Structural Insulted Panels by Eco-Panels, Inc. These panels use polyurethane foam between the OSB "skins." The green exterior oriented strand board is the Huber ZIP System and when taped will become the waterproof exterior layer. The interior OSB layer will be covered with drywall. Interior walls will be framed in the conventional manner. When completed, this house will be much more air-tight and much better insulated than a conventionally framed house.
Photo courtesy of Eco-Panels, Inc.

product will keep a typical attic as much as twenty degrees cooler in summer. It is a worthwhile investment.

Structural Insulated Panels

Commonly called SIPs, structural insulated panels consist of two layers of oriented strand board with rigid foam insulation sandwiched in between. Used primarily for exterior walls, structural insulated panels provide a much better overall wall R-value and are recommended for two reasons. First, there are no studs, so there is much less solid wood going all the way through the wall, thus reducing "thermal bridging." With traditional framing, nearly 15 percent of the wall is solid wood from the interior surface to the exterior surface. Although wood is a better insulator than steel or concrete, it is not nearly as good an insulator as fiberglass batts or foam. The high percentage of solid wood through the wall reduces the wall's effective average R-value considerably. Second, the panels themselves are strong and provide intrinsic bracing. Most SIPs are made with expanded polystyrene foam, i.e. coffee cup foam plastic. A few, such as the ones made by Eco-Panel, are made with rigid polyurethane foam. Polyurethane foam is much stronger than polystyrene, and it will not vaporize in high heat, giving it much more structural stability in a fire.

Advanced Framing Techniques

Because traditional wood framing uses so much wood, there have been studies done to find ways to reduce the wood consumption while still building a strong house. Advanced Framing Techniques were developed from these studies. The idea is to get the wood framing to align from the top to the bottom of the house and eliminate redundant framing around windows, doors, and at building corners. Using this framing method, you can reduce the lumber consumption by five to ten percent. Reducing the wood in the walls increases the area of insulation while reducing thermal bridging. There is a good explanation of advanced framing at www.apawood.org/advanced-framing.

Recycled Wood and Plastic Composite Lumber

It seems like every month, new building products are introduced with recycled wood fiber and plastics. The technology behind these products has advanced quickly, and, in most cases, composite materials with recycled content provide superior performance to their traditional, virgin material counterparts. An example would be the synthetic composite materials used for exterior trim on houses in place of pine or fir materials that had been used for generations. Because the wood fibers in the composite materials are embedded in resins, they provide much better rot-resistance and stability. Other synthetic trim products contain 80 percent fly ash, a waste by-product from the burning of coal in electric generating plants, making productive use of a waste material that is difficult to dispose of safely. Read the product data carefully to gauge the amount of recycled content before making your selection.

Caulking and Sealants

Caulking and sealants are not made from recycled material, and many contain petroleum products, but this does not disqualify them from being considered "green," energy efficient building materials. The energy efficiency lies not in the material production, but rather in the energy savings the product creates after it has been installed. As we discussed earlier, one of the most cost-effective things you can do to make your house consume much less energy is to tighten it up. Fill the gaps and crevices. It is estimated that if you added up the area of all of the gaps and cracks in a conventionally-built house, the total area would be equal to the area of a hole 14 inches square. Can you imagine having that big of a hole in your wall all year long? The impact on your energy efficiency and your electric bill would be dramatic. Chances are, you already have the equivalent of the kind of hole in your house right now.

Indoor Air Quality and VOCs

As we build tighter houses, we unwittingly trap potentially harmful gasses inside the house. Controlled ventilation is important, but proper selection of low or non-emitting building products is the place to start.

Organic compounds are found in all living things. VOCs, or volatile organic compounds, are organic compounds that easily become vapors or gases. Gasoline is a familiar example. VOCs often contain additional elements, such as oxygen, hydrogen, sulfur, bromine, nitrogen, fluorine, and chlorine. VOCs are toxic in your house, and they also contribute to air pollution. Solvents, adhesives, paints, and other products used in construction often emit VOCs. Many of these emitted chemicals,

such as benzene and formaldehyde, are listed as human carcinogens.

There is no federal standard for VOC levels, and most testing is done on single products, not entire houses. Fortunately, many building product manufacturers are responding to the market demand for low- or non-VOC products, making building a healthier house much easier than it was just ten years ago. Products are put through additional curing processes for solvents and adhesives to bring them to a more stable, "non-emitting" state. Look at the manufacturer's labelling when choosing. When in doubt, ask the manufacturer for testing results.

Sustainable Design

Sustainable design is the designing and building of a house with materials and components made from resources that can be replenished at a rate that matches or exceeds the rate of consumption. Bamboo is often referenced as "sustainable"—often without regard to the off-gassing of the resins that bind it—because it re-grows very fast and, at present, grows faster than it is being cut and used. But what about more traditional building products?

Here's where you have to look deeper to understand the whole story. For instance, wood that comes from managed forests or plantations and is only cut at a renewable rate is, in fact, sustainable. But the knee-jerk reaction against the use of wood stems from the claim that trees are being depleted and we are losing forests. However, wood is effectively a renewable crop when it is grown and managed properly.

FOREST STEWARDSHIP COUNCIL

If you are wondering how you can know if the wood you are building with comes from sustainable and environmentally responsible sources, you can do so by only using wood from producers who are FSC Certified. Forest owners and managers gain Forest Stewardship Council certification by maintaining well-managed forests that provide environmental, social, and economic benefits. Many countries participate in this program. Using FSC certified wood products gives you the assurance that each stage of the chain of production, processing, and transformation complies with the Forest Stewardship Council's rigorous standards. You will not be unwittingly helping to decimate the rain forests.

Building materials made from resources that are so vast and plentiful they can never be exhausted, even though they do not replenish, can be considered "sustainable." Clay, for instance, does not replenish. However, we can never use up all that exists on the earth, so bricks and other clay products can be considered to be sustainable.

You might be thinking that bricks require a lot of energy to produce. They do. But because they last so long, they are energy-efficient over their life. The useful life of a product is an important factor in determining if a product is sustainable and green. Products that must be replaced frequently consume energy and labor to manufacture, install, and replace. That would be a mark against them when considering their sustainability. Another factor is disposal. When a product is discarded, does it go to the landfill or can it be recycled efficiently? Materials like brick and concrete not only have long useful lives, they can be recycled into new products. And even if they do end up in the landfill, they are inert, if not painted, and do not pollute the soil and waterways. That makes brick, as well as concrete, an environmentally friendly building material.

Even though bricks consume a good deal of energy to "fire," they are made from clay, an inexhaustible natural material, they require little or no maintenance, and they have an extremely long useful life. Add that up and bricks actually have a small impact on the environment per year of life. Additionally, when not painted, they are benign and non-toxic in the landfill when they are eventually discarded. The same cannot be said of many building materials. Surprisingly, bricks are about as green as it gets.

Using recycled building materials is a major factor in any sustainable design strategy. There are more and more products available made from reprocessed building materials that would have otherwise been headed for the landfill. This means that fewer new resources need to be used, and less waste needs to be disposed of.

One other way to increase the "green-ness" and sustainability of your house is to use reclaimed building materials. These are materials that are reused intact and require little or no processing for their reuse. Reclaimed wood floors, used bricks, reclaimed doors, reclaimed fixtures, and reclaimed roof slate are good examples of building materials that are given an extended life by being used in a new building. Just because a building is no longer useful, it does not mean that all its parts are no longer useful. Every piece of reclaimed building material you use will eliminate the need to produce a piece of new material, thus saving resources. But beyond the environmental benefits, reclaimed building materials and salvaged building parts can be wonderful treasures in your new home. They add warmth, character, and an important link with the past.

Renewable Energy Resources

The fourth step in green building is the use of renewable energy. Photovoltaics, or electricity-producing solar panels, can provide all or part of your electrical needs, depending on your geographical location and consumption. Solar water heating and geothermal equipment may still use electricity to run, but at a lower rate than conventional systems. They make use of the renewable energy of the sun and the earth to reduce power consumption.

Controlling when you use electricity can be an environmental benefit to you and your community. Residential energy management systems can monitor and control your home's peak demand for electricity.

Antique barn beams are reclaimed from collapsing structures that have outlived their usefulness. In their next life, each one of these beams will add beauty and character to another building while eliminating the need to cut one more tree that would have been cut for the purpose. Long ago, a single tree was be put to good use for several centuries and its serviceable life is still not over. That is a great investment in Building Green.

Some electric companies will reward you for not using as much electricity during peak hours by giving you a lower rate, although the list of such companies keeps getting shorter. When power companies offer a demand rate, they do it to encourage the reduction of peak demand across the power grid. This in turn reduces the need to build more power generating facilities. With fewer power generating facilities, less fossil fuel is consumed.

A residential energy management system is a computerized control device that tells what equipment in your home can run and what equipment must wait a couple of minutes to start. By using one of these systems, you can save up to 30 percent on your electric bill without doing any other alterations to your home or changing the way you live. Helping reduce the demand across the power grid qualifies as green building because it helps reduce the number of power plants needed and makes use of excess electricity plants generate in off-peak hours.

HOW DOES A GEOTHERMAL HEATING SYSTEM WORK?

A geothermal HVAC system is actually a heat pump that extracts heat from the ground instead of taking heat from the air. Outdoor air temperatures fluctuate from night to day and seasonally, causing air-to-air heat pumps to lose efficiency during periods of colder outdoor temperatures. But just a few feet below the surface, the temperature of the earth remains around fifty degrees all year long. That is the optimal temperature for heat pumps to operate most efficiently, making geothermal systems ideal energy savers.

Geothermal systems use an "earth loop" that is either laid horizontally in trenches about six feet deep, or vertically in "wells" to take heat from the ground. Neither method extracts any water from the ground. Instead, water is recirculated through the pipes. As the water flows through the pipes, it is warmed (or cooled when in air conditioning mode).

Although geothermal systems are more costly, they have a much longer life. There is no outdoor compressor, so they run quietly. They use a "desuperheater" to preheat water going to your domestic water heater with "waste heat," thus lowering your energy consumption for hot water. Another bonus is the air that comes out of the registers is warm—over ninety degrees—unlike the eighty-degree air that comes from normal heat pumps. That cooler air from heat pumps always feels cold when it blows across your skin. A geothermal system will take many years to pay for itself, but you'll be more comfortable in the meantime.

Because a geothermal system does not actually generate power, it may not seem like it contributes to the overall national reduction in the burning of fossil fuels for electrical generation in the same way as solar electrical panels or wind turbines. However, it does significantly help the effort. In fact, when compared on a cost basis, for every kilowatt hour of electricity a solar and wind system can produce, a geothermal system can reduce electrical demand by four kilowatt hours.

If you employ just some of these green building strategies, your house will be more energy efficient and help improve the local environment. But this list is not completely comprehensive. New information is constantly emerging on this subject. It pays to stay up to date on new developments. Just be sure to use a healthy amount of skepticism. There are a lot of charlatans out there offering green and sustainable materials and methods. Stick with reputable companies and read all of the information before buying. Don't get green-washed.

There is much more to discuss about Building Green. For more on this subject, please check my website, www.about-home-design.com, from time to time.

> *When a man's home is born out of his heart and developed through his labor and perfected through his sense of beauty, it is the very cornerstone of life.*
>
> —GUSTAV STICKLEY

I wish you great success as you design *Your* Perfect House.

There is always more to discuss about home design, homebuilding, and remodeling. My websites are loaded with helpful and hopefully informative articles, blog posts, and videos:

www.about-home-design.com *and* www.designingyourperfecthouse.com

I would welcome any comments or questions. Please let me know whether I need to clarify any topic or whether I have overlooked something you think I should discuss. Drop me a line at bhirsch@williamhirsch.com. I'll either answer your question on the website or I may include the topic in future printings of this book.

I sincerely hope that this book has helped you to realize your dreams and that you will live happily ever after in *Your* Perfect House.

—*William J. Hirsch Jr., AIA*

Additional Reading

The Not So Big House series, by Sarah Susanka, FAIA
www.notsobighouse.com

Home by Design, by Sarah Susanka, FAIA

Creating a New Old House, by Russell Versaci, FAIA

Good House Parts, by Dennis Wedlick, AIA

Get Your House Right, by Marianne Cusato

Index

Numbers in italics refer to sidebars and/or captions.

accountability, *99*
additions, 64–66
adjacent properties, 129–30
aesthetic sense, 90–91
aging, 211–14
"aha!" phenomenon, 22–23
air conditioning, *21*, 115–16, 214, 245
airports, 129–30, 138
Alberti, Leon Battista, 37
allowances, *93*, 94, 114
American Institute of Architects, 106
angles, 54–55, 224
appliances, 195–96, 212
    low energy, 243–245
    Sub-Zero, 218, 228–29
    Viking, 218
architect, 10
    choosing, 98–99
    communication with, 149, 153–54, *160*
    landscape, 103
    registered, *99*, 106
    role of, 66–67, 95–96, *97*, 98, *190*
    spatial thinking of, 158–59
    twenty questions to ask, *102*
    why hire, 95–96, 98
    working with, 23–24, 60, 85, 96, *97*, 98, 100–102, 106–107, 111, 118–19, 233

Architectural Review Committee, 124
architecture
    definition of, 24–25
    eclectic, 27
    grammar of, 28–29
    greatest of fine arts, 91
    language of, 26–28
archways, 28, *59*, *194*, *204*
arrival sequence, *see* SAAPE
artworks, *49*, 58, 69–70, *83*, 197
asymmetry, 50–51, 54
attic, *153*
attic fans, 246
axial corridor, *48*
axis, 46–47, 50–51, 206

backbone, 22, 206
balance, 184
balcony, 199
    Juliet, *38*
Balinese architecture, *30*, 36, 61–63, *76*
basement, *153*
bathrooms, 94–95, 144, *153*, 200, 201–204, 209, 213
    accessibility, 202, *207*
    checklist, *202*
    design of, 203
    government guidelines for, 202–203
    planning questions, *201*

bathtub, 203, 213, 214
Bauhaus, 27
bedrooms, 83, *92*, 94, 144, *152*, 177, 200
    master, 32, *33*, 35, 47, *49*, 132, 200
bedroom suite, 200
beds, 200
Better Homes and Gardens, 66
bonus room, *153*
boulders, 135–36
breakfast room, *55*, *70*, *142*, *191*
brick, *156*, 224, 253
brick mason, 67, 222
Brown, Dan, 52
    The Da Vinci Code, 52
bubble diagram, 158–61, 164, 166
budget, 89, 93–94, 112–13, 150–51, 153–54, 217–33
buildable area, 124–26
builders, 66–67, 95–96, *97*, 105–107, 111, 112–14, 118, 139–40, 151–52, 219–22, 229–33
    questions to ask, *231*
    selection criteria, 229–30
building codes, *97*, 99
building materials, energy efficient, 248–52
    advanced framing techniques, 251
    caulking and sealants, 251–52

insulating concrete forms, 248–49
polyurethane rigid foam, 249
radiant barrier roof sheathing, 250–51
recycled composite lumber, 251
roofing, cool, 249
roofing, metal, 249–250
steel framing, light gauge, 248
structured insulated panels, 251

caregiver, 214
caulking and sealants, 251–52
ceiling fans, 247
ceilings, 78, *88*, 146, 190, 199, 209
    tray, 224
central hall, *21*
chandelier, 82, 197
charrette, *161*
children, 177
chimneys, 186–87
client feedback, 24
closets, 200, 206, 208
code of ethics, 106
Colonial-style house, *72*
columns, 37, 41, 54, *146*, *215*
communal living space, 109–10
compass, *126*
computer bays, 144
construction sites, 230–31
contour lines, 141
contracts, 93, 103, 106, 135
    construction, 232–33
controlling the process, 109–12, 118–19
costs, 89, 90, *93*, *102*, 105–106, 112–13, 115, 118, 135, 140, 147, 208, 209, 218–33
    per square foot, 151–54, 218, 220–21

countertop space, 194–96, *210*
courtyard, *44*, *91*, 129
covenants, 123–24
craftsman style, 28, *39*, *90*, 98, 182
crossing hall, 22
cross slopes, 132
cul-de-sacs, 134
cupola, *67*, *216*
curb appeal, 87, 132
curved cabinets, 218, 226
curves, 54–55

decisions, *190*
demand rate (energy billing), 116
depa asta musti, 36
design, 23–24
    cohesiveness, 48, *49*
    conceptual and theoretical
        aspects, 20–22, 31
    critical questions, 112–14
    details, 70, 71–74, 110
    elements, 149–50
    interior, *104*
    overall, 70, 85
    schematic, 166
    surprises, 74–76
    timeless, 59–60
    unity, 71–72, *73*, *97*
design/build, 105–106, 229
developers, 136, 219
development houses, *122*
Dickens, Charles, 157
dimmers, 224–25
dining room, 35, 36, 82, *83*, 94, 145, *146*, 163, 196–98
direction of approach, 134
display cases, *110*

doors, *207*, 211
    front, 85, 135, 172, *174*, 185, 212
    pocket, *204*
doorways, 28
drainage, 94, 132–33, 136, 138, 139
drip line, *138*
driveway, 94, 124, 130, 132, 162–63, 172, 174–75
drops, 223
ductwork, 115

easements, 125, 140
Ecole des Beaux-Arts, *161*
efficiency of structure, 209
elevators, *152*, 213
energy efficiency, 88, *114*, 115–16, 126, 128, 209, 214, 236–48
energy management system, 116
Energy Star, 243, 249
environmental responsibility, 88, 115–17

façade, *131*, *133*
fads, 59–60
Falling Water, *101*
family room, *194*
farmhouses, 171, 182–83
faucets, 212
fireplaces, *21*, 42, *49*, 56, 100, *104*, 110, 191, 192, 198, *228*
first floor, 157
fixtures, *210*
    low energy, 243–245
flooring, 213
    marble, 57, *58*, 72, 204
    wooden, 57, *58*
floor plan, 158
flow, 80–81, 164

flush wood thresholds, 223
focal points, 58–59
footprint, 124
Forest Stewardship Council, 253
foundation, 184
foyer, 22, 56, 57, *58*, 176, 177, 204, 206
French chateau, 27
French doors, 185, *196*
French Second Empire style, *8*
furniture, 35, 147, 197, 198, 201, 214

gables, 131, 182
garage, *21*, 65, 132, *134*, 135, 162–63,
   170, 172, 175–76, 212
     doors, 175
gardens, 28–29, *108*, 136, *139*
general rules for exterior of house,
   84–85
Georgian-style house, 21–22, *52*, 54,
   72, 100
geothermal heating systems, 236, 255
Gestalt psychology, 80
glass, 100, 209
     storm door, *78*
Goethe, Johann Wolfgang, 19
golden mean, 52
golf courses, 130
grab bars, 203, 213
Great Boston Molasses Flood, *99*
great room, 146, 199
green buiding, 235–256
greenwashing, 235
guest rooms, 95, 200
guest suite, 214
Gullah culture, *53*

hallways, 58, 176
hand-crafted materials, 39–42

heart of the house, 191
heating, 115
heat pumps, 245
height restrictions, 123
Hirsch, Matt, 5
hobbies, 206
hotels, 36
house designer, 98, *99*
house diagram, 169
"house in a hole" syndrome, 130,
   131, *133*
house weight, *187*
human interactions, 80
human scale, 34–37, 42, *49*, *57*
HVAC units, 115–16, 214
hyphens, 54

indoor air quality, 252
inlays, 42, *59*
insulation, 116, 240–43
   R-values, 242
interior designer, 103
International Style, 27

Japanese architecture, 36
Jefferson, Thomas, 26, 41, 147
John Chad house, *64*
Johnson, Herbert "Hib," *100*
Johnson, Philip, 31

kitchen, 37, 47, 79, 144, 151, *153*,
   163–64, 191–96, 212
     checklist, 195
     country, 192, *193*
     galley, 194
     island-type, 194
     planning, *192–93*

lanai, *155*
land use ordinances, 123
landings, 178
"last settler" syndrome, 129
Le Corbusier, 45, 54, 217
LEED certification, 249
Leonardo da Vinci, 51
"less is more," 37
library, 37, 56, *79*, *150*, 199
life-style costing, 220
lifestyle issues, 109–10
lighting
   artificial, *21*, 82–84, *210*, 213, 214
   control systems, 82–84
   layered, 82, *83*
   LED, 243
   natural, 56, 58, *59*, *67*, *70*, 71, 81–
     82, 128, 200, 203, 209, *216*,
     245–246
living room, 146–47, 164, 198–99
Longfellow, Henry Wadsworth, 109
lot size, 124
Lutyens, Sir Edward, *86*, 87
Lyndon, Donlyn, 37, 39

magazine clippings, 149
mansard roof, *27*
Mansart, François, *27*
massing, 182
mass-produced houses, 219–20
master bedroom, *see* bedroom, master
materials, 57, 85, 115, 117, 184, 186–
   87, 209
McAlester, Virginia and Lee, 182
   *A Field Guide to American
     Houses*, 182
meditation loft, 75–76
Mies van der Rohe, Ludwig, 71, 169
mirror, *7*

misunderstandings, 92–94, 118

modernism, 27–28, 54

Mona Lisa, 51

Monticello, 24

motor court, *139*

Mount Vernon, 26

mud room, 177

multivalence, 69–70

National Arbor Day Foundation, *137*

natural energy efficiency, 236–48
    comfortable temperatures, 237–40
    fixtures and appliances, 243–45
    insulation, 240–43
    natural light, 245–46
    orientation, 238–39
    roof overhangs, 238–39
    ventilation, 246–48

neighbors, 128–30

New England-style house, *188*

"new old house," 148

noise, 138

nostalgia, 60, 77–79, 110, 148, 150, 172

ogee curve, 52

optical illusions, *23*, *126*

options, 222–29

orientation, 122, 126–28, *134*, 209, 238–39

other guy syndrome, 211, 222, 228

outlets, *225*

Oval Office, 26

Palladian-style house, 54

Palladio, Andrea, 56

Parthenon, 52

passive solar design, 115, 128, 171, 237
    heat sink, 240
    orientation, 238–39
    roof overhangs, 238–39
    thermal mass, 240

patio, *see* terrace

pavilions, 61–63

perc tests, *123*

photovoltaics, 236

pineapples, *72*

plan
    axes, *22*
    crazy-quilt, 22, 85
    developing, 84, 181–82
    four-square, 21, 22
    "L" shaped, 55
    open, 100
    purposefulness, 21
    standardized, 106

planned and unplanned places, 38

planned communities, 123–24, 136–37

planning, 92–93, 147
    questions, 144

point of arrival, 172

pool house, *138*

porches, 21, 32–33, *77*, 110, 227–28

portal gate, *76*

powder room, 94, 206

priorities, 87, 150–52

privacy, 127, 209

problem lots, 139–40

programming, 143–55, 161, *193*, 198, 218

property lines, 125, 138, 140

railings, 178, *179*, *181*

reality test, 152–55

recycled composite lumber, 251

refrigerators, *see* appliances

registers, *225*

Registry of Historical Buildings, 63

renewable energy, 254–255

resale houses, 219

resale value, 206, 211, 220, 222, 228

retainage, 232

risers, 179–80

rock, 135–36, 139

rock clause, 135

roof, 130–31, *133*, 183
    cool, 249
    line, *8*, 182
    metal, 249–50
    overhangs, 127, 238–39
    pitch, *183*
    radiant barrier sheathing, 250–51

rooms
    function of, 190
    height of, 56
    layouts of, 208–209
    list of, 143, 147, 151
    "non-view," 161
    orientation of, 200
    sequence of, 163–64
    size of, 145

roots, *137*

rules of composition, 182–83

SAAPE, 173–76

Saarinen, Eliel, 235

sapele pomele, *59*, *73*

scale, 56

sconces, 82, *83*

secret passageway, 76

selective perception, 218

septic system, *123*

sequential progressions, 32

setback restrictions, 124, 141
shell, 146
shopping mall, 41
shower, 203, 213
shutters, 38, 185
side entrances, 177
sidewalk superintendents, 118–19
sink, 193–94, 215
site, 67, 94, 106–107, 112, *120*, 121–41, 161–62, 170
    analysis, 125–26, 128, 136, 160
    filling in, 170
    level, *126*
    plan, 140–41, *162*, 169
sitting area, 200
sketches, *20, 23, 160*
skylights, *100,* 246
sliding glass doors, *155*
Sloane, Eric, 65
slopes, *122*, 125–26, 130–33, 139–41, 170
soils, 136, *137*
solar chimney, 247
solar panels, 236
sound, 112, 199
    insulation, 222–23
spaces, 24–26, 88, 112, 209
    changes in, 71
    defining, *40*
    designing, 33–36
    function of, 145–46
    high, 226
    outdoor, 153–54
    "peopling," 37–42, 185
    personal, 35
    public vs. private, 32–33
    relations between, 145
    types of, 25
    vs. places, 26
spine, *see* backbone

square footage, 152–54, 157, 227
    calculating, *221*
staircases, 32, 54, 56, 63, *77*, 144, *150*, 160, 165, 177–80, *181*, 213, *225*, *226*, 230
    curved, 178
    floating, *205*
    guidelines for, 179–80
    terminology, *180*
steel beams, 223–24
Stern, Robert A. M., 143
Stickley, Gustav, 256
stock house, 106
stone, *156*
storage, *195*, 208, 213
structural engineer, 98, 104
stucco, *156*, 187
study, 146, 199
style, 84, 147–50
    Carolandrick, 148
subcontractors, 66–67, 96, *97*, 118, 229
Sullivan, Louis, 69
sunroom, *168*
survey, 141
Susanka, Sarah, FAIA
    Home by Design, 234
    The Not So Big House series, 234
sustainable design, 252–254
swimming pool, 124, *142*, 211
symmetry, 50–51, 184

"telescope" house, 182–83
television, 198–99, 215
terrace, 25, 38–39, 71, *108*
test holes, 135–36
three-dimensional models, 84
tiles, 215
toilet, 203, 213
topography, 126, 140–41
trade-offs, 150–51, 208

traffic, *137*, 138
treads, 179–80
trees, 128, 135–38, 139, 174
Twain, Mark, 99

universal design, 202–203, *207*
University of Virginia, 24, 26, 37, 41
U.S. Green Building Council, 249

ventilation, 246–248
    ceiling fans, 247
    solar chimneys, 247
veranda, *8, 53*, 66, *70, 111, 142*, 227–28
Versaci, Russell, FAIA
    Creating a New Old House, 234
videotape, *210*
view easement, 130
views, *24, 44, 57, 68*, 111, *127*, 128–30, 131, 134–35, 198, *205*, 209, 214
    of your house, 128–29
Villa Rotunda, *56*
Villa Savoye, 54
visual logic, *186*
VOCs (volatile organic compounds), 252
volute, *52*

walls, 100, 146, 151
    brick, 67, 80–81
    curved, 225–26
    glass, 28
    sample, *92*
    stone, 73, 226–27
    thickness of, 73–74
    wood, 73
wall space, 208
Washington, George, 26
Washington Monument, 34, 35

water heaters, tankless, 244
weather, 171
Wedlick, Dennis, AIA
    Good House Parts, 234
whirlpool, 203
wind, 138–39
windbreaks, 171
windows, *21*, 37, *38*, 58, 63, *64*, *68*,
    81, 89, *91*, 100, 111, 115, 126–27,
    176, *178*, *179*, 184–85, 197, 200,
    203, 209, 219–20, 241, 242, 245
        bay, *57*, 186
        dormer, 131, *133*, 186
        groups of, 215
        proportions of, 84
        Zen, 29, 76
window seats, *78*, 80, 200–201
wine cellar, *117*
woodland cottage, 27
woodworking, *75*, *199*
work triangle, 193–94
Wright, Frank Lloyd, 100–102, 121,
    189, 191
why build a house?, 90–95

your opinion, 23–24

zone of influence, 34–35
zone of retreat, 79–80
zoning, 123, 133

Purchase an Author-Signed Copy of

DESIGNING YOUR PERFECT HOUSE
LESSONS FROM AN ARCHITECT

by ordering from our websites.

www.about-home-design.com

and

www.designingyourperfecthouse.com

Please visit our websites
for more useful advice about
home design, home building, and remodeling;
you will find many articles and videos
to help you learn more and be a
well-informed client and customer.